Also available at all good book stores

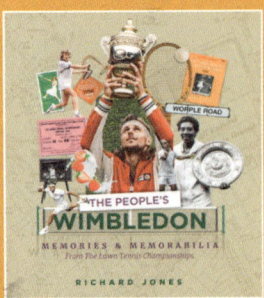

9781785316357

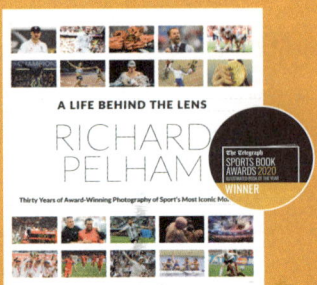

9781785315466

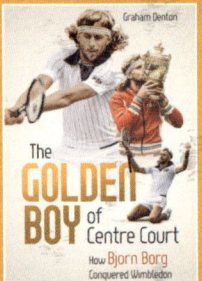

9781785317774

9781785313868

9781785313837

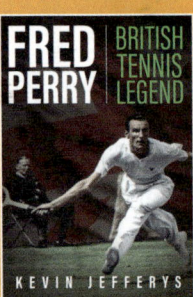

9781785312908

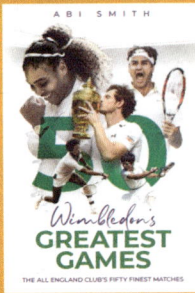

9781785318443

9781785313608

Beyond SW 19

Beyond SW 19

World Class
Tennis in England
since the 1880s

Kevin Jefferys

First published by Pitch Publishing, 2021

Pitch Publishing
A2 Yeoman Gate
Yeoman Way
Worthing
Sussex
BN13 3QZ
www.pitchpublishing.co.uk
info@pitchpublishing.co.uk

A CIP catalogue record is available for this book
from the British Library.

ISBN 978 1 78531 776 7

Typesetting and origination by Pitch Publishing
Printed and bound in India by Replika Press Pvt. Ltd.

Contents

Preface   7

Acknowledgements   9

Introduction   11

1. **Queen's Club**   21
   The London Grass Court Championships   22
   London Grass Court Championships Results   30
   The British Covered Court Championships   34
   British Covered Court Championships Results   42
   The Grass Court Championships since the 1970s   46
   Queen's Grass Court Championships Results   50

2. **Surbiton**   52
   The Surrey Grass Court Championships   53
   Surrey Grass Court Championships Results   60
   The Surbiton Trophy   64
   Surbiton Trophy Results   66

3. **Beckenham**   68
   The Kent All-Comers' Championships Results   78

4. **Eastbourne**   84
   The South of England Championships   85
   South of England Championships Results   95
   The Eastbourne International   100
   Eastbourne International Results   105

5. **Bournemouth**   108
   The British Hard Court Championships Results   123

6. **The West of England**   127
   The West of England Championships   129
   West of England Championships Results   138
   The Palace Hotel Tournament, Torquay   142

Palace Hotel Tournament Results 148

7. **The Northern** 151
Northern Tournament Results 166

8. **Scarborough** 172
The North of England Championships 174
Hoylake 182
North of England Championships Results 184

9. **Midland Counties** 190
The Midland Counties Championships 191
Midland Counties Championships Results 201
Edgbaston Priory and the Birmingham Classic 205
Birmingham Classic Results 209
Nottingham 210
Nottingham Open Results 212

10. **Wembley, the Albert Hall and the O2 Arena** 214
The Empire Pool, Wembley 215
Wembley Professional Championships Results 223
The Royal Albert Hall 225
Rothmans International Results 226
Dewar Cup Results 229
The O2 Arena 231
ATP World Tour Finals Results 234

Abbreviations 236
Notes 239
Select Bibliography 247

Preface

SOME BOOK titles are self-explanatory. Readers are unlikely to be surprised by what they find between the covers of, say, *The A-Z of London*, or an A-Z of any major city. Other titles are more difficult to second-guess. *Half Asleep in Frog Pajamas*, for example, might leave uninitiated readers intrigued as to what's to come in the novel by American author Tom Robbins. My chosen title and sub-title fall somewhere between these two opposite extremes and so perhaps require an explanation at the outset.

Even those with only a passing interest in the sport of tennis will know that the annual summer gathering held at Wimbledon in London SW19 is special. One of Britain's finest competitors of the 20th century, Bunny Austin, wrote in his memoir *A Mixed Double*, 'All players will agree there is no tournament experience to equal "The Championships" at Wimbledon. The vast attendance, the excitement of the crowd, the perfection of the conditions, the efficiency of the management, all combine to lift it above any other tournament or championship in the world [see p. 94].' Austin's view as a player is no doubt shared by the hosts of officials, coaches, journalists, media outlets and spectators who flock to London from around the world each summer, and could be applicable to any period in Wimbledon's illustrious history – from the early days of the Victorian pioneers through to the modern era of Federer, Nadal, Djokovic and Murray.

But however enduring, significant and popular it is, Wimbledon does not tell the whole story of high-quality tennis played on English shores. At the start of 2020 the game's domestic governing body, the Lawn Tennis Association (LTA), looked forward to another year of 'world-class tennis around the country', having in mind tournaments such as those at Queen's Club, Eastbourne, Edgbaston, Nottingham and Manchester, as well as at the highlight of the grass-court season in London SW19. The LTA's hopes for the summer were of course dashed – in common with much of the nation's sporting and social life – by the global COVID-19 pandemic, but the underlying sentiment and reasoning stands. As this study sets out to demonstrate, international-standard tennis has long been on display *Beyond SW19*, at a range of locations and tournaments in addition to the revered showcase at Wimbledon.

As for the sub-title, this alludes to the scope and timescale of the book's coverage. My main focus is on tennis featuring top stars of the sport played primarily, but not exclusively, at tournaments such as those referred to above. Because venues such as Queen's and Eastbourne (and several less-well-known settings, the likes of Bristol and Scarborough) have also staged other forms of international competition that are included in what follows, notably numerous Davis Cup ties, a sub-title along the lines of 'a history of leading tournaments apart from Wimbledon' would not altogether encompass the content of the main chapters. Instead, what readers will find in these pages, one hopes, is an overview, assessment and celebration of the various forms of world-class tennis played at key locations around the country from the 1880s to the present day.

Acknowledgements

FOR HELP during the course of researching and preparing my text, I'd especially like to thank Dr Matt Cole, for his assistance in relation to the history of Edgbaston; David Baker at Beckenham Sports Club; and staff at the Bristol Reference Library. My debt to the writings and recollections of formers players, journalists and officials is suitably acknowledged, I hope, in the Notes at the end of the book. I'd also like to express my gratitude to the many excellent websites that have aided the research process. These include:

    www.beckenhamtennisclub.co.uk;
    www.britishnewspaperarchive.co.uk;
    www.eastbournetennis.com;
    www.thenorthern.co.uk; www.surbiton.org;
    www.tennisarchives.com;
    www.thetennisbase.com; www.tennisforum.com;
    and www.westhants.co.uk.

While appreciative to all those concerned for their valuable assistance, it should be added that responsibility for any errors or omissions rests with the author alone.

I'm grateful once more to the support and expert guidance of Pitch Publishing in bringing the project to fruition, notably to Jane Camillin, Paul Camillin, Duncan Olner and Graham Hales. Thanks also to Andrea Dunn.

For permission to use the photographs reproduced on the cover and inside the book I'd like to thank Getty Images and Alamy.

The front jacket photographs show (clockwise from the top): Jimmy Connors with the men's singles trophy at Queen's Club, 1982; Althea Gibson holding the women's singles trophy at Surbiton, 1956; Dan Evans in action at Surbiton, 2019 (when he won the men's singles); The British Hard Court Championships in progress at Bournemouth, 1969; Martina Navratilova with the trophy at Eastbourne, 1983; Dorothy Round competing at Beckenham, 1931.

The inside front cover photograph shows Andy Murray and Feliciano Lopez (nearest to camera) in action against Joe Salisbury and Rajeev Ram in the men's doubles final at the Queen's Championships in June 2019. The inside back image is an aerial view of the South of England Championships at Devonshire Park, Eastbourne, taken in 1905.

The back jacket cover features Billie Jean King, holding the Manchester Silver Challenge Tray after winning the Northern tournament in 1966, and Vijay Amritraj, winner of the Bristol Open in 1986.

The running order of the images inside the book, it might be added, follows the structure of the main chapters/tournaments, rather than being arranged in, say, chronological date order.

Finally, I'd like to say a big thank you, during these challenging pandemic times, to Sue, Pete, Kate, Katie and James for their ongoing love, support and inspiration.

Kevin Jefferys
February 2021

Introduction

FOR A sport that originated as a genteel English garden-party pursuit – and was derided by critics in its formative years as mere 'pat-ball' – lawn tennis has a surprisingly long history of keen competition. The knockout tournament, pitting players one against the other and embedding a strong culture of winning and losing, has been a staple of the game since it began and started to spread in the 1870s. This book sets out to illustrate the longevity, high quality and variety of competitive tennis that has taken place on English shores outside of Wimbledon.

Before saying more about the tournaments and locations that provide the focus of the individual chapters, it's important to set the scene by outlining the framework in which top-tier meetings operated. Looking back with the benefit of hindsight, we can see that in the 140-year history of lawn tennis so far there have been three overlapping but quite distinct phases in the evolution of what the LTA in 2020 described as 'world-class tennis around the country'.

The first phase runs from the 1880s through to the First World War in 1914, and witnessed the emergence and development of a flourishing tournament scene, such that the United Kingdom – as might be expected of the nation that pioneered the sport – led the world in the hosting of highly regarded open tournaments. In the late-Victorian period and beyond, the term 'open' referred to events in which any amateur player was eligible to compete, as distinct from the 'closed' meetings, or parts of meetings, restricted to those from a particular locality, club or county (these closed events were themselves popular and widespread, but are not a central concern in these pages). It was axiomatic, in a game governed from the start by strict amateur rules, that no paid professionals – in this era primarily tennis coaches – were allowed to participate in the same events as amateurs.

A revealing insight into the expansion of tournament competition is provided by F.R. (Fred) Burrow, the chain-smoking referee at scores of meetings of variable size and quality (including Wimbledon) before and after the 1914–18 war. Burrow recalled in a book of reflections that in his own playing days, when he was a student at Oxford in the early 1880s, there were only a handful of tournaments in existence. Most of them, he noted, had small numbers of entrants and they were nearly all played on grass courts and concentrated into a few summer weeks in June and July. But within a few years, the numbers being organised and of those participating started to rise sharply, and it's worth outlining in detail his recollection of a single season, that of 1889, to appreciate the speed and scale of growth.

Burrow's list of elite-level events taking place in the UK that year included the Irish Championships, Bath, Cheltenham, Whitehouse, Waterloo, the Welsh Championships, the Scottish Championships, Macclesfield, Beckenham, the Northern Championships, Edgbaston, Blackheath, The Championships (Wimbledon), Stafford, Hull, Nottingham, Chiswick, Leamington, Leicester, Whitby, Market Harborough, Taunton, Torquay, Darlington, East Grinstead, Exmouth, Keswick, Sheffield, Buxton, Teignmouth, Bournemouth, Scarborough, Weston-super-Mare, Leyton, Brighton and Eastbourne. All these, he noted, were 'played in the order given'.[1]

Burrow's overview was not fully comprehensive, but it indicates that with additions – we know of several other tournaments that took place in 1889 – regular annual fixtures in the summer season, running from May to early September, totalled at least 40 each year;

a figure that, by Burrow's estimation, thereafter more than trebled to over 140 by the time hostilities broke out in Europe in 1914 (after which tournament play went into abeyance for the duration of the conflict). Exact numbers are hard to pin down, depending on which types of gathering are counted, but the upward trajectory prior to the Great War is clear. What characterises this first stage, ultimately, was the rapid geographical spread of tournaments, to cover all regions of the country, and the sheer variety of meetings on offer. These ranged from short, after-work or seaside holiday gatherings, where local club and county players often mingled with wealthy visiting hopefuls, to the longer, highest-level tournaments dominated by the crème de la crème, the so-called 'cracks', of the day.

In the second of our three phases, the half-century between 1918 and 1968, the UK experienced the golden age of its tournament history beyond SW19. With lawn tennis rising sharply in popularity across much of the globe after the First World War, England, especially, of the home nations developed a much longer playing season – stretching over six months from spring to late autumn – and hosted a range of meetings that showcased world-class tennis for both men and women. Hence, as the following chapters show, prestigious events on different types of court surface became commonplace, including one of the most important indoor tournaments in Europe (at Queen's); a national hard-court championships that attracted strong international contenders (at Bournemouth); and popular grass-court meetings such as those seen as essential dress rehearsals for Wimbledon and those among the largest tournaments anywhere in the world (at Beckenham and Eastbourne respectively).

One young overseas player, South African left-hander Gordon Forbes, kept a 1950s diary indicating that the English tournament scene was renowned for being both competitive and fun at the same time. Despite the presence of irritating ex-military-type referees, who Forbes wrote 'used to lay down the law in a very British way' – and notwithstanding some inevitable poor weather – he described with affection his 1954 tour around numerous meetings ahead of Wimbledon: at Bournemouth, Hurlingham, Paddington, Newcastle, Manchester, Surbiton, Beckenham and Roehampton. Amateur rules continued to officially ban prize money (except for inexpensive shopping vouchers), but Forbes noted that there were other compensations, including free accommodation with welcoming local families and small-scale, permissible expenses. In addition to 50 shillings in cash and second-class rail fares, players were given, he said, 'books of lunch tickets which enabled us to eat egg and ham pie and lettuce in dampish tents. Blissfully happy, we played for our lives'.[2]

Throughout this period, smaller meetings in particular (as they had before 1914) tended to come and go. Tournaments were discontinued for a range of reasons. The retirement of a key organiser might affect a club's ability to continue hosting; entry numbers could suddenly or unexpectedly fall away; bad weather sometimes ruined finals, so contributing to a financial loss that made future meetings unviable. But the upward trend in overall tournament numbers continued, at least for a couple of decades after the Great War. Precise figures are again not easy to collate owing to different methods of calculation, but one authoritative source claims that the LTA sanctioned 155 senior tournaments in England and Wales in 1934.[3] This peak was never to be surpassed, but there was another mini revival after the Second World War. Starting from a low base – as competitive tennis was again severely curtailed during the 1939–45 war – about 100 tournaments took place in 1953, followed by a small drift downwards thereafter; 83 were reported as going ahead in 1966. The number of entrants between these two dates fell from over 14,000 to around 9,400.[4]

Despite the continued vibrancy of larger gatherings in particular – several of which were regularly covered by national newspapers and also by the emerging medium of television – the dwindling number of events and entrants indicated strains in the system by the

1950s. As the global tennis calendar became more congested, and with air travel allowing elite players to move more easily across the world all year round, English tournaments beyond SW19 found it ever harder to attract the best to their own meetings. It was an open secret that – in contravention of the creaking amateur rulebook – top stars sought and were offered generous inducements to appear at concurrent events taking place in the United States or mainland Europe. Unless willing to emulate such practices, tournament committees in England found it hard, doubly so after Wimbledon was finished each summer, to continue attracting the calibre of player who would bring in the large paying crowds necessary to cover costs. While most of the gatherings featured in these pages managed to stay afloat going into the 1960s, for others the writing was already on the wall.

In the third and final of our chronological stages, running from the early 1970s to the present day, we find the non-Wimbledon tournament scene contracting sharply, before eventually adapting and reinventing itself. The number of top-tier senior meetings around the country fell to 56 by the end of the 1970s, and the decline continued apace thereafter.[5] What gradually emerged after a period of protracted upheaval was the more streamlined tournament structure of today, with world-class tennis still on offer but now mostly concentrated into a short grass-court swing of five to six weeks ahead of Wimbledon. The elongated English season stretching from March to November, characteristic of the former heyday, now shrunk and almost disappeared, although not entirely. London, as we will see, remained the home of several important autumn meetings held indoors, ranging from the Rothmans International and Dewar Cup competitions at the Albert Hall in the 1970s through to the hugely prestigious men's tour World Finals at the O2 Arena in recent years.

The chief cause of the diminished scale of high-quality tennis beyond SW19 was the long-term impact of professionalism following the arrival of Open tennis. After 1968, the definition of open and closed events, as used in former times, was superseded by the notion that elite events were open to all categories of players, whether amateur or professional. Prior to this, since the 1920s, the small bands of professional players who toured the world receiving above-board payment for their endeavours were barred from all amateur meetings, including the grand slams. The seismic effects of the move to Open tennis were not immediately apparent when the international authorities gave the go-ahead for ten experimental tournaments to take place across the world in 1968. It was an illustration of the hard-earned global status of English tournaments that four of these ten Open events took place on home shores: at Bournemouth, Beckenham, Queen's Club and Wimbledon.

Within a few years, however, several long-standing and cherished meetings (including Bournemouth and Beckenham) had gone out of business. The reality was that the Open era saw the elite game transformed in a multi-million dollar enterprise, attracting massive TV and media interest and making it difficult for home events outside of Wimbledon to offer the rocketing levels of prize money required to attract the world's best. As will be shown in the individual chapters that follow, some tournaments secured good sponsorships deals, enabling them to continue in adapted forms, becoming valued parts of separate men's and women's tours overseen by the Association of Tennis Professionals (ATP) and the Women's Tennis Association (WTA) respectively. But for others, large-scale sponsorship was difficult to find and sustain as configurations elsewhere in the global calendar – notably on European clay courts in the spring and American hard courts ahead of the US Open – consolidated their hold and contributed to squeezing the life out of traditional English gatherings.

By the end of the 1980s Wimbledon was the only grand slam event still played on grass (the US and Australian Opens having switched to hard surfaces), further reducing the appeal of the UK's formerly extended grass-court season. Yet the story of recent decades is not entirely one of gloom and doom. With assistance from the LTA, the fittest of the English meetings not only survived but were able to flourish. By the end of the 20th century a strong schedule of high-quality tournaments remained an established part of the annual circuit, some ATP events showcasing the skills of top men (as at Queen's) and other WTA meetings featuring leading women stars – at Eastbourne, for example, which moved with the times by abandoning its old September date in favour of a pre-Wimbledon slot. Hence, today, the LTA is still able to promise tennis fans, coronavirus aside (at the time of writing the fate of the 2021 summer season remained unclear), the prospect of witnessing – if not on the scale of yesteryear – 'world-class tennis around the country'.

* * *

Moving from the general historical picture to the specific, the ten chapters that follow look to explore a range of venues and competitions (including Davis and Wightman Cup ties as well as individual tournaments) that have featured international-standard tennis in the past and/or the present day. The aim is to shed fresh light not only on some of the best-known annual gatherings, at the likes of Queen's, Eastbourne and Edgbaston, but also on once high-profile but now-defunct and largely forgotten meetings in places such as Torquay, Scarborough and Wembley Arena.

Each chapter, drawing from materials including tennis journals and magazines, newspapers and memoirs by players, officials and journalists, includes background about the geographical setting and the origins of the tournament concerned. This is followed by discussion of the highs and lows in the evolution of the event (all the tournaments covered, we shall see, experienced ebbs and flows at various points in time) and by stories about key matches and the top stars who participated and lifted the main trophies. Particular attention is paid to examining why certain meetings managed to adapt to the demands of commercialism that came with the Open era, whereas others faltered and were consigned to the record books.

The running order of chapters is determined not by the relative status of individual tournaments but rather takes the form of a round-the-country journey, starting in the heartland of British tennis, at Queen's Club in London, and then working outwards and onwards in a roughly (though not precisely) clockwise fashion around England. These travels take us far and wide across regions, towns and cities, from Eastbourne and Bournemouth on the south coast to Bristol in the west country, and to Manchester, Liverpool and Scarborough in the north before returning via Birmingham to the capital to end by focusing on major indoor venues in London including Wembley and the O2 Arena.

Ireland, Scotland and Wales all have creditable records in staging top-quality tennis (including, in the contemporary era of Andy and Jamie Murray, several crucial Davis Cup encounters), but those areas of the UK are not covered in these pages, partly because of space constraints and partly as they warrant and have received separate treatment in their own right. The Irish Championships – which began only two years after Wimbledon and for a couple of decades had strong claims to rival the All England Club meeting in terms of prestige – has attracted much attention from historians in recent years.[6] Detailed coverage can also be found elsewhere of the Welsh and Scottish Championships, the latter of which has been described in Max Robertson's authoritative *Encyclopedia of Tennis* as holding for many years a place 'of high esteem in the British calendar'.[7]

Interspersed in the text of the ten chapters – with the aim of allowing readers to gauge tournament outcomes for every year covered – are lists of results for the men's and women's singles at the meetings under discussion, ranging from the London Grass Court Championships in chapter 1 to the ATP World Finals in the last chapter. Many tournaments in their early years adopted (as did

Wimbledon) the practice of stipulating that reigning champions who chose to defend their title only had to face one 'challenge round' final against the best of the 'all-comers', the remainder of the entrants who played through the draw. All the lists embedded in the chapters, it should be noted, show winners of all-comers' finals in cases where the title holder did not defend; this avoids excessive usage of the technically correct term 'walkover', as there were numerous examples where reigning champions did not take part at the challenge round stage.

The results lists, compiled from multiple published and online sources, bear witness to the scale and significance of international-standard play that has characterised English tennis history. Nearly all of the great names of the sport over the past century and more – from the likes of the Renshaw brothers in the 1880s to Roger Federer today – can be found on the roll of honour at one or more of the tournaments featured. In general terms, overseas victors became increasingly regular and numerous from the time of the First World War onwards. For ease of reference, the winners and runners-up named in the results lists are from the UK unless indicated otherwise; a guide to the abbreviations used for players of other nationalities follows on at the end of the last chapter.

Also interspersed in the body of each main chapter – with the intention of providing additional texture and colour – are a series of descriptions, in italicised text, of some unusually short or excessively long contests, and of quirky, humorous or controversial moments associated with individual tournaments. Most of the categories covered in these vignettes are self-explanatory (e.g. 'memorable match'), although it's worth mentioning that 'underrated champion' refers not to a player's career achievements across the board but rather to giving fuller recognition to that man or woman's record at top-level English tournaments other than Wimbledon.[8]

By including a wealth of anecdotes alongside extensive lists of winners, *Beyond SW19* seeks to avoid the pitfall once identified by

Times correspondent Rex Bellamy, namely that tennis enthusiasts were sometimes 'saturated with facts and figures' in coverage of their sport at the expense of 'more character and peripheral detail'.[9] This book hopefully combines, and keeps in appropriate balance, both 'facts and figures' and 'character'. The main objective is to describe and do justice to the great tennis played on home soil: from those far-off Victorian times when the keen, wealthy amateur might embark on a 'western tour', taking in meetings at a string of coastal resorts such as Exmouth, Torquay and Teignmouth, through to today's ultra-professional players, chasing ranking points and huge prize money at the likes of Queen's and the ATP Finals, two of the most stellar tournaments on the world stage.

1

Queen's Club

OF ALL the leading tennis locations in England outside of SW19, Queen's Club is the most iconic. The Fever-Tree Championships (as known since 2018, after the name of the current sponsors) sits close to the pinnacle of the modern global circuit, one of a handful of ATP Tour meetings immediately below the level of the grand slams. Many of the world's leading men stars – including Britain's Andy Murray, who holds the record for the number of victories in the singles – regularly vie for honours every June. The tournament is seen as both highly valued in its own right, offering some £2m in prize money, and as a vital warm-up for Wimbledon, which takes place a couple of weeks later. Attracting around 50,000 spectators annually and bolstered by extensive BBC television coverage, the Queen's Championships has several times been voted the ATP Tournament of the Year and has been described by one of its former sponsors, Stella Artois, as a 'shining jewel in the UK tennis crown'.[1]

Part of the successful formula of the tournament is its rich heritage and distinctive setting. Queen's Club in Palliser Road, West Kensington, in the heart of London, claims to be the world's oldest multi-sport venue. Founded on a ten-acre site in the mid-1880s, and named after its first patron, Queen Victoria, the club hosted over 20 different sports before becoming more exclusively identified as a playing and administrative hub for lawn tennis (as well as for real tennis and rackets). For many years marked out by its socially exclusive membership, which included royalty, aristocracy and wealthy businessmen, the club suffered serious damage during the Second World War and was taken over in the 1950s, at a time of financial difficulties, by the LTA, which located its headquarters there until 2007. After that, the governing body moved to the National Training Centre at Roehampton, while also granting to Queen's a long lease, which meant club members once more owned and operated facilities including the instantly recognisable Victorian clubhouse and large numbers of top-quality outdoor and indoor courts, currently around 40 in total.

Many of the great legends of the sport from the 1880s to the present day have displayed their skills at Queen's, which for decades also staged a highly esteemed indoor tournament, the British Covered Court Championships (BCCC). Because the grass-court event is so widely known and revered today, it's easy to assume this has always been the case. But, as this chapter will show, Queen's Club has a more chequered, nuanced tournament past than the glittering present might suggest, with notable low points as well as towering highs. The reputation of both main tournaments at Queen's fluctuated over time and, at certain points, as we shall see, the annual outdoor gathering had its critics and was less well regarded than its indoor counterpoint. Nor should it be forgotten, as we examine the pre-1970s history of the two great flagship meetings in turn, that neither of them actually started life in West Kensington.

The London Grass Court Championships

The London Athletic Tournament, the precursor to the famous Queen's grass-court annual summer gathering, was initially established in the early 1880s at Stamford Bridge, west London, where it remained until the end of the decade. There were some distinguished winners, Wimbledon champions among them, in the early years: Herbert Lawford (a committee member at Queen's) claimed the men's title three times in succession and Maud Watson was a two-time winner of the women's singles. But the meeting had yet to build a settled, distinct identity. Its timing each summer varied – ranging from early June to mid-July in different years – and entry levels fluctuated in quality and depth. No women's singles event was held in 1882 or 1883, and in 1885 (when it was renamed the London Championships) there were only 15 men and seven ladies in the draw.

In 1890 the tournament was switched to Queen's, where lawn tennis was becoming more fashionable among the various sports on offer. The new, more central location (and the subsequent opening of a nearby underground station at Barons Court) helped to ensure the attendance of many top 'cracks'. Victors on the men's side in the 1890s included stars such as Pim, Mahony and Laurence Doherty, although the great R.F. Doherty never lifted the trophy, losing to Mahony in the 1896 final. That same year Charlotte Cooper claimed the first of what would be five London Championship titles. Some onlookers felt it might have been six, but for bad line calls that went against her when she lost to old adversary Edith Austin 9-7 in the deciding set of the 1899 women's final. Other controversies also received unwelcome publicity. The journal *Pastime* aired complaints by some players that because Queen's hosted other games such as winter football on the same turf the grass courts were of variable quality, and in very hot weather especially could be 'fiery and bumpy'.[2]

During the Edwardian period the London Championships acquired a more established look. The challenge round was abolished in 1904; a fixed position in the annual calendar (the week before Wimbledon) was finally agreed; and a more international entry became characteristic, at least on the men's side. The singles title went overseas on six out of ten occasions before the First World War. The legendary New Zealander Tony Wilding beat Queen's Club member Major Ritchie comfortably in 1907 and never dropped a set throughout three later campaigns where he retained the title. In 1907 and 08, early illustrations were seen of shock results that would, in later times, be widely commented upon. The women's title in both of those years went to Wiltshire-born Violet Pinckney, who never progressed beyond the last eight at Wimbledon but who, at Queen's, twice got the better of Dorothea Lambert Chambers, usually unassailable at most tournaments outside of SW19 in which she took part. According to the *Evening Standard*, Miss Pinckney's 'wonderfully safe' game saw her through in 1907,[3] while the following year Mrs Chambers was much perturbed by a strong wind blowing across the centre court.

THE WINNERS WHO ALMOST NEVER MADE IT

In 1905 the London Championships was dominated, on the men's side, by players from the American Davis Cup squad. The first overseas winner of the singles was Holcombe Ward, whose opponent in the final – team-mate Beals Wright – conceded without hitting a ball. To the annoyance of organisers at Queen's, both men wanted to preserve energy for Davis Cup encounters ahead after coming through strenuous semi-finals. Ward and Wright did contest, as a pair, the doubles final, where they lost to two further members of the US squad, William Larned and W.J. Clothier. The Larned-Clothier combination had lady luck on their side, and might well not have made it to finals day. Called upon to play a first-round match not long after disembarking from their Atlantic voyage, they came off court after losing two sets to love. When they reported the score, the referee told them it was a best-of-five contest and they needed to finish it properly. Upon returning to action, the Americans won the next three sets; they survived and thrived, going on a few days later to claim the title.

At first sight, the roll of honour for the men's singles between the wars suggests the London Championships had developed into one of the most sought-after titles in world tennis. No fewer than six

Wimbledon champions, five of them American, triumphed in Palliser Road, starting with 'Little Bill' Johnston in 1920. In an era when the USA fully arrived as a pre-eminent force in the sport, other winners at Queen's included 'Big Bill' Tilden, a two-time champion in the late 1920s, Ellsworth Vines, Sidney Wood and Donald Budge. The powerful-hitting Budge beat his compatriot David Jones in straight sets in 1936; this, despite Jones hitting 22 aces, almost half the total number of points he garnered in the whole match. Budge easily retained the title in 1937 when he crushed Britain's Bunny Austin for the loss of just three games.

While any event featuring so many global stars clearly offered 'world-class tennis' (to adopt LTA phraseology), Queen's was not generally regarded around this time as the leading pre-Wimbledon grass-court tournament of the English summer. Criticism of the standard of the courts only subsided when football and rugby departed from the club in the late 1920s, and a few years of poor weather in the 1930s generated some adverse headlines. Above all, it was the scheduling of the meeting, in the week immediately preceding Wimbledon, that held the key to the tournament's ambiguous status. On the one hand, the timing meant serious contenders for honours in SW19 were in London and keen to find good grass-court practice. But on the other hand, journalists and tennis insiders felt Queen's had an air of artificiality. Often entrants were highly anxious to avoid any injury that would prevent them appearing a few days later at the venue that most mattered – the All England Club – so did not always pull out all the stops in West Kensington.

The consequence was that the London Championships became associated with many difficult-to-explain results. According to Queen's Club historian Roy McKelvie, when Johnston surprised Tilden to win the 1920 men's final, 'there were suggestions that neither player tried his hardest or best'.[4] Tilden's form was certainly transformed when he proceeded to take the Wimbledon title a

IN A HURRY

Many a jaw dropped at the sight of Gottfried von Cramm crushing Bobby Riggs 6-0, 6-1 in the semi-finals of the London Championships in June 1939. Although the German aristocrat was a three-time Wimbledon finalist, he had not long been released from a spell in prison under Hitler's Nazi regime, whereas the dynamic, up-and-coming American was considered the favourite for Wimbledon that summer. Words like 'thrashing' were bandied about when, instead of a close contest between two accomplished titans, von Cramm barely broke sweat in winning the first 11 games of the match. Riggs held on in the next game, but the German quickly completed the rout. The whole thing was over in less than half an hour. Before long, rumours were circulating that Riggs 'threw' the match in order to get improved betting odds on himself at Wimbledon the week following, and it was later revealed that he had backed himself to win the singles and two doubles events at The Championships. When he duly did so, he pocketed handsome winnings. By contrast, although von Cramm went on to claim the 1939 Queen's title, his fortunes rapidly took a turn for the worse. He was summoned back to Germany and not allowed to compete in SW19, clearing the path for Riggs to achieve his Wimbledon hat-trick of titles.

couple of weeks later. In 1928 it was widely felt that the famous 'Musketeers', Cochet and Lacoste, subsided tamely against their American opponents in the men's doubles at Queen's because the Frenchmen were holding themselves in reserve for a later Davis Cup final against the USA (which they won). Upsets of a similar order were not unknown in the women's singles at Queen's. The legendary Helen Wills Moody, in her second appearance at the meeting (she shared the title in 1933 when rain intervened), suffered an extremely rare defeat at the semi-final stage in 1938, and yet cruised to her eighth title at Wimbledon a fortnight afterwards. Arguably the most out-of-kilter result yet, however, came in the men's event in 1939 (see *In a Hurry* opposite).

In the two decades after the Second World War, the strongly international flavour of the London Championships continued. The powerful American presence seen prior to 1939 was for a while maintained with victories in the men's singles for Pancho Segura, Bob Falkenburg and Ted Schroeder. On the women's side, every final between 1946 and 1951 was an all-USA affair. Improved air travel, however, facilitated the arrival of much larger numbers than before of Australian men especially (as it did at all the leading English tournaments). In 1952 six of the eight quarter-finalists at Queen's were from down under; the eventual winner was Frank Sedgman, who triumphed without dropping a set all week. The following year, Lew Hoad won the battle of the Aussie teenagers by beating Ken Rosewall in two tight sets. Rosewall turned the tables on his compatriot in 1955, although on this occasion Hoad had the excuse that he got married on the morning of the final. In the 1960s Roy Emerson won at Queen's four years in succession and the last meeting before the arrival of Open tennis, in 1967, was won by another Australian, John Newcombe. He defeated Roger Taylor, the first British player to reach the men's final since the war.

Australian influence also made itself felt, though less overwhelmingly, in the women's singles. The leading Americans often confined themselves to doubles after 1955, leaving room for others to make a mark in the singles, including British winners such as Angela Buxton and Christine Truman. The most successful player during and after the 1960s, however, was Aussie Margaret Smith, who in due course won four times at Queen's. Her most remarkable success came in 1970 when – as Mrs Court – she was firm favourite against Scotland's Winnie Shaw. A major upset looked on the cards when Shaw took the first set 6-2 and then rushed into a 5-1 lead. With service to follow, a home victory looked almost certain. But

Mrs Court called upon all her resourcefulness and determination to break back twice. She edged the set 8-6 and then showed glimpses of her supremely clean ball-striking to take the decider 6-3.

With such an array of talent on display every year, the status of the London Championships had never been higher. And yet the tournament still had its critics, not least some of the overseas arrivals. South Africa's Gordon Forbes wrote in his diary account that he found 'aloof management and damp changing rooms' at the famous old venue in 1962. Lunch and tea tickets were provided by organisers but not the level of expenses which amateurs were permitted under the rules. Forbes noted that the elderly attendants tended to eye competitors suspiciously, handing out towels for showering 'as though they thought the players mightn't return them'.[5] Mutterings about players being desperate to avoid strains or injuries that would harm their chances at Wimbledon persisted. Two of Roy Emerson's four titles were secured when his opponents in the final granted walkovers and British hopeful Mike Sangster described the atmosphere at the meeting as 'generally light-hearted', albeit laced with occasional 'temperamental eruptions'.[6]

Following the onset of Open tennis, Queen's, like other tournaments, had to find fresh ways of attracting the top contenders, professionals now seeking handsome prize money wherever it was to be found. Sponsorship deals to support what became the Rothmans London Grass Court Championships ensured that, for a few years, the entry lists remained impressive. On the men's side, winners in the late 1960s and early 1970s included well-known greats such as Rod Laver and Stan Smith, as well as Jimmy Connors (and after him Ilie Nastase). Similarly, in the women's singles, the list of champions remained highly distinguished. Britain's Ann Jones triumphed in 1969, crushing Winnie Shaw for the loss of just one game before going on to capture the Wimbledon crown two weeks later. Margaret Court's spell of dominance was followed by success in 1972 and 1973

EARLY BATH

The 1972 London Championships was marked by shocks and alarums. Britain's John Paish, son of Davis Cup stalwart Geoff, distinguished himself by reaching the men's singles final, where he lost to emerging superstar Jimmy Connors, claiming the first main title of his career. Paish made it to finals day after a stunning victory in the last eight over Stan Smith (who went on to claim the Wimbledon title just two weeks later), and a more hollow triumph in the semi-finals over Pancho Gonzales. The veteran American, winner of the US Championships back in the late 1940s before becoming a formidable presence on the pre-1968 pro circuit, was a set up on Paish when he disputed a series of line calls in one of his service games. His vociferous demands for the official to be replaced brought the tournament referee to the court. In Bea Seal, a former British Wightman Cup captain, Gonzales met his match. When he refused to play on, she promptly disqualified him.

respectively for America's soon-to-be world number one Chrissie Evert and for Russia's Olga Morozova.

Morozova's victory over Evonne Goolagong turned out to be the last occasion the world's top women stars appeared in competition at Queen's. The global circuit was in a state of flux in the early Open years, with vying interest groups pushing for generally separate men's and women's tournaments outside of the grand slams. Eastbourne became the preferred location for a major pre-Wimbledon women's meeting after 1973, exacerbating what was already a thorny issue at Queen's: how to ensure the long-term viability of its flagship summer meeting as the support of Rothmans came to an end. In 1974, when key sponsor John Player decided to prioritise a men's gathering in Nottingham, no tournament of any sort – for either men or women – took place in West Kensington. Top-quality international tennis at Queen's was suddenly in limbo, especially as just a few years before this the club's other main showcase – its long-standing annual indoor meeting – had been wound up altogether.

London Grass Court Championships

Men's Singles

Year	Winner	Runner-up	Score
1881	Frederick Rawson	George Hill	1-6, 6-1, 6-2, 6-3
1882	Herbert Lawford	Otway Woodhouse	6-1, 4-6, 6-2, 6-3
1883	Herbert Lawford	Teddy Williams	6-2, 6-1, 6-0
1884	Herbert Lawford	Frederick Bowlby	6-3, 6-1, 3-6, 6-2
1885	Charles Ross	Ernest Lewis	3-6, 8-6, 1-6, 6-2, 6-3
1886	Ernest Lewis	Charles Ross	7-5, 6-1, 6-3
1887	Ernest Lewis	Herbert Chipp	6-1, 6-4, 6-0
1888	Ernest Lewis	Harry Barlow	6-0, 6-1, 6-2
1889	Harry Barlow	Charles Eames	5-7, 7-5, 3-6, 6-1, 7-5
1890	Harry Barlow	Wilfred Baddeley	3-6, 6-8, 6-1, 6-2, 6-2
1891	Harry Barlow	Joshua Pim	6-4, 2-6, 6-0, 7-5
1892	Ernest Lewis	Joshua Pim	6-4, 6-4, 3-6, 4-6, 6-1
1893	Joshua Pim	Harold Mahony	9-7, 1-6, 6-1, 6-8, 6-3
1894	Harold Mahony	Harry Barlow	6-2, 6-3, 6-3
1895	Harry Barlow	Manliffe Goodbody	6-4, 7-5, 5-7, 5-7, 10-8
1896	Harold Mahony	Reginald Doherty	11-9, 6-4, 6-4
1897	Laurence Doherty	Major Ritchie	6-2, 6-2, 6-2
1898	Laurence Doherty	Harold Mahony	6-3, 6-4, 9-7
1899	Harold Mahony	Arthur Gore	8-10, 6-2, 7-5, 6-1
1900	Arthur Gore	Arthur Lavy	6-0, 6-2, 6-3
1901	Charles Dixon	George Greville	6-1, 6-0, 4-6, 6-4
1902	Major Ritchie	George Simond	6-3, 6-4, 6-0
1903	George Greville	George Simond	6-1, 6-4, 7-9, 5-7, 6-4
1904	Major Ritchie	Harold Mahony	6-3, 6-1, 6-1
1905	Holcombe Ward (USA)	Beals Wright (USA)	walkover
1906	Major Ritchie	John Flavelle	6-0, 6-1, 7-5
1907	Anthony Wilding (NZ)	Major Ritchie	6-2, 6-1, 6-0
1908	Hare William Powell (USA)	Major Ritchie	6-4, 3-3 retd
1909	Major Ritchie	Harry Parker (NZ)	11-13, 6-4, 6-1, 6-0
1910	Anthony Wilding (NZ)	Major Ritchie	6-4, 6-3, 2-0 retd
1911	Anthony Wilding (NZ)	Alfred Beamish	7-5, 6-2, 6-3
1912	Anthony Wilding (NZ)	Otto Froitzheim (Ger)	walkover

1913	Gordon Lowe	Wallace Johnson (USA)	7-5, 6-4, 4-6, 4-6, 6-4
1914	Gordon Lowe	Percival Davson	6-2, 7-5, 6-4
1915–18	No tournament held		
1919	Pat O'Hara Wood (Aus)	Louis Raymond (SA)	6-4, 6-0, 2-6, 7-5
1920	Bill Johnston (USA)	Bill Tilden (USA)	4-6, 6-2, 6-4
1921	Zenzo Shimidzu (Jpn)	Mohammed Sleem (Ind)	6-2, 6-0
1922	Henry Mayes (Can)	Donald Greig	6-8, 6-2, 6-2, 6-1
1923	Vincent Richards (USA)	Sydney Jacob	6-2, 6-2
1924	Algernon Kingscote	Gordon Lowe	3-6, 8-6, 6-3, 6-2
1925	Gordon Lowe	Henry Mayes (Can)	6-2, 9-7
1926	Henry Mayes (Can)	Gordon Lowe	6-3, 6-2
1927	Henry Mayes (Can)	David Evans	6-3, 6-3
1928	Bill Tilden (USA)	Francis Hunter (USA)	6-3, 6-2, 6-1
1929	Bill Tilden (USA)	Francis Hunter (USA)	title shared
1930	Wilmer Allison (USA)	Gregory Mangin (USA)	6-4, 8-6
1931	John Olliff	Ted Avory	3-6, 6-4, 6-2
1932	Jack Crawford (Aus)	Hendrik Timmer (Ned)	1-6, 6-3, 6-3, 6-4
1933	Ellsworth Vines (USA)	Lester Stoefen (USA)	title shared
1934	Sidney Wood (USA)	Frank Shields (USA)	11-9, 6-0
1935	Wilmer Allison (USA)	David Jones (USA)	title shared
1936	Donald Budge (USA)	David Jones (USA)	6-4, 6-3
1937	Donald Budge (USA)	Bunny Austin	6-1, 6-2
1938	Bunny Austin	Kho Sin-Kie (Chn)	6-2, 6-0
1939	Gottfried von Cramm (Ger)	Ghaus Mohammed	6-1, 6-3
1940–45	No tournament held		
1946	Pancho Segura (USA)	Dinny Pails (Aus)	6-4, 0-6, 6-4
1947	Bob Falkenburg (USA)	Colin Long (Aus)	6-4, 7-5
1948	Bob Falkenburg (USA)	Eric Sturgess (SA)	title shared
1949	Ted Schroeder (USA)	Gardnar Mulloy (USA)	8-6, 6-0
1950	John Bromwich (Aus)	Art Larsen (USA)	6-2, 6-4
1951	Eric Sturgess (SA)	Frank Sedgman (Aus)	6-4, 5-7, 6-2
1952	Frank Sedgman (Aus)	Mervyn Rose (Aus)	10-8, 6-2
1953	Lew Hoad (Aus)	Ken Rosewall (Aus)	8-6, 10-8
1954	Lew Hoad (Aus)	Mervyn Rose (Aus)	8-6, 6-4
1955	Ken Rosewall (Aus)	Lew Hoad (Aus)	6-2, 6-3
1956	Neale Fraser (Aus)	Ken Rosewall (Aus)	7-5, 3-6, 9-7
1957	Ashley Cooper (Aus)	Neale Fraser (Aus)	6-8, 6-2, 6-3
1958	Malcolm Anderson (Aus)	Robert Mark (Aus)	1-6, 11-9, 6-3
1959	Ramanathan Krishnan (Ind)	Neale Fraser (Aus)	6-3, 6-0

1960	Andres Gimeno (Spn)	Roy Emerson (Aus)	8-6, 6-3
1961	Bob Hewitt (Aus)	Robert McKinley (USA)	6-2, 6-3
1962	Rod Laver (Aus)	Roy Emerson (Aus)	6-4, 7-5
1963	Roy Emerson (Aus)	Owen Davidson (Aus)	6-1, 6-2
1964	Roy Emerson (Aus)	Toomas Leius (USSR)	12-10, 6-4
1965	Roy Emerson (Aus)	Dennis Ralston (USA)	walkover
1966	Roy Emerson (Aus)	Tony Roche (Aus)	walkover
1967	John Newcombe (Aus)	Roger Taylor	7-5, 6-3
1968	Clark Graebner (USA)	Tom Okker (Ned)	title shared
1969	Fred Stolle (Aus)	John Newcombe (Aus)	6-3, 22-20
1970	Rod Laver (Aus)	John Newcombe (Aus)	6-4, 6-3
1971	Stan Smith (USA)	John Newcombe (Aus)	8-6, 6-3
1972	Jimmy Connors (USA)	John Paish	6-2, 6-3
1973	Ilie Nastase (Rom)	Roger Taylor	10-8, 6-3
1974–76	No tournament held		

Women's Singles

Year	Winner	Runner-up	Score
1881	M. Raikes	Miss Burleigh	5-0, 5-2
1882–83	No women's tournament held		
1884	Maud Watson	Edith Cole	6-4, 6-2, 2-6, 6-1
1885	Maud Watson	Lilian Watson	6-2, 6-3
1886	Blanche Bingley	Edith Davies	6-1, 6-1
1887	Blanche Bingley	B. James	6-4, 6-3
1888	Blanche Hillyard	May Jacks	6-4, 6-3
1889	May Jacks	Maud Shackle	6-2, 6-2
1890	May Jacks	Maud Shackle	6-2, 6-1
1891	Maud Shackle	May Jacks	6-2, 4-6, 6-3
1892	Edith Austin	Charlotte Cooper	6-4, 8-6
1893	Maud Shackle	Edith Austin	6-2, 6-1
1894	Edith Austin	Charlotte Cooper	8-6, 11-9
1895	Maud Shackle	Edith Austin	6-2, 7-5
1896	Charlotte Cooper	Agatha Templeman	6-3, 6-2
1897	Charlotte Cooper	Edith Austin	2-6, 6-2, 6-2
1898	Charlotte Cooper	Edith Austin	6-4, 3-6, 8-6
1899	Edith Austin	Charlotte Cooper	12-10, 2-6, 9-7
1900	Charlotte Cooper	Edith Greville	6-4, 6-1
1901	Edith Greville	Ethel Thomson	6-1, 6-1
1902	Charlotte Sterry	Ruth Durlacher	6-0, 6-0

1903	Agnes Morton	Edith Greville	6-4, 5-7, 6-0
1904	Agnes Morton	Ellen Stawell-Brown	6-2, 6-3
1905	Ethel Thomson	Edith Greville	6-3, 6-4
1906	Ethel Thomson	Mildred Coles	6-2, 6-1
1907	Violet Pinckney	Dorothea Lambert Chambers	2-6, 6-3, 6-4
1908	Violet Pinckney	Dorothea Lambert Chambers	6-3, 6-2
1909	Aurea Edgington	Madeline O'Neill	6-2, 1-6, 6-3
1910	Gladys Lamplough	Edith Johnson	6-2, 6-0
1911	Dorothea Lambert Chambers	Mildred Coles	6-2, 6-0
1912	Ethel Larcombe	Dorothy Holman	6-1, 6-0
1913	Ethel Larcombe	Aurea Edgington	6-2, 10-8
1914	Ethel Larcombe	Beryl Tulloch	6-1, 6-2
1915–18	No tournament held		
1919	Ethel Larcombe	Dorothy Holman	6-4, 8-6
1920	Dorothy Holman	Ethel Larcombe	walkover
1921	Mabel Clayton	Dorothy Holman	6-4, 8-6
1922	Mabel Clayton	Winifred Keays	6-3, 6-4
1923	Elizabeth Ryan (USA)	Geraldine Beamish	6-2, 1-6, 6-2
1924	Elizabeth Ryan (USA)	Doris Craddock	6-1, 6-1
1925	Elizabeth Ryan (USA)	Ermyntrude Harvey	6-0, 6-1
1926	Doris Kemmis-Betty	Eileen Bennett	7-5, 6-2
1927	Doris Kemmis-Betty	Enid Broadbridge	6-0, 6-1
1928	Joan Ridley	Helene Contostavios (Gre)	4-6, 6-1, 6-0
1929	Elizabeth Ryan (USA)	Elsie Goldsack	6-2, 2-6, 6-2
1930	Madge List	Margaret Stocks	6-1, 6-3
1931	Elsie Pittman	Kitty Godfree	9-7, 6-4
1932	Dorothy Burke (USA)	Jadwiga Jedrzejowska (Pol)	1-6, 7-5, 6-4
1933	Helen Wills Moody (USA)	Elsie Pittman	title shared
1934	Jacqueline Goldschmidt (Fra)	Dorothy Burke (USA)	5-7, 6-2, 6-0
1935	Anita Lizana (Chl)	Sylvie Henrotin (Fra)	title shared
1936	Jadwiga Jedrzejowska (Pol)	Susan Noel	6-2, 6-4
1937	Jadwiga Jedrzejowska (Pol)	Kay Stammers	6-3, 6-0
1938	Jadwiga Jedrzejowska (Pol)	Hilde Sperling (Ger/Den)	6-3, 6-0
1939	Jadwiga Jedrzejowska (Pol)	Hilde Sperling (Ger/Den)	6-1, 6-4
1940–45	No tournament held		
1946	Pauline Betz (USA)	Margaret Osborne (USA)	6-8, 6-3, 6-3
1947	Louise Brough (USA)	Margaret Osborne (USA)	6-4, 6-0
1948	Doris Hart (USA)	Margaret du Pont (USA)	title shared
1949	Louise Brough (USA)	Margaret du Pont (USA)	3-6, 6-1, 6-3

1950	Doris Hart (USA)	Margaret du Pont (USA)	4-6, 6-4, 6-4
1951	Shirley Fry (USA)	Nancy Chaffee (USA)	6-3, 8-6
1952	Hazel Redick-Smith (SA)	Elizabeth Wilford	7-5, 6-1
1953	Jean Rinkel-Quertier	Heather Nicholls (Ber)	6-1, 4-6, 6-2
1954	Louise Brough (USA)	Shirley Fry (USA)	6-1, 6-4
1955	Louise Brough (USA)	Jean Forbes (SA)	6-3, 6-1
1956	Angela Buxton	Pat Ward	6-4, 6-0
1957	Mimi Arnold (USA)	Suzie Kormoczy (Hun)	6-1, 5-7, 6-3
1958	Bernice Carr (SA)	Margaret Varner (USA)	6-4, 5-7, 8-6
1959	Yola Ramirez (Mex)	Christiane Mercelis (Bel)	2-6, 6-1, 6-3
1960	Christine Truman	Karen Susman (USA)	6-4, 6-3
1961	Margaret Smith (Aus)	Nancy Richey (USA)	6-0, 4-6, 6-2
1962	Rita Bentley	Lorna Cawthorn	7-5, 7-5
1963	Robyn Ebbern (Aus)	Rita Bentley	6-3, 6-3
1964	Margaret Smith (Aus)	Ann Jones	6-3, 6-2
1965	Annette Van Zyl (SA)	Christine Truman	6-3, 4-6, 6-4
1966	Francoise Durr (Fra)	Judy Tegart (Aus)	4-6, 6-3, 7-5
1967	Nancy Richey (USA)	Kerry Melville (Aus)	2-6, 6-2, 6-4
1968	Nancy Richey (USA)	Ann Jones	title shared
1969	Ann Jones	Winnie Shaw	6-0, 6-1
1970	Margaret Court (Aus)	Winnie Shaw	2-6, 8-6, 6-2
1971	Margaret Court (Aus)	Billie Jean King (USA)	6-3, 3-6, 6-3
1972	Chris Evert (USA)	Karen Krantzcke (Aus)	6-4, 6-0
1973	Olga Morozova (USSR)	Evonne Goolagong (Aus)	6-2, 6-3

The British Covered Court Championships

As pioneer of the new pastime of lawn tennis in the Victorian period, it was fitting that England should stage the world's first regular indoor (or 'covered', in the parlance of the day) tournament. The inaugural meeting of the BCCC was held in 1885 at the Hyde Park Club in Porchester Square, London, and consisted of men's singles only. The winner was the energetic Herbert Lawford, credited with developing topspin as standard in the forehand groundstroke.

When organisers looked to expand the meeting, introducing women's singles and men's doubles in 1890, Queen's was selected for these additional events on the basis of the extra capacity it provided;

the club's two inter-connected East and West Courts were opened in 1888. The men's singles, meanwhile, remained at Hyde Park for a decade until the tournament was consolidated into a single spring gathering at Queen's. The 1896 men's final in West Kensington saw a dramatic last-gasp win for Ernest Lewis, who beat Wilberforce Eaves despite temporarily collapsing when 5-1 ahead in the fifth set; he lost four games in a row, but then recovered to clinch victory 7-5.

UNDERRATED CHAMPION

Ernest Lewis won the Covered Court Championships seven times between 1887 and 1896 and belonged to that small band of players who – with better fortune – might have become Wimbledon champions and achieved greater lasting recognition. His pedigree was evident in his two triumphs in 1890 and 1981 at the highly competitive Irish Championships. Lewis took many of his opponents by surprise with his persistent use of the half-volley, especially on fast wooden courts such as those at Queen's. Players tended to resort to this shot when caught in the wrong position, with the ball dipping at their feet. But Lewis, gifted with tremendous hand-to-eye coordination, deliberately employed it as an attacking weapon, pushing opponents on to the defensive and enabling him to reach the net to put away winning volleys. There were those who, when seeing Lewis using the shot initially, thought it must have been unplanned or a fluke. But they soon realised it was a key ingredient of his strategy. On grass he employed the half-volley less frequently, knowing that the bounce was less reliable than indoors and therefore the margin for error higher. Even so, his record outdoors at Queen's was impressive: Lewis won the Grass Court Championships four times.

The entry for the BCCC was mixed in size and quality in the formative years, but its reputation soared as it increasingly attracted top amateurs keen to find good spring-time competition. Although beaten early in his career in the 1898 final (by Eaves, a three-time champion), the peerless Laurie Doherty took advantage of the challenge round provision in use to claim six successive men's titles between 1901 and 1906. The Doherty brothers won the men's doubles seven times and the elder sibling, Reginald, also triumphed in the mixed doubles – introduced in 1898 – on four occasions. On the women's side, four pre-1914 BCCC winers were also Wimbledon champions. The ultra-competitive Dorothea Lambert Chambers established what would be a women's record of seven victories; this might have been eight but for a sprained ankle that prevented her taking part in the challenge round in 1914.

The prestige of the meeting was further enhanced in the Edwardian period when overseas contenders began to challenge for honours, particularly in the men's singles. Anthony Wilding, the talented New Zealander, became the first winner from outside the UK in 1907, although he was surprisingly beaten in four sets by home-favourite Arthur Gore the following year. Until after the First World War, most leading lights from beyond Europe did not arrive to compete in England until the start of the summer grass-court season; Wilding was an exception, someone who studied and worked in the country. There were, however, rising numbers of entrants from the continent, especially from France, willing and able to make the short trip across the Channel to London. The men's final in 1912 was the first to be an all-overseas affair (see *Memorable Match* opposite).

Having witnessed many encounters featuring the world's best, as in the 1912 final, the long-time secretary at Queen's, E.B. Noel, claimed that the BCCC was the more important of the two annual meetings hosted by the club. It certainly got into its stride quickly after the Great War. The gathering of April 1919 was the first leading tournament staged in England after the end of hostilities, and the large crowds that flocked to Barons Court were once again treated to world-class tennis on home shores. Adding to his two pre-war wins,

MEMORABLE MATCH

The 1912 final was one of the most thrilling in the history of the Covered Court Championships. Three-time Wimbledon champion Tony Wilding, powerful and fluent in his all-court play, had not dropped a set en route to the final. His opponent there was young Frenchmen André Gobert, winner of the BCCC the previous year and an outstanding exponent of covered court tennis (in due course a five-time winner at Queen's). Gobert's serve was so strong that opponents were forced almost into the back netting to return it, and off the ground he generated fearsome pace from his exquisite timing. Wilding was the favourite having won when they last met, and for the first two sets he was in irresistible form, displaying a customary mix of fine attack and sound defence. Gobert's weakness was a sometimes suspect temperament, and Wilding may have miscalculated in thinking a 'safety first' approach would suffice to finish things off. But as he eased up slightly, the Frenchman's confidence grew. Gobert's deep drives and sharp volleying allowed him to level the match at two sets each. The packed gallery witnessed further twists and turns in the final set. Gobert squandered a 4-0 lead, and at 4-4 it looked as though Wilding had regained the initiative. Instead, the Frenchman took the next two games to retain his title amid loud cheering. He fully deserved his win, one reporter observed, by virtue of the variety of his shot-making, the penetration of his serving, and the 'enterprise and audacity of his generalship'.[7]

André Gobert claimed a hat-trick of victories; the last of these, in 1922, saw him beat South Africa's Brian Norton, despite travelling overnight from Paris and arriving in time for only the briefest of knock-ups. Dorothea Lambert Chambers demonstrated she was still a force to be reckoned with by triumphing in 1919, but the following year she retired on medical advice, thereby ensuring that the winner of the all-comers, California's Elizabeth Ryan, became the first overseas player to claim the women's singles.

The entry in 1923 (the year the challenge round was abolished) was felt to be the weakest for a while and there was concern that, on the women's side especially, top stars from outside Europe were reluctant to attend because of the spring timing. This prompted the first of what would be several switches of date. For several years the BCCC was moved to October, though without significantly altering the mostly all-British nature of the women's singles. Fortunately, renewed energy was injected into the BCCC by the regular appearance of the stylish Musketeer – and two-time Wimbledon champion – Jean Borotra. In 1928 the charismatic beret-wearing Frenchman, renowned for catching the eye of female spectators during play and bounding across the net at the conclusion of his matches, embarked on a six-year winning streak, emulating – without the benefit of often having to play only one challenge round match – the Edwardian record set by Laurie Doherty. The profile of the tournament benefited considerably from the duelling for several seasons between the 'Bounding Basque' and one of the rising stars of British tennis (and another figure with matinee idol looks), Bunny Austin.

By the end of the inter-war period, E.B. Noel's claim that the covered-court event was the superior of the two Queen's tournaments was more difficult to sustain. It could not, like the London Grass Court Championships, claim a string of Wimbledon champions (on the men's side) among its post-1918 winners. On the other hand, the BCCC remained distinctive – if no longer unique, following the start of the Wembley professional gathering in 1934 – in providing international-standard competition indoors. In 1934 women's doubles was added to the portfolio of individual titles contested, and the following year the LTA sanctioned the Barons Court meeting as one of its official championships; it was sometimes thereafter referred to as the National Covered Court Championships. This confirmed

THE WILY FRENCH CHAMPION

Between 1930 and 1934 Borotra and Austin played out three long, close indoor finals at Queen's. The French crowd-pleaser deployed his acrobatic volleying skills to edge the first of these in five sets, and repeated the feat in 1933, but only after a controversial ending. Austin looked to be cruising to the title at 4-0 in the deciding set, at which point his exhausted-looking opponent fell over bending for a low volley. After crashing into the net post, the Frenchman lay prone on the court amid gasps from the crowd. Austin rushed to help Borotra to his seat, where – unusually for that era – he was allowed to recuperate quietly for several minutes. The Englishman thought an imminent retirement was on the cards, but instead Borotra not only returned to the court but claimed the point on a technicality. The Englishman conceded, thinking that victory was close. Instead, he never won another game. The wily old champion was revitalised and transformed, capturing 12 of the last 14 points. Austin, it seems, resolved not to be fooled again. The following year he won 6-2 in the decider to break Borotra's stranglehold on the title.

its place as the acknowledged indoor leg of a trio of senior English tournaments held on different surfaces during the 1930s, alongside Wimbledon and the hard-court championships held annually in Bournemouth.[8]

Partly as a result of bomb damage in Palliser Road during the Second World War, the BCCC had to wait until 1947 to resume, but it then gave every appearance of picking up where it left off. Despite controversy surrounding his wartime activities, Jean Borotra was as popular as ever among spectators when he returned to claim his tenth and 11th titles at Queen's in 1948 and 1949; at the latter point he was aged 51, the oldest winner of a men's singles title at any of the tournaments featured in this book. After losing in three successive finals, Surrey's Geoff Paish got his hands on the trophy in 1951 (a year when he also won the men's and mixed doubles), but he was the only British winner of the men's event in ten years. The Borotra ascendancy was replaced by a spell of dominance by another global star, grand slam-winning Jaroslav Drobny, whose swinging left-hand serve was well suited to the green-stained wooden courts in West Kensington, where he triumphed four years out of five in the first half of the 1950s.

Behind the scenes, however, all was not well. Indeed, the BCCC was among the first of the frontline meetings discussed in these pages to experience a notable fall from grace, declining both in its strength of entry and its reputation. At the heart of the problem was the need to adapt to circumstances in which top amateurs could more easily travel across the world than in the past. In choosing what tournaments to attend (and which, in consequence, drew large crowds and remained profitable), star players were influenced by the extent to which generous expenses were on offer, often contravening the limits specified in amateur regulations. As breaches of the rules rose year-on-year, with organisers desperate to attract the crème de la crème, the BCCC suffered; the LTA was extremely wary of being accused of supporting one of its official championships with expenses in excess of the International Lawn Tennis Federation (ILTF) rules. Another cause of malaise was that tennis fans looking for an alternative autumn meeting to patronise in the capital turned in increasing numbers to the London Professional at Wembley, which during the late 1950s featured many of the acknowledged legends of the men's game.

In the face of such challenges, Queen's was unable to stage the BCCC in 1957. When it resumed, and in the years that followed, the number of overseas contenders dwindled markedly, leaving the tournament mostly as the preserve of established or aspiring British competitors. Angela Mortimer, having secured a hat-trick of women's singles titles from 1952 to 1954, repeated the feat between 1959 and 1961; in each of her six finals her opponents were home-based.

The men's event became mainly a showcase for those looking to burnish their Davis Cup credentials. Bobby Wilson was a four-time champion between 1959 and 1965 and also lost in two further finals in that period. He was beaten in 1964 by Mike Sangster, who said a break of serve in the first game of the match gave him an important psychological edge. Sangster admitted this was a rare indoor victory for him over Wilson, whom he described as 'the uncrowned king of British covered court tennis'.[9]

In the mid-1960s attempts were made to breathe new life into the BCCC, but to little avail. The LTA offered subsidies to make it financially viable; additional indoor facilities were provided; and further changes of timing were introduced, from autumn to spring and vice versa. But attendances remained low other than for finals and a decision was made not to go ahead in 1966, the second cancellation within a decade. Such was the diminished status of the tournament that the following year the LTA – despite negotiating reasonable terms with sponsors and securing approval for TV coverage – still struggled to attract international stars. Tennis commentator Jimmy Jones, who long before warned of the 'slow death' of the BCCC, pointed out that the need for generous expenses to draw in leading names from overseas had never been faced. In the view of Jones, 'The appeal of London in February at only £5 per day plus travel expenses was simply non-existent.'[10] With top British players also absent, training and competing in warmer climes abroad, the tournament committee had no option but to scrap the meeting again.

After dormancy for a couple of years, the BCCC returned in 1968 as part of the Dewar Cup indoor initiative (discussed in more detail in chapter 10). But there was to be no fairytale revival. Although a three-year sponsorship deal was in due course agreed with Wills, critics argued that, in the unfolding Open era, facilities for indoor competition at Queen's were outdated and in desperate need of modernisation. It was agreed that the 1969 meeting would start in West Kensington and then relocate to Wembley Arena for finals, and this proved a prelude – for the remainder of the Wills-sponsored years – to a full relocation which saw Wembley rather than Queen's as the setting for leading professionals to ply their trade. Australian legend Rod Laver claimed the rebranded Embassy Championships twice (and was narrowly denied a trio of wins when defeated by Ilie Nastase in 1971), and his achievement was matched on the women's side by Billie Jean King, who triumphed in 1970 and 1971. The following year, when leading men attached to the influential World Championship Tennis (WCT) group of professionals were contracted to play elsewhere, Wills declined to provide any further sponsorship and the Covered Court Championships – once the flagship of the tournament portfolio at Queen's – finally lost its rearguard battle for survival.

RECORD BREAKERS: BCCC

Most titles – Men: Jean Borotra (11), Ernest Lewis (7), Laurence Doherty (6), André Gobert (5), Jaroslav Drobny (4), Bobby Wilson (4)

Most titles – Women: Dorothea Lambert Chambers (7 – twice as Dorothea Douglass), Angela Mortimer (6), Edith Austin (5), Dorothy Holman (4), Ann Jones (4 – once as Ann Haydon)

Number of Covered Court champions who also won Wimbledon singles

Men: 7; Women: 9; Total: 16

British Covered Court Championships

Men's Singles

Year	Winner	Runner-up	Score
1885	Herbert Lawford	Charles Ross	7-5, 6-3, 6-0
1886	Teddy Williams	Herbert Lawford	6-2, 1-6, 5-7, 6-4, 6-4
1887	Ernest Lewis	Teddy Williams	6-2, 6-2, 6-1
1888	Ernest Lewis	Ernest Meers	6-3, 6-0, 6-0
1889	Ernest Lewis	James Crispe	6-1, 6-1, 6-1
1890	Ernest Lewis	Ernest Meers	6-2, 6-3, 6-2

1891	Ernest Lewis	Ernest Meers	6-4, 8-6, 6-3
1892	Ernest Meers	Ernest Lewis	6-3, 3-6, 6-1, 6-2
1893	Harold Mahony	Ernest Meers	6-2, 6-2, 6-4
1894	Harold Mahony	Ernest Meers	6-4, 6-4, 6-3
1895	Ernest Lewis	Wilberforce Eaves	8-6, 7-5, 6-3
1896	Ernest Lewis	Wilberforce Eaves	6-4, 6-1, 6-8, 4-6, 7-5
1897	Wilberforce Eaves	Ernest Lewis	6-3, 6-3, 7-5
1898	Wilberforce Eaves	Laurence Doherty	6-4, 7-5, 6-3
1899	Wilberforce Eaves	Harold Mahony	6-2, 6-4, 6-8, 3-6, 6-4
1900	Arthur Gore	Major Ritchie	6-1, 7-5, 6-3
1901	Laurence Doherty	Arthur Gore	6-3, 6-1, 6-1
1902	Laurence Doherty	Major Ritchie	6-4, 6-3, 5-7, 6-3
1903	Laurence Doherty	George Hillyard	6-1, 4-6, 6-4, 6-2
1904	Laurence Doherty	Major Ritchie	6-2, 8-10, 5-7, 6-4, 6-3
1905	Laurence Doherty	Major Ritchie	6-1, 8-6, 6-2
1906	Laurence Doherty	Arthur Gore	6-2, 6-4, 8-6
1907	Anthony Wilding (NZ)	George Carida	6-2, 6-3, 6-2
1908	Arthur Gore	Anthony Wilding (NZ)	4-6, 8-6, 6-0, 8-6
1909	Major Ritchie	Arthur Gore	7-5, 8-6, 6-3
1910	Gordon Lowe	Arthur Lowe	6-4, 6-0, 6-1
1911	André Gobert (Fra)	Gordon Lowe	6-3, 7-5, 6-3
1912	André Gobert (Fra)	Anthony Wilding (NZ)	3-6, 5-7, 6-4, 6-4, 6-4
1913	Percival Davson	Erik Larsen (Den)	5-7, 6-2, 6-3, 6-2
1914	Major Ritchie	Percival Davson	8-6, 6-3, 6-1
1915–18	No tournament held		
1919	Percival Davson	Major Ritchie	6-2, 6-3, 8-6
1920	André Gobert (Fra)	Percival Davson	6-4, 7-5, 6-2
1921	André Gobert (Fra)	Walter Crawley	6-2, 6-4, 4-6, 0-6, 7-5
1922	André Gobert (Fra)	Brian Norton (SA)	4-6, 6-1, 6-8, 6-4, 6-2
1923	Patrick Wheatley	Hassan Ali Fyzee (Ind)	1-6, 6-2, 6-4, 6-4
1924	Patrick Spence (SA)	Patrick Wheatley	6-2, 6-2, 4-6, 6-1
1925	Sydney Jacob	Patrick Spence (SA)	3-6, 7-5, 6-0, 3-6, 6-3
1926	Jean Borotra (Fra)	Donald Greig	6-3, 6-2, 6-4
1927	Edward Higgs	Gordon Crole-Rees	6-4, 6-3, 6-4
1928	Jean Borotra (Fra)	Gordon Crole-Rees	4-6, 6-1, 6-2, 6-3
1929	Jean Borotra (Fra)	Nigel Sharpe	7-5, 6-2, 6-2
1930	Jean Borotra (Fra)	Bunny Austin	6-1, 0-6, 2-6, 6-2, 6-4
1931	Jean Borotra (Fra)	Jiro Satoh (Jpn)	10-8, 6-3, 0-6, 6-3

1932	Jean Borotra (Fra)	Harry Lee	6-2, 6-3, 6-3
1933	Jean Borotra (Fra)	Bunny Austin	6-3, 5-7, 6-4, 1-6, 6-4
1934	Bunny Austin	Jean Borotra (Fra)	6-2, 4-6, 6-0, 6-8, 6-2
1935	Jean Borotra (Fra)	Nigel Sharpe	6-0, 6-2, 6-0
1936	Karl Schroeder (Swe)	Jean Borotra (Fra)	8-6, 6-1, 9-7
1937	Bunny Austin	Karl Schroeder (Swe)	6-2, 3-6, 7-5, 6-2
1938	Jean Borotra (Fra)	Don Butler	6-0, 4-6, 6-4, 6-2
1939–46	No tournament held		
1947	Ivo Rinkel (Ned)	Ernest Wittman (Pol)	3-6, 7-5, 7-5
1948	Jean Borotra (Fra)	Geoff Paish	6-3, 6-3, 6-2
1949	Jean Borotra (Fra)	Geoff Paish	6-4, 6-3, 6-3
1950	Jaroslav Drobny (Egy)	Geoff Paish	6-3, 6-2, 6-0
1951	Geoff Paish	Ignacy Tloczynski (Pol)	6-4, 6-4, 6-1
1952	Jaroslav Drobny (Egy)	Tony Mottram	6-3, 6-4, 8-6
1953	Jaroslav Drobny (Egy)	Bobby Wilson	6-2, 7-5, 6-2
1954	Jaroslav Drobny (Egy)	Wladyslaw Skonecki (Pol)	7-5, 7-5, 7-9, 6-4
1955	Wladyslaw Skonecki (Pol)	Billy Knight	5-7, 7-5, 6-4, 9-7
1956	Alfred Huber (Aut)	Geoff Paish	7-5, 7-5, 7-9, 6-4
1957	No tournament held		
1958	Mike Davies	Sven Davidson (Swe)	5-7, 6-1, 6-2, 6-2
1959	Bobby Wilson	Kurt Nielsen (Den)	6-3, 8-6, 6-2
1960	Billy Knight	Bobby Wilson	6-3, 6-4, 8-6
1961	Tony Pickard	Manuel Santana (Spa)	6-1, 6-3, 6-3
1962	Bobby Wilson	Billy Knight	3-6, 6-3, 8-6, 2-6, 6-2
1963	Bobby Wilson	Roger Taylor	16-14, 6-2, 9-7
1964	Mike Sangster	Bobby Wilson	6-3, 8-6, 6-4
1965	Bobby Wilson	Mark Cox	6-3, 3-6, 6-3, 6-4
1966–67	No tournament held		
1968	Bob Hewitt (SA)	Robert Lutz (USA)	4-6, 6-2, 6-4, 10-8
1969	Rod Laver (Aus)	Tony Roche (Aus)	6-4, 6-1, 6-3
1970	Rod Laver (Aus)	Cliff Richey (USA)	6-3, 6-4, 7-5
1971	Ilie Nastase (Rom)	Rod Laver (Aus)	3-6, 6-3, 3-6, 6-4, 6-4

Women's Singles

Year	Winner	Runner-up	Score
1890	May Jacks	Maud Shackle	6-0, 6-1
1891	Maud Shackle	May Jacks	7-5, 6-2
1892	Maud Shackle	May Arbuthnot	6-3, 3-6, 6-2

1893	Maud Shackle	May Arbuthnot	6-2, 1-6, 7-5
1894	Edith Austin	May Arbuthnot	2-6, 6-4, 7-5
1895	Charlotte Cooper	Edith Austin	6-4, 3-6, 6-1
1896	Edith Austin	Charlotte Cooper	6-2, 3-6, 6-3
1897	Edith Austin	Ruth Dyas	9-11, 6-4, 12-10
1898	Edith Austin	Ruth Pennington-Legh	6-3, 2-6, 6-2
1899	Edith Austin	Charlotte Cooper	6-2, 6-4
1900	Toupie Lowther	Edith Greville	2-6, 7-5, 6-4
1901	Blanche Hillyard	Toupie Lowther	6-2, 6-3
1902	Toupie Lowther	Blanche Duddell	6-3, 6-1
1903	Toupie Lowther	Adine Masson (Fra)	6-1, 6-0
1904	Dorothea Douglass	Edith Greville	6-2, 6-3
1905	Hilda Lane	Gladys Eastlake-Smith	6-4, 8-6
1906	Dorothea Douglass	Hilda Lane	6-2, 6-0
1907	Gladys Eastlake-Smith	Mildred Coles	6-3, 6-3
1908	Dorothea Lambert Chambers	Gladys Eastlake-Smith	6-3, 6-3
1909	Dora Boothby	Madeline O'Neill	6-1, 6-3
1910	Dorothea Lambert Chambers	Madeline O'Neill	6-4, 6-3
1911	Dorothea Lambert Chambers	Helen Aitchison	6-3, 6-1
1912	Dorothy Holman	Aurea Edgington	6-2, 6-0
1913	Dorothea Lambert Chambers	Dorothy Holman	6-2, 6-3
1914	Dorothy Holman	Dorothea Lambert Chambers	walkover
1915–18	No tournament held		
1919	Dorothea Lambert Chambers	Dorothy Holman	6-3, 6-3
1920	Elizabeth Ryan (USA)	Dorothea Lambert Chambers	walkover
1921	Dorothy Holman	Irene Peacock (SA)	6-1, 3-6, 6-4
1922	Dorothy Holman	Doris Craddock	6-2, 6-1
1923	Mabel Clayton	Aurea Edgington	6-3, 6-2
1924	Geraldine Beamish	Doris Craddock	6-4, 6-4
1925	Joan Reid-Thomas	Blanche Colston	6-2, 7-5
1926	Peggy Saunders	Betty Dix	6-4, 6-2
1927	Eileen Bennett	Cristobel Hardie	6-4, 6-0
1928	Kitty Godfree	Eileen Bennett	6-1, 6-2
1929	Peggy Michell	Joan Ridley	6-4, 6-4
1930	Joan Ridley	Joan Fry	6-2, 6-2
1931	Mary Heeley	Jeanette Morfey	6-1, 6-0
1932	Peggy Scriven	Kay Stammers	6-2, 6-4
1933	Phyllis King	Kay Stammers	10-12, 6-1, 6-3

1934	Phyllis King	Mary Hardwick	6-3, 4-6, 6-2
1935	Peggy Scriven	Ermyntrude Harvey	6-2, 6-2
1936	Anita Lizana (Chl)	Mary Hardwick	6-3, 6-0
1937	Peggy Scriven	Phyllis King	6-1, 6-2
1938	Peggy Scriven	Alexandra McKelvie	6-3, 4-6, 6-1
1939–46	No tournament held		
1947	Gem Hoahing	Peggy Dawson-Scott	8-6, 6-3
1948	Gem Hoahing	Joan Curry	1-6, 6-3, 7-5
1949	Joan Curry	Jean Quertier	6-1, 6-0
1950	Jean Quertier	Joan Curry	3-6, 7-5, 6-3
1951	Susan Partridge	Jean Walker-Smith	6-4, 6-4
1952	Angela Mortimer	Susan Partridge	6-3, 3-6, 6-3
1953	Angela Mortimer	Georgie Woodgate	6-3, 6-2
1954	Angela Mortimer	Shirley Bloomer	6-2, 6-3
1955	Anne Shilcock	Pat Ward	6-2, 6-4
1956	Angela Buxton	Anne Shilcock	6-2, 6-2
1957	No tournament held		
1958	Anne Shilcock	Christine Truman	6-2, 6-2
1959	Angela Mortimer	Pat Ward	6-2, 6-3
1960	Angela Mortimer	Ann Haydon	7-5 retd
1961	Angela Mortimer	Christine Truman	2-6, 6-1, 6-4
1962	Ann Haydon	Christine Truman	6-4, 4-6, 9-7
1963	Deidre Catt	Renee Schuurman (SA)	4-6, 6-3, 6-3
1964	Ann Jones	Fay Toyne (Aus)	6-3, 6-3
1965	Ann Jones	Fay Toyne (Aus)	6-2, 6-1
1966–67	No tournament held		
1968	Margaret Court (Aus)	Virginia Wade	10-8, 6-1
1969	Ann Jones	Billie Jean King (USA)	9-11, 6-2, 9-7
1970	Billie Jean King (USA)	Ann Jones	8-6, 3-6, 6-1
1971	Billie Jean King (USA)	Francoise Durr (Fra)	6-1, 5-7, 7-5

The Grass Court Championships since the 1970s

The demise of the BCCC, combined with the uncertainty facing the Grass Court Championships, meant the future for world-class tennis at Queen's Club looked perilous in the mid-1970s. Unable to offer a showcase summer meeting for three successive seasons, between

1974 and 1976, club chairman Clive Bernstein worked tirelessly to find a sponsor generous enough to ensure top players would attend and with enough clout to ensure Queen's would be included as part of the Grand Prix, the generic name used in the early Open era for the top-tier circuit below the grand slams. Bernstein – with backing from the LTA – eventually secured his goal (courtesy of Rawlings, the soft drinks section of Whitbread Brewery), allowing a men's event to return in 1977. The tournament was not an unbridled success. Many leading stars were absent and poor weather took its toll on attendances. But the sponsors were happy enough to support the gathering for another year; the renamed Queen's Club Championship was back in business.

The next couple of years proved crucial in catapulting Queen's from near oblivion to the top of the pre-Wimbledon tournament tree. A shift in start date to earlier in June meant the revived meeting quickly established a firm sense of identity; more a top-drawer event in its own right, rather than, as in the case of the earlier London Championships, last-minute practice before moving on to SW19. In 1978, the BBC, looking to expand its summer tennis portfolio, began regular coverage from Queen's, thereby significantly raising the profile of the club and the tournament. The following year a substantial, long-term sponsorship deal was secured, helping to ensure that the Stella Artois Championships became embedded within the men's Grand Prix circuit. Finally, although Bjorn Borg never competed, the Stella – as many called it – found favour with household-name performers who kept the turnstiles ticking over and the TV viewers watching in large numbers. The stand-out figure in this regard was the immensely talented but controversial John McEnroe, who first reached the final in 1978, where he was narrowly beaten by Australia's Tony Roche.

As a result of a mixture of hard graft and good fortune, Queen's was therefore able to establish itself in the 1980s as *the* key pre-Wimbledon men's warm-up tournament – a position it has not since relinquished – although not without some further bumps in the road. The weather in the following few years was frequently disruptive and occasioned grumbling from players and also broadcasters looking to fill their schedules. On court, the early 1980s witnessed some fine-quality tennis as well as renewed ructions (the latter welcomed by much of the media, which regarded it as good box office). Despite winning three times in succession, John McEnroe's volatile temper was never far from the surface. His hat-trick of wins was secured in 1981 when, in the process of beating fellow American Brian Gottfried in straight sets, McEnroe spent much time sniping about the positioning of a linesman. Gottfried, not best pleased, told him to stop baiting the female umpire and questioning so many line calls.

In 1982 and 1983 McEnroe accepted defeat in the final quite calmly, by his standards, both times losing to his great rival Jimmy Connors, another leading crowd-puller in his own right. In 1984 the top three world-ranked men – Connors, McEnroe and Lendl – all competed at the Stella Artois, and the tournament's profile was sharpened by fresh uproar. Lendl, having beaten McEnroe at the French Open days before to win his first grand slam title, lost in the first round to American Leif Shiras, who despite being outside the world top 100 worked his way through one side of the draw to reach the final. McEnroe, putting the setback in Paris behind him, beat Connors in the last four to reach his seventh final in a row at Queen's. He easily won the first set against Shiras, but then at 4-1 down in the second he exploded after the umpire overruled a line call, leading to a lengthy delay during which the American called the official a 'moron'. McEnroe lost the set but recovered to win in three; front as well as back-page headlines the following day were again dominated by discussion of the New Yorker's antics.

In 1985 – when McEnroe stayed away prior to Wimbledon, citing media 'harassment' – the spotlight fortuitously fell on another big tennis personality, 17-year-old West German Boris Becker. The talented newcomer stole the show by storming through to become the youngest man to take the Stella title, a feat he repeated in SW19 a few weeks later. With club membership at a record high and tournament profits soaring, Queen's went from strength to strength. Becker went on to triumph four times, and was followed on the winner's rostrum by a string of fellow grand slam champions including Lendl, Edberg, Stich and Sampras.

The roll call of illustrious victors continued between 2000 and 2007 when Lleyton Hewitt and Andy Roddick matched McEnroe's record by each winning four times. Roddick praised the grass surface at Queen's as possibly the best in the world and, for good measure, he sent down in 2004 what was then a world record for the fastest serve, timed at 153mph.

A final factor underpinning the rise and rise of the Stella Artois (after 2009 the Aegon, and currently the Fever-Tree) Championships was the sustained level of British interest. Tim Henman came close in three finals between 1999 and 2002, but was thwarted by Pete Sampras and by Lleyton Hewitt (twice). Andy Murray burst into public consciousness when, as an 18-year-old newly turned professional, he memorably won through two rounds at Queen's in 2005. When he lifted the trophy four years later, beating America's James Blake in the final, he became the first home man to do so since Bunny Austin in 1938. Murray proceeded to claim the title five times over eight years. His win over Canada's Milos Raonic in 2016 meant he became the only man in the history of the famous event thus far – stretching all the way back to its original form in the 1880s – to become a five-time singles champion. The capacity crowd at Queen's cheered Murray more loudly than ever when, after hip surgery and agonisingly long spells out through injury, he returned to West Kensington in 2019 to win the men's doubles alongside his Spanish partner (and winner of the singles that year), Feliciano Lopez.

RECORD BREAKERS: GRASS COURT CHAMPIONSHIPS SINCE 1881

Most titles – Men: Andy Murray (5), Ernest Lewis (4), Harry Barlow (4), Major Ritchie (4), Anthony Wilding (4), Roy Emerson (4), John McEnroe (4), Boris Becker (4), Lleyton Hewitt (4), Andy Roddick (4)

Most titles – Women: Ethel Larcombe (6 – twice as Ethel Thomson), Charlotte Sterry (5 – four as Charlotte Cooper), Edith Greville (4 – three as Edith Austin), Elizabeth Ryan (4), Jadwiga Jedrzejowska (4), Louise Brough (4), Margaret Court (4 – twice as Margaret Smith)

Number of Grass Court/Queen's champions who also won Wimbledon singles

Men: 23 (1881–1973), 8 (1977–2020); Women: 13; Total: 44

Queen's Grass Court Championships

Year	Winner	Runner-up	Score
1977	Raul Ramirez (Mex)	Mark Cox	9-7, 7-5
1978	Tony Roche (Aus)	John McEnroe (USA)	8-6, 9-7
1979	John McEnroe (USA)	Victor Pecci (Par)	6-7, 6-1, 6-1
1980	John McEnroe (USA)	Kim Warwick (Aus)	6-3, 6-1
1981	John McEnroe (USA)	Brian Gottfried (USA)	7-6, 7-5
1982	Jimmy Connors (USA)	John McEnroe (USA)	7-5, 6-3
1983	Jimmy Connors (USA)	John McEnroe (USA)	6-3, 6-3
1984	John McEnroe (USA)	Leif Shiras (USA)	6-1, 3-6, 6-2
1985	Boris Becker (WG)	Johan Kriek (USA)	6-2, 6-3
1986	Tim Mayotte (USA)	Jimmy Connors (USA)	6-4, 2-1 retd
1987	Boris Becker (WG)	Jimmy Connors (USA)	6-7, 6-3, 6-4
1988	Boris Becker (WG)	Stefan Edberg (Swe)	6-1, 3-6, 6-3
1989	Ivan Lendl (Czh)	Christo van Rensburg (SA)	4-6, 6-3, 6-4
1990	Ivan Lendl (Czh)	Boris Becker (WG)	6-3, 6-2
1991	Stefan Edberg (Swe)	David Wheaton (USA)	6-2, 6-3
1992	Wayne Ferreira (SA)	Shuzo Matsuoka (Jpn)	6-3, 6-4
1993	Michael Stich (Ger)	Wayne Ferreira (SA)	6-3, 6-4

1994	Todd Martin (USA)	Pete Sampras (USA)	7-6, 7-6
1995	Pete Sampras (USA)	Guy Forget (Fra)	7-6, 7-6
1996	Boris Becker (Ger)	Stefan Edberg (Swe)	6-4, 7-6
1997	Mark Philippoussis (Aus)	Goran Ivanisevic (Cro)	7-5, 6-3
1998	Scott Draper (Aus)	Laurence Tieleman (Ita)	7-6, 6-4
1999	Pete Sampras (USA)	Tim Henman	6-7, 6-4, 7-6
2000	Lleyton Hewitt (Aus)	Pete Sampras (USA)	6-4, 6-4
2001	Lleyton Hewitt (Aus)	Tim Henman	7-6, 7-6
2002	Lleyton Hewitt (Aus)	Tim Henman	4-6, 6-1, 6-4
2003	Andy Roddick (USA)	Sebastien Grosjean (Fra)	6-3, 6-3
2004	Andy Roddick (USA)	Sebastien Grosjean (Fra)	7-6, 6-4
2005	Andy Roddick (USA)	Ivo Karlovic (Cro)	7-6, 7-6
2006	Lleyton Hewitt (Aus)	James Blake (USA)	6-4, 6-4
2007	Andy Roddick (USA)	Nicolas Mahut (Fra)	4-6, 7-6, 7-6
2008	Rafael Nadal (Spn)	Novak Djokovic (Srb)	7-6, 7-5
2009	Andy Murray	James Blake (USA)	7-5, 6-4
2010	Sam Querrey (USA)	Mardy Fish (USA)	7-6, 7-5
2011	Andy Murray	Jo-Wilfried Tsonga (Fra)	3-6, 7-6, 6-4
2012	Marin Cilic (Cro)	David Nalbandian (Arg)	6-7, 4-3 default
2013	Andy Murray	Marin Cilic (Cro)	5-7, 7-5, 6-3
2014	Grigor Dimitrov (Bul)	Feliciano Lopez (Spn)	6-7, 7-6, 7-6
2015	Andy Murray	Kevin Anderson (SA)	6-3, 6-4
2016	Andy Murray	Milos Raonic (Can)	6-7, 6-4, 6-3
2017	Feliciano Lopez (Spn)	Marin Cilic (Cro)	4-6, 7-6, 7-6
2018	Marin Cilic (Cro)	Novak Djokovic (Srb)	5-7, 7-6, 6-3
2019	Feliciano Lopez (Spn)	Gilles Simon (Fra)	6-2, 6-7, 7-6
2020	No tournament held		

2

Surbiton

ALTHOUGH THE best known, Queen's is far from being the only home to what the LTA calls 'world-class tennis' in London outside of Wimbledon. The fledgling game of lawn tennis expanded and thrived in the middle-class suburbs of the capital and so it comes as no surprise that leading clubs within a few miles of central London became closely associated with the rise of tournament play from Victorian times onwards. Whereas indoor meetings such as the British Covered Court Championships at Queen's tended to base themselves in central parts of the metropolis (see chapter 10 for discussion of other indoor venues such as the O2 Arena), suburban and outer London has been the site of several high-profile outdoor events, some now defunct but others still thriving as modern variants of tournaments going back to the earliest years of the sport.

North of the River Thames, distinguished entry lists were common at tournaments staged at Harpenden (30 miles or so out of London, in Hertfordshire) and at clubs such as Cumberland in Hampstead and Connaught in Chingford. But the lion's share of top gatherings traditionally took place south of the river. Fred Burrow observed of his long years refereeing before and after the First World War that it was a curious feature of London tournaments that elite players flocked to meetings south of the city centre but were not 'nearly so eager to go a little to the north'.[1] Burrow was at a loss to explain this trend, saying that transport links were equally good both sides of the river. Whatever the cause, his view was borne out by the number of high-quality meetings that regularly took place during his era in the historic counties of Surrey and Kent, including at the likes of Epsom (won by charismatic New Zealander Tony Wilding in 1906), Sutton, Roehampton and Blackheath.

While the fortunes of many such events – as elsewhere in the country – tended to wax and wane, two tournaments south of the Thames stand out in terms of longevity and renown. In the next chapter the focus will be on Beckenham in Kent, which for decades occupied a central place in the pre-Wimbledon schedule. But here, as we begin working outwards from central London on our journey nationwide around key tennis venues, the spotlight falls on a gathering which was long regarded as the first important tournament of the English grass-court season: at Surbiton, formerly in Surrey and now in the Greater London Borough of Kingston upon Thames, just a few miles to the south-west of the All England Club.

The Surrey Grass Court Championships

The inaugural meeting of what was initially called the Surrey Counties tournament took place not in Surbiton but at Old Deer Park in Richmond. Some 400 competitors entered in June 1890 for 11 events including open singles for men and women and a range of handicaps. Despite some heavy rain during the week, the courts were in good shape for finals, 'a false bound being rarely observable'.[2] These were the words of the weekly publication *The Field*, sub-titled *The Country Gentlemen's Newspaper*, which provided the most extensive coverage of English tournaments prior to much of the national and regional press assuming greater interest in lawn tennis in the Edwardian era. In the most entertaining match of the finals day in 1890 Harry Barlow won the men's singles, overcoming Wilfred Baddeley, later to be a three-time Wimbledon champion. A second tournament was held at the same venue in 1892, again won by Barlow, but it was not until almost a decade later that the Surrey Championships became more firmly established.[3]

The long-term home for the tournament turned out to be Surbiton Lawn Tennis Club, founded originally in 1881 as the Berrylands Club. With about ten grass courts on a narrow strip of land in the leafy residential area surrounding Berrylands Road, the club boasted a steadily rising membership, helping to facilitate the construction of a handsome new pavilion around the turn of the century.[4] *The Field* reported that Surbiton had previously hosted gatherings restricted to local or county-only entrants, but in 1900 it 'blossomed forth into a full-blown open tournament'.[5] The donation of challenge cups meant the main prize on offer became known as the Surrey Grass Court Championships, won in 1900 by two 'cracks' of the day, Charles Dixon and Charlotte Cooper. The latter was a club member at Surbiton, and her ties with the area were reinforced a generation later when her daughter, Gwen Sterry, took the singles title in 1932.

Being close to central London and easily accessible by train, and with play taking place on a 'half-day' basis (starting in the afternoon and continuing until early evening), the Surrey Championships quickly built in popularity and esteem. The main honours in the Edwardian era went to some of the best British players of the time. Charlotte Cooper, Mrs Sterry after her marriage in 1901, became a five-time winner, and – in an indication of the high standard of the women's competition – she was joined before 1914 by three other Wimbledon champions, each of whom won at Surbiton in the same year as triumphing in SW19: Dora Boothby (1909), Ethel Larcombe (1912) and Dorothea Lambert Chambers (1914).

On the men's side, two players featured strongly, each claiming five titles. Charles Dixon, a two-time winner of the men's doubles at Wimbledon, used his strong volleying to good effect on the fast grass at Berrylands, notably when he beat the odds-on favourite Anthony Wilding in the 1911 final. Major J.G. Ritchie, a stylish all-court player who claimed multiple titles at home and abroad (and who came within a set of taking the Wimbledon crown in 1909), won the singles at Surbiton for three years in succession from 1908 to 1910. Each of his victories was hard earned, over – respectively – Wimbledon champion Arthur Gore, Dixon, after a tough five-setter, and Canadian newcomer Robert Powell.

SURPRISE DEFEATS

A huge crowd gathered at Surbiton in 1911, many drawn by the prospect of seeing the reigning Wimbledon champion, Tony Wilding, contest the singles final. The stylish New Zealander, considered one of the sport's first superstars, was a strong favourite to lift the Surrey title, but he was badly affected on the day by a knee injury and was beaten in four sets by Charles Dixon. Although he was in due course to win Wimbledon four times, Wilding never claimed the Surrey title despite reaching the final twice. Five years before he lost to Dixon, in 1906, he proceeded serenely to the final without dropping a set, and was due to face Sydney Smith. But the timing of the match clashed with his commitment to meeting his parents as they arrived for a visit from New Zealand. He also qualified for the men's doubles final and the tournament committee remained hopeful to the last moment that he might turn up at least for the singles. Wilding, however, was not to be moved and scratched from both events. In the words of The Field's correspondent, 'What should have been two splendid matches came to nought – a very great disappointment all round.'[6]

Surbiton's burgeoning reputation as the acknowledged curtain-raiser of the English grass-court season – taking place each year in the second half of May, sometimes tipping into early June – helped to attract growing numbers of overseas competitors in the run-up to the First World War, especially on the men's side. By 1910 contenders included not only Canadians such as finalist Robert Powell but also South Africans, New Zealanders, Americans, Germans and Indians, and in 1914 Australia's Norman Brookes became the first winner from outside the UK, beating Gordon Lowe in the men's final. The meeting of May 1919 had the distinction of being the first premier grass-court tournament held in England after the war, and featured its most distinguished entry list yet. The dynamic left-handed Aussie Gerald Patterson swept to victory, a feat he was to repeat at Wimbledon a few weeks later.

GOING UP IN SMOKE

As well as witnessing the unexpected defeat of Tony Wilding, the Surbiton crowd in 1911 was treated to a moment of high drama in the men's doubles final. Early in the match a spectator seated close to courtside carelessly threw away a match (smoking among the crowd being permissible in those times). This promptly set fire to the green canvas surround behind the umpire's chair. The four finalists all rushed forward to help, and one of them, Herbert Roper Barrett, swiftly took the initiative by picking up the tall glass of brandy and soda belonging to his partner, Arthur Gore. Barrett poured all the contents over the small fire, dousing it fully. Gore, however, looked none too pleased at the disappearance of his chosen brand of liquid refreshment, and the crowd responded by roaring with laughter. It wasn't really Barrett and Gore's day: they lost the final in a long five-setter.

The early years after the Great War marked, with hindsight, a pinnacle for the Surrey Championships in terms of drawing some of the world's very best to Berrylands. South African Brian 'Babe' Norton took the men's title in 1921 and almost matched Gerald Patterson's triumph shortly afterwards in SW19. Norton had match points against Bill Tilden in the Wimbledon final that summer but eventually lost in five sets. On the women's side, American Elizabeth Ryan set a record by becoming a six-time winner at Surbiton, culminating in a closely contested three-set victory over Britain's Wimbledon champion Kitty McKane in 1925. This, in the view of the *Illustrated Sporting and Dramatic News*, was the best ladies final yet seen at Berrylands, a further instalment in the struggle between the two stars for supremacy 'in these islands'.[7]

For the remainder of the inter-war period, Surbiton continued to hold its own. Top amateurs, some of whom barely competed in the winter months, enjoyed the chance to get together in congenial surroundings in south-west London and to get their new grass-court season under way. But the tournament also encountered challenges and difficulties. After club officials agreed to take over additional ground for new courts, necessary to help cope with larger entry numbers than hitherto, the weather made some unwelcome interventions. A period of unusually dry conditions made the bounce on the newly laid grass unreliable and several players, allocated to the new courts in the early rounds, were forthright in their criticism. At the other meteorological extreme, the meeting then suffered a run of overcast, damp summers; heavy rain forced the abandonment of finals in 1931 and 1933.

The Surbiton club also lost members during the economic depression of the early 1930s and had to fall back on support from the local district council, which bought the land and leased it back to the club.[8] These factors, combined with sharper competition from other venues at home and abroad as tennis expanded globally, took their toll. The Surrey Championships retained an international flavour, but now found it harder to attract grand slam contenders as in former times, particularly on the men's side. Winners of the men's singles in the 1930s were a mixture of young British aspirants and strong but not world-beating overseas players, often from newly emerging tennis nations. Four players from Asia lifted the trophy during the decade, starting with Japan's Yoshiro Ohta, who in 1930 beat the up-and-coming 21-year-old Fred Perry in three tight sets.

UNDERRATED CHAMPION

The British number two during the first half of the 1950s (behind similarly underrated Tony Mottram, winner of five of the tournaments featured in these pages) was Geoff Paish. Born in Croydon in 1922 and a stalwart of Surrey tennis – he became a leading county administrator after his playing days were over – Paish served in the RAF during the Second World War before combining a civil service career with tournament play as circumstances allowed. In view of his work commitments, and the fact that amateur competition was in abeyance while he was in his mid-20s because of the war, Paish had a respectable record at top-level events. His best result at Surbiton came in 1948 when he shared the title (after rain intervened) with Australia's John Bromwich, but elsewhere he won the British Covered Court title at Queen's in 1951 and triumphed five times in succession at the South of England Championships in Eastbourne. According to one tennis journalist, Paish managed all this – as well as regularly turning out for Britain in the Davis Cup - without – because of his work routines – being able to devote the time necessary to 'hit world-class'.[9]

On the other hand, Surbiton was able to boast consistently strong entries on the women's side during the mid-to-late 1930s. Whereas Gerald Patterson in 1919 became the third and last man to win both the Surrey Championships and Wimbledon, the number of women who achieved that sought-after double was much higher in the long run, 13 altogether including both finalists in the abandoned 1954 final. Ahead of the outbreak of the Second World War, Dorothy Round defeated Chile's Anita Lizana at Berrylands in 1936 (one of several close encounters between these two on English soil), and Helen Wills Moody triumphed in 1938 a few weeks ahead of claiming her eighth and final Wimbledon crown. Another American star, reigning US champion Alice Marble, also contested the Surbiton final in 1937, but was surprisingly beaten by Freda James.

After 1945 the elevated standard of women's competition remained a notable feature of the Surrey Championships. Among the new generation of grand slam champions from across the Atlantic, Maureen Connolly triumphed at Surbiton in 1952, Shirley Fry and Doris Hart shared the honours when rain intervened in 1954, and Althea Gibson won three finals in a row (1956–58) without dropping a set. Britain's post-war Wimbledon champions also made their mark at Surbiton. The first of Angela Mortimer's two titles, in 1960, came after she and arch rival Christine Truman fought out a fluctuating three-set final, the Devon woman coming through 9-7 in the decider. Ann Jones was also a two-time victor, on both occasions beating American opponents in the final, Carole Caldwell in 1964 and Patti Hogan in 1970.

Having undertaken improvements to the infrastructure of the site in the 1950s (and increasing the number of grass courts further to around 20), Surbiton was well placed initially to adapt to the arrival of Open tennis. The tournament became part of the elite-level Grand Prix circuit for a while, and the roll of honour in the 1970s included some fine world-ranked players: Owen Davidson, Peter McNamara and Brian Gottfried among the men; Wendy Turnbull, Sue Barker and Evonne Cawley in the women's event. But organisers found, as was common elsewhere, that securing and maintaining the high-grade sponsorship required to offer attractive prize money was far from easy. No meeting was possible in 1976 and by the start of the 1980s Surbiton found that – for the moment at least – it could no longer command a slot in the condensed, crowded pre-Wimbledon grass-court schedule.

RECORD BREAKERS

Most titles – Men: Charles Dixon (5), Major Ritchie (5), Sydney Smith (3), Roger Becker (3)
Most titles – Women: Elizabeth Ryan (6), Charlotte Sterry (5 – one as Charlotte Cooper), Althea Gibson (3)
Number of Surrey Grass Court champions who also won Wimbledon singles
Men: 3; Women: 13; Total: 16

Surrey Grass Court Championships

Men's Singles

Year	Winner	Runner-up	Score
1890	Harry Barlow	Wilfred Baddeley	5-7, 6-3, 7-5, 6-2
1891	No tournament held		
1892	Harry Barlow	Horace Chapman	6-2, 6-2, 6-1
1893–99	No tournament held		
1900	Charles Dixon	Major Ritchie	6-3, 1-6, 6-3, 6-2
1901	Charles Dixon	Philip Pearson	walkover
1902	Major Ritchie	David Hawes	6-1, 6-0
1903	Major Ritchie	Charles Finlason	6-1, 6-3, 6-4
1904	Sydney Smith	Major Ritchie	6-3, 6-3, 6-3
1905	Sydney Smith	Edward Allen	6-2, 6-3, 6-1
1906	Sydney Smith	Anthony Wilding (NZ)	walkover
1907	Arthur Gore	Major Ritchie	6-3, 6-2, 6-3
1908	Major Ritchie	Arthur Gore	6-3, 6-4, 6-2
1909	Major Ritchie	Charles Dixon	4-6, 6-2, 6-4, 0-6, 6-4
1910	Major Ritchie	Robert Powell (Can)	6-3, 6-1, 2-6, 6-3
1911	Charles Dixon	Anthony Wilding (NZ)	7-5, 3-6, 6-0, 6-1
1912	Charles Dixon	Major Ritchie	6-2, 6-2, 6-3
1913	Charles Dixon	Theodore Mavrogordato	6-2, 8-6, 6-3
1914	Norman Brookes (Aus)	Gordon Lowe	6-1, 6-1, 5-7, 6-8, 6-3
1915–18	No tournament held		
1919	Gerald Patterson (Aus)	Herbert Roper Barrett	6-2, 6-3, 6-2
1920	Frank Fisher (NZ)	Theodore Mavrogordato	6-4, 6-4, 6-1
1921	Brian Norton (SA)	Sydney Jacob	6-2, 6-2, 6-3
1922	Brian Norton (SA)	Randolph Lycett (Aus)	9-7, 7-5, 1-6, 6-1

1923	Randolph Lycett (Aus)	Brian Norton (SA)	3-6, 6-4, 6-1, 2-6, 7-5
1924	Jack Hillyard	Henry Mayes (Can)	6-4, 1-6, 10-12, 6-3, 6-2
1925	Gordon Crole-Rees	Athar Ali-Fyzee (Ind)	3-6, 7-5, 3-6, 6-2, 6-4
1926	Charles Kingsley	Gordon Crole-Rees	6-4, 6-2 retd
1927	Gordon Crole-Rees	Nigel Sharpe	6-1, 6-0
1928	Henry Mayes (Can)	Patrick Spence (SA)	6-2, 6-4
1929	Eric Peters	Oswald Turnbull	3-6, 6-1, 6-1, 6-3
1930	Yoshiro Ohta (Jpn)	Fred Perry	6-3, 4-6, 6-3
1931	Iwao Aoki (Jpn)	Harry Lee	title shared
1932	Nigel Sharpe	Iwao Aoki (Jpn)	7-5, 6-3
1933	David Williams	Herman David	title shared
1934	Jiro Yamagishi (Jpn)	Hideo Nishimura (Jpn)	6-3, 6-3
1935	Buster Andrews (NZ)	Patrick Spence (SA)	6-2, 6-3
1936	Cam Malfroy (NZ)	Harry Lee	6-2, 9-11, 6-0
1937	Robert Tinkler	Pat Sherwood	9-7, 6-3
1938	John Olliff	Eric Filby	2-6, 6-4, 6-3
1939	Kho Sin-Kie (Chn)	Jack Doloford	6-2, 6-4
1940–45	No tournament held		
1946	Hans van Swol (Ned)	David Butler	4-6, 6-4, 7-5
1947	Claude Lister	Marcel Coen (Egy)	7-5, 6-2
1948	John Bromwich (Aus)	Geoff Paish	title shared
1949	Czeslaw Spychala (Pol)	Geoff Paish	6-3, 6-0
1950	Narendra Nath (Ind)	Czeslaw Spychala (Pol)	6-2, 6-4
1951	Czeslaw Spychala (Pol)	David Samaai (SA)	1-6, 7-5, 6-3
1952	Ian Ayre (Aus)	Bryan Woodroffe (SA)	6-4, 6-2
1953	George Worthington (Aus)	Roger Becker	6-3, 6-1
1954	John Barry (NZ)	Abe Segal (SA)	title shared
1955	Mal Anderson (Aus)	Ramanathan Krishnan (Ind)	6-3, 6-4
1956	Ian Vermaak (SA)	Gordon Forbes (SA)	6-4, 6-3
1957	Roger Becker	Alan Mills	7-9, 6-2, 6-3
1958	Roger Becker	Mike Davies	4-6, 6-2, 6-2
1959	Mike Davies	Warren Jacques (Aus)	9-7, 6-2
1960	Roger Becker	Keith Diepraam (SA)	6-4, 6-1
1961	Marty Mulligan (Aus)	Warren Jacques (Aus)	9-7, 6-2
1962	Marty Mulligan (Aus)	Mark Otway (NZ)	6-3, 6-4
1963	Roger Taylor	Jaidip Mukerjea (Ind)	10-8, 9-11, 10-8
1964	David Phillips (SA)	Bob Carmichael (Aus)	2-6, 6-4, 8-6
1965	Jan-Erik Lundqvist (Swe)	Roger Taylor	9-7, 6-3

1966	Keith Wooldridge	Peter Curtis	7-5, 6-4
1967	Roger Taylor	Bobby Wilson	2-6, 6-4, 6-2
1968	Keith Wooldridge	Ken Fletcher (Aus)	3-6, 6-3, 7-5
1969	Gerald Battrick	John Cooper (Aus)	6-2, 6-1
1970	Robert Maud (SA)	Frew McMillan (SA)	6-4, 6-3
1971	Anand Amritraj (Ind)	Paul Hutchins	6-2, 6-2
1972	Premjit Lall (Ind)	Ross Case (Aus)	6-4, 8-6
1973	Owen Davidson (Aus)	Tony Roche (Aus)	4-6, 6-4, 10-8
1974	Bob Giltinan (Aus)	Syd Ball (Aus)	6-3, 6-2
1975	Peter McNamara (Aus)	Steve Docherty (Aus)	4-6, 9-8, 6-4
1976	No tournament held		
1977	Peter Lawlor (Ire)	Chris Wells	4-6, 6-3, 8-6
1978	David Lloyd	Willie Davies	6-4, 6-7, 6-5
1979	Victor Amaya (USA)	Mark Edmondson (Aus)	6-4, 7-5
1980	Brian Gottfried (USA)	Sandy Meyer (USA)	6-3, 6-3

Women's Singles

Year	Winner	Runner-up	Score
1890	May Arbuthnot	Elizabeth Mocatta	6-2, 6-2
1891	No tournament held		
1892	May Arbuthnot	Ivy Arbuthnot	6-3, 6-1
1893–99	No tournament held		
1900	Charlotte Cooper	Ellen Evered	6-2, 6-2
1901	Charlotte Sterry	Edith Bromfield	6-1, 6-3
1902	Charlotte Sterry	Agnes Morton	6-3, 6-3
1903	Toupie Lowther	Edith Bromfield	3-6, 6-1, 6-3
1904	Connie Wilson	Ellen Stawell-Brown	6-4, 7-5
1905	Connie Wilson	Agnes Morton	6-2, 6-0
1906	Toupie Lowther	Dora Boothby	5-7, 6-4, 8-6
1907	Charlotte Sterry	Dorothea Lambert Chambers	6-4, 6-3
1908	Alice Greene	Charlotte Sterry	3-6, 6-2, 6-2
1909	Dora Boothby	Edith Johnson	6-0, 6-4
1910	Dora Boothby	Agnes Morton	6-3, 6-3
1911	Helen Aitchison	Agnes Morton	6-3, 6-4
1912	Ethel Larcombe	Dora Boothby	7-5, 6-3
1913	Charlotte Sterry	Madeline O'Neill	8-6, 6-1
1914	Dorothea Lambert Chambers	Ethel Larcombe	6-3, 2-6, 6-4
1915–18	No tournament held		

1919	Elizabeth Ryan (USA)	Dorothea Lambert Chambers	walkover
1920	Dorothea Lambert Chambers	Elizabeth Ryan (USA)	6-4, 6-2
1921	Elizabeth Ryan (USA)	Dorothy Holman	6-0, 6-0
1922	Elizabeth Ryan (USA)	Irene Peacock (SA)	10-8, 6-2
1923	Elizabeth Ryan (USA)	Eleanor Rose	3-6, 6-3, 6-2
1924	Elizabeth Ryan (USA)	Aurea Edgington	6-3, 6-4
1925	Elizabeth Ryan (USA)	Kitty McKane	7-9, 6-1, 6-3
1926	Joan Fry	Phoebe Watson	3-6, 6-1, 6-2
1927	Bobbie Heine (SA)	Irene Peacock (SA)	1-6, 6-3, 7-5
1928	Elsie Goldsack	Joan Ridley	6-4, 6-2
1929	Betty Nuthall	Elizabeth Ryan (USA)	7-5, 6-1
1930	Jenny Sandison (Ind)	Betty Nuthall	3-6, 7-5, 6-4
1931	Dorothy Jameson	Joan Lycett	title shared
1932	Gwen Sterry	Peggy Saunders Michell	7-5, 6-4
1933	Peggy Michell	Elsie Pittman	title shared
1934	Elsie Pittman	Patricia Brazier	6-3, 6-3
1935	Joan Hartigan (Aus)	Phyllis Mudford King	6-4, 6-3
1936	Dorothy Round	Anita Lizana (Chl)	6-2, 6-3
1937	Freda James	Alice Marble (USA)	6-4, 6-3
1938	Helen Wills Moody (USA)	Margot Lumb	6-3, 6-4
1939	Mary Hardwick	Margot Lumb	6-4, 6-4
1940–45	No tournament held		
1946	Kay Menzies	Gay Chandler	6-4, 6-3
1947	Kay Menzies	Joan Curry	6-4, 6-3
1948	Joan Curry	Jean Walker-Smith	title shared
1949	Patricia Todd	Jean Walker-Smith	6-3, 9-7
1950	Jean Walker-Smith	Jean Quertier	6-2, 7-5
1951	Helen Fletcher	Joan Curry	6-3, 6-1
1952	Maureen Connolly (USA)	Patricia Todd (USA)	3-6, 6-3, 6-4
1953	Patricia Ward	Shirley Bloomer	6-2, 6-3
1954	Shirley Fry (USA)	Doris Hart (USA)	title shared
1955	Rosemary Walsh	Daphne Seeney (Aus)	6-4, 7-5
1956	Althea Gibson (USA)	Anne Shilcock	6-3, 13-11
1957	Althea Gibson (USA)	Thelma Long (Aus)	8-6, 7-5
1958	Althea Gibson (USA)	Mimi Arnold (USA)	6-1, 6-0
1959	Sally Moore	Ann Haydon	6-4, 6-2
1960	Angela Mortimer	Christine Truman	3-6, 6-4, 9-7
1961	Deidre Catt	Edda Buding (WG)	5-7, 6-3, 7-5

1962	Angela Mortimer	Carole Caldwell (USA)	6-4, 6-4
1963	Deidre Catt	Darlene Hard (USA)	1-6, 9-7, 8-6
1964	Ann Jones	Carole Caldwell (USA)	6-3, 6-1
1965	Christine Truman	Rita Bentley	7-5, 6-1
1966	Winnie Shaw	Mary-Ann Eisel (USA)	6-4, 4-6, 6-3
1967	Lynn Abbess (USA)	Robin Blakelock-Lloyd	6-4, 6-3
1968	Judy Tegart (Aus)	Christine Truman	10-8, 6-4
1969	Mary-Ann Curtis (USA)	Judy Tegart (Aus)	4-6, 6-4, 8-6
1970	Ann Jones	Patti Hogan (USA)	2-6, 6-3, 6-4
1971	Judy Tegart-Dalton (Aus)	Joyce Barclay	9-8, 6-2
1972	Joyce Williams	Patti Hogan (USA)	6-4, 6-3
1973	Wendy Turnbull (Aus)	Ann Kiyomura (USA)	6-2, 6-0
1974	Sue Barker	Sue Mappin	6-2, 7-5
1975	Greer Stevens (SA)	Patti Hogan (USA)	6-1, 6-4
1976	No tournament held		
1977	Winnie Shaw	Gwen Sammel (SA)	6-3, 7-6
1978	Evonne Cawley (Aus)	Winnie Wooldridge	6-1, 6-1
1979	Cynthia Doerner-Seiler (Aus)	Kym Ruddell (Aus)	6-1, 6-2
1980	No tournament held		
1981	Betsy Nagelsen (USA)	Barbara Hallquist (USA)	6-4, 3-6, 6-3

The Surbiton Trophy

Unlike a number of the gatherings examined in later chapters (including at fellow suburban London venue, Beckenham), Surbiton made a comeback. Following a successful men's exhibition held in 1997, the Surbiton Rackets and Fitness Club – as it was by then called – again became the setting for regular international-standard tennis.

The reconstituted Surbiton Trophy quickly became a well-regarded event in the pre-Wimbledon calendar, popular with a new generation of players from around the world, many attracted by the welcoming and informal atmosphere cultivated by tournament organisers.

Good crowds routinely turned out to watch, if not the grand slam champions of the moment, then quality performers and some up-and-coming megastars of the future. In 1999 the 17-year-old Roger

Federer made his senior professional grass-court debut at Surbiton, falling at the semi-final stage.

LONG DRAWN-OUT

Back in 1975 an unusual record was set in a first-round tournament encounter at Surbiton between Surrey county player Keith Glass and his Rhodesian opponent A.G. Fawcett. The opening exchanges were nip and tuck, and after a tie-break the British player took the first set. Glass was serving at 3-1 down in the second when the match got stuck in a rut. Neither player could finish the game off as they moved from deuce to advantage and back again, over and over. The umpire called 'deuce' 37 times before the deadlock was broken; Glass heaved a sigh of relief as he finally held serve. In contrast to the speed of some entire matches (particularly before players could sit down at change of ends), in this instance a single game took 31 minutes, spanning 80 individual points. The episode appeared, however, to have had a draining effect on the local man. Tony Fawcett thereafter took control of proceedings, easily winning the second and deciding sets to march into the next round. Speaking afterwards, the winner was convinced the historic deuce game won him the match. His opponent, he said, was finished after that.

In the early years of the 21st century, although it was sometimes referred to as 'the warm-up to the warm-up'[10] (the latter, by this point in time, alluding to Queen's as the most important precursor to Wimbledon), the Surbiton Trophy was claimed by some well-known stars of the game. Winners of the men's singles included top-ten world-ranked players such as American Mardy Fish (2006) and France's Jo-Wilfried Tsonga (2007). After a further five-year hiatus between 2009 and 2014, when a shake-up of the calendar saw the LTA give priority to the concurrent meeting at Nottingham, high-level competitive play resumed in 2015 when Surbiton again became part of the lower tier Challenger tour for men and the International

Tennis Federation (ITF) circuit for women. In 2019, Dan Evans, who also won at Nottingham that summer, grabbed the headlines by becoming the first British man to lift the modern Surbiton Trophy; by doing so, he emulated the achievement of another Birmingham-based player, Louise Latimer, who won the women's singles at the turn of the century.

Surbiton Trophy

Men's Singles

Year	Winner	Runner-up	Score
1998	Gianluca Pozzi (Ita)	Kevin Ullyet (Zim)	6-4, 6-3
1999	Sargis Sargsian (Arm)	Martin Damm (CR)	7-6, 7-5
2000	Wayne Arthurs (Aus)	Laurence Tieleman (Ita)	4-6, 7-6, 6-4
2001	Taylor Dent (USA)	Neville Godwin (SA)	4-6, 7-6, 6-2
2002	Jeff Morrison (USA)	Wesley Moodie (SA)	7-6, 5-7, 7-6
2003	Wesley Moodie (SA)	Alex Bogdanovic	6-4, 6-7, 6-1
2004	Karol Beck (Slo)	Wesley Moodie (SA)	6-4, 6-4
2005	Daniele Bracciali (Ita)	Ivo Karlovic (Cro)	6-7, 7-6, 7-6
2006	Mardy Fish (USA)	Wesley Moodie (SA)	6-2, 7-6
2007	Jo-Wilfried Tsonga (Fra)	Ivo Karlovic (Cro)	6-3, 7-6
2008	Frank Dancevic (Can)	Kevin Anderson (SA)	4-6, 6-3, 7-6
2009–14	No tournament held		
2015	Matthew Ebden (Aus)	Denis Kudla (USA)	6-7, 6-4, 7-6
2016	Lu Yen-hsun (Tai)	Marius Copil (Rom)	7-5, 7-6
2017	Yuichi Sugita (Jpn)	Jordan Thompson (Aus)	7-6, 7-6
2018	Jeremy Chardy (Fra)	Alex de Minaur (Aus)	6-4, 4-6, 6-2
2019	Dan Evans	Victor Troicki (Srb)	6-2, 6-3
2020	No tournament held		

Women's Singles

Year	Winner	Runner-up	Score
1997	Tamarine Tanasugarn (Tha)	Aleksandra Olsza (Pol)	5-7, 7-6, 5-0 retd
1998	Amelie Cocheteux (Fra)	Seda Noorlander (Ned)	6-2, 6-4
1999	Tamarine Tanasugarn (Tha)	Surina de Beer (SA)	6-4, 5-7, 6-2
2000	Louise Latimer	Tamarine Tanasugarn (Tha)	7-5, 6-3
2001	Rika Fujiwara (Jpn)	Kristina Brandi (PR)	6-3, 6-3

2002	Janet Lee (Tai)	Laura Granville (USA)	4-6, 6-4, 6-4
2003	Kristina Brandi (PR)	Cho Yoon-Jeong (SK)	6-1, 6-3
2004	Akiko Morigami (Jpn)	Anna Chakvetadze (Rus)	6-4, 1-6, 6-1
2005	Kristina Brandi (PR)	Laura Granville (USA)	6-3, 6-1
2006	Kristina Brandi (PR)	Laura Granville (USA)	7-5, 6-0
2007	Brenda Schultz-McCarthy (Ned)	Ayumi Morita (Jpn)	4-6, 6-4, 7-6
2008	Marina Erakovic (NZ)	Anne Keothavong	6-4, 6-2
2009–14	No tournament held		
2015	Vitalia Diatchenko (Rus)	Naomi Osaka (Jpn)	7-6, 6-0
2016	Marina Melnikova (Rus)	Stephanie Foretz (Fra)	6-3, 7-6
2017	Magdalena Rybarikova (Slo)	Heather Watson	6-4, 7-5
2018	Alison Riske (USA)	Conny Perrin (Sui)	6-2, 6-4
2019	Alison Riske (USA)	Magdalena Rybarikova (Slo)	6-7, 6-2, 6-2
2020	No tournament held		

3

Beckenham

THE KENT All-Comers' Championships has several claims to fame. In 1963 the meeting became the first tournament in Britain to be sponsored, by tobacco company Rothmans, following a loosening of rules by the LTA. Five years later, in the wake of the decision to introduce Open tennis, Beckenham was the venue for the world's first grass-court tournament in which amateurs and professionals could compete against each other (as distinct from the groundbreaking hard-court meeting held a couple of months earlier, at Bournemouth). Another landmark moment came in 1972 when the men's and women's events were won by Alex Metreveli and Olga Morozova respectively: the first time two Russians had captured singles titles at the same frontline British tournament.

More broadly, across a long time frame, Beckenham held an exalted place in the English summer season. For much of its 110-year existence, from 1886 to 1996, it was the Kent All-Comers – more so than the likes of the pre-Open London Grass Court Championships at Queen's – that was regarded as special by players, officials and spectators alike. It was Beckenham that was routinely referred to as *the* 'dress rehearsal for Wimbledon'.[1]

How did Beckenham acquire such elevated status? The answer lies partly in the attractive setting of the tournament. Situated in an affluent suburb south of the River Thames, Beckenham was referred to by *The Field* as one of the 'prettiest spots devoted to sports in the London district'.[2] A cricket club had been founded in Foxgrove Road in 1866, and when tennis courts were laid out on adjoining land some years later the Beckenham Cricket and Tennis Club came into existence. In terms of accessibility, the club was only a few hundred yards from Beckenham Junction train and tram stations, providing speedy links to central London and beyond. This helped to ensure that large crowds flocked to Foxgrove Road after the club hosted the first Kent All-Comers' event in 1886, giving organisers the benefit of gate receipts that were the envy of many tournament committees elsewhere. Saturdays in particular at Beckenham, when finals took place, developed a reputation as a significant social/sporting day out, drawing fashionable society in sufficiently large numbers to draw comparisons with other prominent summer occasions such as racing at Ascot or the Eton versus Harrow cricket match at Lord's.

Beckenham also had familiarity and stability in its favour. Unlike many comparable meetings in their infancy, it had a name that was recognisable and unchanging from the outset; the Kent All-Comers' Championships was adopted in the first instance to avoid confusion with the Kent Championships, the latter confined to county players only, which took place for many years at nearby Blackheath. Also in contrast to other tournaments – Queen's, we have seen, falls into this category, being initially held at Stamford Bridge – Beckenham remained constantly at one venue, its appeal enhanced by the construction around 1896 of a stylish timber-framed pavilion (still in existence today as a Grade II-listed building).

The All-Comers further benefited from a settled and coveted place in the tennis calendar. Whereas the timing of several tournaments shifted or took years to find a suitable niche, Beckenham almost always took place a fortnight before Wimbledon. This in itself was a major draw for the top players of the day. Home 'cracks', and later overseas stars when they started arriving in larger numbers, were equally keen to adjust to the surface and the weather conditions in the knowledge that their grass-court skills would soon be put to the test in SW19. Most were determined not to miss the 'dress rehearsal'.

LONG DRAWN-OUT

The inaugural men's singles final at Beckenham, in June 1886, has sometimes been described as a 'tedious' affair. Both protagonists, Herbert Chipp – who later became secretary of the LTA – and Edward Avory, a member of the club's tournament committee, camped on the baseline and engaged in numerous long rallies. After the first four sets were shared, the ambidextrous Chipp got the upper hand in the decider, coming through 6-3 to take the title. The tone of reporting in The Field, however, did not give the impression that the large crowd was bored by proceedings. All week, it insisted, spectators had enjoyed close encounters, and the men's finale was no different; the match was described as 'protracted' (rather than 'tedious') and culminated in an 'exciting finish'.[3] The losing finalist remained a club stalwart for the rest of his life. He was in attendance almost half a century later to watch the All-Comers' title being won in 1932 by his grandson – E.R. (Ted) Avory.

The ability of Beckenham to attract the world's best, both men and women, was evident from early on in its history. In the first 15 years the entry lists regularly featured the Renshaw brothers – who often confined themselves to the men's doubles, though William Renshaw was a losing finalist in the singles in 1893 – and also the Baddeleys, residents of nearby Bromley. These illustrious siblings were followed by the Dohertys; Laurie Doherty took the singles title three years in succession as he entered his era of primacy on the global stage. American competitors arrived for the first time in 1898 to add an international dimension and their numbers increased steadily during the Edwardian period. In 1905 rising Australian star Norman Brookes became the first overseas winner, although his victory over Arthur Gore did not take place at Foxgrove Road.

Finals day was badly disrupted by thunderstorms, and it was agreed that the challenge round (in place at the Kent All-Comers until 1911) would be held during the Wimbledon fortnight. Brookes duly claimed the Beckenham title without dropping a set.

In the run-up to the First World War the men's entry at Foxgrove Road was often as strong as found at Wimbledon shortly afterwards. Most serious contenders for individual honours in SW19 had arrived in town, and the quality and depth of the draw at Beckenham was also enhanced by the appearance of national squads from countries such as South Africa and Canada, due to compete in Davis Cup fixtures on English soil. Local newspapers were therefore not exaggerating when they claimed in 1910 that the 'pick of the lawn tennis world' had arrived on their doorstep.[4] All the stars in the firmament could be found on display at Beckenham, it was claimed, as was underlined when the men's title went to Beals Wright, a former winner of the US National Championships.

IN A HURRY

In 1914 the final of the men's doubles at Beckenham was over in a flash. The formidable Australasian pairing of Norman Brookes and Tony Wilding, neither of whom competed in the singles that year, thrashed the usually competitive home combination of Arthur Gore and Herbert Roper Barrett. The match was timed (in an era with no sit down at change of ends) as lasting for just 16 and a half minutes. Many spectators went off for tea, assuming they could return to watch some good tennis later, only to find when they got back that the players had finished and left the court.

On the women's side, although a handicap event was arranged for a couple of years when the meeting started, it was not until 1888, following the donation of a challenge cup, that the first open singles took place. In a small entry of 11, Fulham resident May Jacks beat Edith Gurney of Staines to become the inaugural champion. For some while, the women's event was dominated by two further local players, Maud Shackle (four-time winner) and Edith Austin (six-time champion), and it was only around the turn of the century that the intensity of the competition rose sharply. Austin's ascendancy was interrupted in 1898 with a three-set defeat at the hands of Charlotte Cooper, the first of four Beckenham champions before 1914 who also triumphed at Wimbledon. The formidable Dorothea Douglass had a particular liking for Foxgrove Road, where the intimate setting allowed spectators to get close up to legends of the sport. In 1901 Miss Douglass beat Edith Greville (formerly Miss Austin) 6-4 in the deciding set; this was the first of four wins in six years.

It was just months after marriage in 1907 that Dorothea, as Mrs Lambert Chambers, experienced her most serious setback at the Kent All-Comers, losing to her arch American rival May Sutton. Unlike in the men's game, few leading women travelled the globe in search of honours before the Great War, but Miss Sutton was an exception, having burst on the scene to claim the Wimbledon crown in 1905. One newspaper reported that Mrs Lambert Chambers was 'not at her best' in the 1907 Beckenham final;[5] it came at a time when she was taking a break from her usual routine of intensive practice. Whatever the reason, the American was able to deploy to good effect her powerful topspin forehand (accompanied by regular loud grunts, still at that time unusual in women's tennis), beating her opponent in straight sets – a feat she repeated at Wimbledon a couple of weeks later. Marriage and defeat in 1907 had little impact on the stranglehold Dorothea exercised at Beckenham during the Edwardian era. Her relentless accuracy and fierce desire to win carried her to three further titles; the three-setter against Austin in 1901 was the only time in her seven victorious finals that she dropped a set.

Two players dominated proceedings for several years when the Kent All-Comers resumed after the war: Britain's Algernon Kingscote and American Elizabeth Ryan (each discussed in more detail as *Underrated Champions*, below and in chapter 7). As record crowds gathered, both were involved in high-quality finals in 1919. Kingscote prevailed against New Zealand's Frank Fisher, each man having chances to win a hard-fought five-setter, while Miss Ryan won a see-saw encounter against Mrs Lambert Chambers, still a tough competitor at the age of 40. Fred Burrow, referee at Beckenham from 1912 to the mid-1930s, described the latter clash as one of the best finals he ever witnessed. During the thrilling climax, he recalled, the spectators were 'almost beside themselves with excitement'.[6] The following year Saturday's showcase proceedings were disrupted by a prolonged downpour. Kingscote was fortunate that his opponent, Japanese newcomer Shimidzu, sportingly retired despite being only one set down when the storm burst. As the women's finalists never got on court, Ryan shared the honours with Winifred McNair.

UNDERRATED CHAMPION

The record for the most titles won at Beckenham in men's singles (six) is held by the relatively obscure figure of Algernon Kingscote. Decorated with the Military Cross for distinguished service on the Western Front, 'Algy' Kingscote won the Kent All-Comers' Championships four times in a row after the First World War. Despite being over 30 by this point, and regularly confronted with younger, swifter opponents, Kingscote's tactical awareness and good all-court game enabled him to carry the flag for British tennis with understated distinction. Shortly after his success at Beckenham in 1919, he reached the All-Comers' final at Wimbledon, where he lost to eventual champion Gerald Patterson. As well as winning the Australasian Championships, in 1920 Kingscote retained his Beckenham title before being the only man to take Bill Tilden to five sets, as the great American advanced to the first of his three Wimbledon crowns. In 1924, when Kingscote recorded his final victory at Beckenham, he also won the London Grass Court Championships.

The exceptionally high standard of play seen at Beckenham dipped slightly on the men's side for a while, but not by much. American 'Little Bill' Johnston was the only man between the wars to achieve the Kent-Wimbledon double (in 1923), and several of the men's finals were all-British affairs rather than featuring overseas contenders. In 1930 Britain's two future world stars, Bunny Austin and Fred Perry, were both to the fore. Perry, still a raw talent at that point, lost in the semi-final to the holder, Harold Lee, who in turn had no answer to the more accomplished strokeplay of Austin, who was also to win a second Beckenham title in 1934. Perry had to be content in 1930 with winning the men's and the mixed doubles, the latter with Miss Ryan – one of the large number of doubles wins she accumulated at the venue alongside her singles titles (11 in the women's doubles alone).

In the women's event, the entry at Beckenham continued to have a strong international flavour, although this varied in alternate years for a specific reason. The venue for the Anglo-American Wightman Cup fixture switched between the competing nations every year. When the USA hosted on home soil, the cup was contested in August, but when held in England it tended to coincide with the Kent All-Comers. Although this restricted the availability of top players from the two nations concerned, the honours board at Beckenham during the inter-war period still featured several of the world's very best. In addition to Elizabeth Ryan, overseas winners included Spain's Lili de Alvarez, Anita Lizana of Chile, Poland's Jadwiga Jedrzejowska (a three-time grand slam finalist) and American legends Helen Wills and Alice Marble. The home flag was kept flying by Kitty McKane, who beat Ryan to take the title in 1922, and by Dorothy Round, with two victories in the 1930s.

When the Kent All-Comers resumed after the Second World War in 1946, the loudest cheers were reserved for Vera Dace, who, in beating compatriot and former US champion Betty Nuthall, became the only Beckenham club member to lift the women's singles trophy.

More so than several of the tournaments featured in other chapters, Beckenham was characterised by world-class tennis throughout its history. No fewer than five of the women who triumphed at Foxgrove Road between 1946 and the arrival of Open tennis were also Wimbledon champions. The quarter-final line-up in 1965

MEMORABLE MATCH/SURPRISE DEFEAT

The doyen of British tennis journalists before the Second World War, Arthur Wallis Myers, included in his 1937 book Great Lawn Tennis the 'amazing' defeat at Beckenham in 1935 of the legendary Helen Wills Moody. Already a six-time Wimbledon champion, Mrs Moody had not suffered a singles defeat in Europe since 1924, yet she had little answer to the clean-hitting of Kay Stammers. The rising young English star was in prime form, having won the Hard Court Championships at Bournemouth a few weeks earlier, and the 4,000-strong crowd looked on in astonishment as she took the first set from the American to love in around 15 minutes. Stammers possessed a particularly potent forehand, which, when working well, could put any opponent under pressure. Her margin for error in going for winners from the baseline was slim, however, and early in the second set Mrs Moody looked to be in command. When the American secured a 4-1 lead, one spectator was heard to say, 'Now she will soon polish her off!' But the pinpoint accuracy of the English left-hander suddenly returned. It was true that Mrs Moody seemed reluctant to risk injury on a slightly damp surface, and she was to triumph in SW19 yet again within a matter of weeks. But this did not detract from the adept manner in which Miss Stammers regained the initiative and finished the job. She took five games in a row, the final one to love, thereby securing a famous 6-0, 6-4 victory. 'The cheers,' Wallis Myers reported, 'were heard at the railway station, a quarter of a mile away.'[7]

contained nearly all the contenders for the Wimbledon crown that year; victory went to Aussie Margaret Smith, who beat Brazilian star Maria Bueno in a thrilling final (as she did in SW19 a few weeks later). As for the men during this period, Beckenham became a site in the tussle for supremacy – seen on the global stage in the Davis Cup – between the USA and Australia. Americans claimed the men's title five times, but this was trumped by Australian victories on 16 occasions. John Newcombe won three years in succession in the 1960s, and it was a measure of the enduring quality of the meeting that other Aussie greats such as Rosewall, Hoad, Laver and Emerson all competed yet never triumphed.[8]

Beckenham's reputation was underlined when it was chosen to be the first grass-court tournament of the Open era in the summer of 1968. The Kent All-Comers was the third of the ten experimental Open meetings sanctioned that year, coming in the calendar after the British Hard Court Championships at Bournemouth and the French Open in Paris. The leading Australians once more turned out in force, Fred Stolle winning the men's title and Margaret Court the women's. But despite being at a pinnacle of prestige and popularity, Beckenham was not immune from the challenges that developed as the sport moved into its new age of professionalism. An efficiently run, crowd-pulling and profitable week at Foxgrove Road had been the order of the day for generations, but was no longer sufficient alone to ensure long-term viability. Large-scale sponsorship deals were now essential in order for tournaments to offer the escalating prize money required to attract top stars and prevent them opting for other events in an increasingly crowded summer schedule.

At the start of the 1970s Beckenham faced serious questions about its future. Fortunately, following dedicated and sustained efforts by club officials, a series of significant sponsorships deals were agreed: first with Peter West & Associates and later with the likes of the *Kentish Times* newspaper and the Direct Line Insurance

Company. As a result, a new generation of top talents arrived to grace the courts at Foxgrove Road. The men's roll of honour featured a fresh host of Wimbledon champions: from Stan Smith, Arthur Ashe and Jimmy Connors in the 1970s through to Pat Cash and John McEnroe in the 1980s. McEnroe, although he won in straight sets in 1989, made headlines by temporarily losing control of his legendary temper following a disputed line call.[9] Leading American women including Andrea Jaeger and Pam Shriver were serial winners at Beckenham during this period, and the tournament also played a unique part in the career of all-time great Billie Jean King. In 1961, as Ms Moffitt, she made her grass-court debut in England, aged 17, and over two decades later her victory over fellow American Barbara Potter in the All-Comers' final proved to be the last high-level singles title of her sparkling career.

The Beckenham bubble did, however, eventually burst. The tournament found it increasingly hard to compete for attention in the packed pre-Wimbledon schedule against Queen's Club, which by the 1980s had become a high-profile, lucrative televised affair. Nor did Foxgrove Road, a multi-sport site reliant on temporary stands, have the benefit of a bespoke, modernised venue dedicated solely to tennis as did the likes of Eastbourne, to which many of the top women players gravitated ahead of Wimbledon. With no new sponsorship deals in the offing, the end of the road came after the staging of the Direct Line Insurance Beckenham Open in 1996. An unsuccessful attempt at revival was made in 2005.[10] The curtain thus came down on Beckenham, although more so than other defunct meetings featured in these pages it is fondly remembered today as holding a cherished place in the nation's tennis history. By the time it bowed out, a total of 33 Kent All-Comers' winners, men and women, were also crowned as Wimbledon champions – a higher figure than at any other English grass-court tournament except Queen's.

RECORD BREAKERS

Most titles – Men: Algernon Kingscote (6), Harry Barlow (4), Ernest Meers (3), Laurence Doherty (3), Anthony Wilding (3), John Newcombe (3)

Most titles – Women: Dorothea Lambert Chambers (7 – four as Dorothea Douglass), Elizabeth Ryan (7 including one shared title), Edith Greville (6 – five as Edith Austin), Maud Shackle (4), Margaret Court (4 – three as Margaret Smith)

Number of Beckenham champions who also won Wimbledon singles

Men: 16; Women: 17; Total: 33

Kent All-Comers' Championships

Men's Singles

Year	Winner	Runner-up	Score
1886	Herbert Chipp	Edward J. Avory	6-4, 3-6, 6-3, 2-6, 6-3
1887	Frederick Bowlby	Herbert Chipp	1-6, 8-6, 6-4, 6-1
1888	Ernest Meers	Frederick Bowlby	5-7, 3-6, 9-7, 6-3, 6-2
1889	Harry Barlow	Ernest Meers	6-4, 1-6, 6-2, 9-7
1890	Ernest Meers	Harry Barlow	5-7, 8-6, 6-3, 6-3
1891	Ernest Meers	Arthur Gore	6-0, 6-2, 6-2
1892	Harry Barlow	Ernest Meers	4-6, 2-6, 8-6, 6-2, 6-3
1893	Harry Barlow	William Renshaw	2-6, 6-3, 6-1, 6-4
1894	Horace Chapman	Harry Barlow	3-6, 3-6, 6-3, 6-4, 6-3
1895	Harry Barlow	Horace Chapman	2-6, 6-3, 6-3, 4-6, 6-3
1896	Manliffe Goodbody	Harry Barlow	6-1, 6-2, 2-6, 6-0
1897	George Greville	Manliffe Goodbody	4-6, 6-3, 4-6, 6-4, 6-4
1898	Wilberforce Eaves	George Greville	6-0, 6-0, 6-1
1899	Harold Mahony	Wilberforce Eaves	6-1, 6-1, 6-8, 3-6, 8-6
1900	Arthur Gore	Harold Mahony	6-4, 6-4, 6-4
1901	Laurence Doherty	Arthur Gore	6-1, 6-3, 3-6, 6-4
1902	Laurence Doherty	George Simond	6-4, 6-0, 6-3
1903	Laurence Doherty	Arthur Gore	6-1, 6-2, 6-3
1904	Harold Mahony	Brame Hillyard	6-3, 8-6, 7-9, 4-6, 6-3
1905	Norman Brookes (Aus)	Arthur Gore	6-3, 9-7, 6-2

1906	Arthur Gore	Alfred Bentley	6-0, 6-2, 6-1
1907	Anthony Wilding (NZ)	Arthur Gore	9-7, 6-2, 3-6, 0-6, 6-1
1908	Herbert Roper Barrett	Charles Dixon	6-0, 9-7, 6-2
1909	Herbert Roper Barrett	Major Ritchie	abandoned due to rain
1910	Beals Wright (USA)	Herbert Roper Barrett	4-6, 7-5, 12-10, 6-4
1911	Anthony Wilding (NZ)	Major Ritchie	6-0, 6-0, 6-3
1912	Anthony Wilding (NZ)	Herbert Roper Barrett	6-2, 4-6, 6-2, 1-6, 6-2
1913	Alfred Beamish	George Thomas	6-3, 6-3, 3-6, 7-5
1914	Algernon Kingscote	Hope Crisp	7-5, 2-6, 3-6, 6-2, 6-2
1915–18	No tournament held		
1919	Algernon Kingscote	Frank Fisher (NZ)	4-6, 6-4, 9-7, 3-6, 6-2
1920	Algernon Kingscote	Zenzo Shimidzu (Jpn)	7-5, 3-2 retd
1921	Algernon Kingscote	Sydney Jacob	6-4, 4-6, 6-0, 6-3
1922	Algernon Kingscote	Randolph Lycett (Aus)	6-3, 3-1 retd
1923	Bill Johnston (USA)	Donald Greig	6-2, 6-3
1924	Algernon Kingscote	Jack Hillyard	8-6, 9-7, 6-2
1925	Randolph Lycett (Aus)	Harry Lewis Barclay	6-3, 6-1, 5-7, 6-4
1926	Gordon Crole-Rees	Patrick Spence (SA)	6-4, 6-2
1927	Donald Greig	Charles Kingsley	4-6, 6-2, 6-3
1928	Charles Kingsley	Patrick Spence (SA)	2-6, 6-4, 8-6
1929	Harry Lee	Charles Kingsley	7-5, 6-4, 6-2
1930	Bunny Austin	Harry Lee	6-2, 2-6, 6-4, 6-2
1931	Colin Gregory	John Olliff	3-6, 6-3, 7-9, 6-3, 6-0
1932	Edward R. Avory	Buster Andrews (NZ)	6-1, 6-4
1933	Vernon Kirby (SA)	Colin Robbins (SA)	8-6, 6-4
1934	Bunny Austin	Yiro Yamagishi (Jpn)	6-3, 6-0
1935	Yiro Yamagishi (Jpn)	Ian Collins	6-3, 6-1
1936	David Jones (USA)	Frank Wilde	11-9, 6-3
1937	Yiro Yamagishi (Jpn)	Raymond Tuckey	8-6, 1-6, 7-5
1938	John Olliff	Nigel Sharpe	6-2, 6-3
1939	Murray Deloford	Donald McPhail	3-6, 6-2, 9-7
1940–45	No tournament held		
1946	Geoff Brown (Aus)	Hans van Swol (Ned)	6-1, 6-4
1947	Bill Sidwell (Aus)	Torsten Johansson (Swe)	6-2, 10-8
1948	Frank Sedgman (Aus)	Jack Harper (Aus)	6-4, 6-4
1949	Gardnar Mulloy (USA)	Earl Cochell	2-3 retd
1950	Geoff Brown (Aus)	Bill Sidwell (Aus)	8-6, 7-9, 17-15
1951	Don Candy (Aus)	Gardnar Mulloy (USA)	3-6, 6-4, 6-2

1952	Ham Richardson (USA)	Don Candy (Aus)	6-2, 6-8, 6-2
1953	George Worthington (Aus)	Gardnar Mulloy (USA)	6-4, 4-6, 6-3
1954	Abandoned due to rain		
1955	Tony Trabert (USA)	Herb Flam (USA)	6-4, 6-2
1956	Mal Anderson (Aus)	Sammy Giammalva (USA)	
	Abandoned due to rain		
1957	Mal Anderson (Aus)	Herb Flam (USA)	6-2, 4-6, 8-6
1958	Neale Fraser (Aus)	Kurt Nielsen (Den)	6-4, 6-4
1959	Alex Olmedo (USA)	Kurt Nielsen (Den)	8-6, 3-6, 6-4
1960	Robert Mark (Aus)	Butch Buchholz (USA)	6-3, 6-4
1961	Jack Douglas (USA)	Lew Gerrard (NZ)	4-6, 6-3, 6-3
1962	Barry Phillips-Moore (Aus)	Owen Davidson (Aus)	6-4, 8-6
1963	Ken Fletcher (Aus)	Marty Mulligan (Aus)	6-3, 6-2
1964	John Newcombe (Aus)	Fred Stolle (Aus)	6-2, 5-7, 12-10
1965	John Newcombe (Aus)	Lew Gerrard (NZ)	6-3, 6-1
1966	John Newcombe (Aus)	Premjit Lall (Ind)	6-4, 15-13
1967	Owen Davidson (Aus)	Ken Fletcher (Aus)	3-6, 6-2, 6-3
1968	Fred Stolle (Aus)	Roy Emerson (Aus)	6-3, 6-1
1969	Ove Bengston (Swe)	Tom Gorman (USA)	6-4, 7-5
1970	Clark Graebner (USA)	Robert Maud (SA)	6-4, 10-8
1971	Stan Smith (USA)	Premjit Lall (Ind)	7-9, 6-4, 6-2
1972	Alex Metreveli (USSR)	Vijay Amritraj (Ind)	6-2, 7-5
1973	Alex Metreveli (USSR)	Bjorn Borg (Swe)	6-3, 9-8
1974	Vijay Amritraj (Ind)	Tom Gorman (USA)	6-7, 6-2, 6-4
1975	Arthur Ashe (USA)	Roscoe Tanner (USA)	7-5, 6-4
1976	Roscoe Tanner (USA)	Jimmy Connors (USA)	6-3, 6-4
1977	Mark Edmondson (Aus)	Tim Gullikson (USA)	6-3, 6-4
1978	Jimmy Connors (USA)	Stan Smith (USA)	9-8, 6-3
1979	Peter Fleming (USA)	Roscoe Tanner (USA)	3-6, 6-3, 7-5
1980	Onny Parun (NZ)	Sandy Mayer (USA)	6-4, 4-6, 9-7
1981	Kevin Curren (SA)	Chris Lewis (NZ)	6-2, 6-3
1982	Kevin Curren (SA)	Buster Mottram	7-6, 6-4
1983	Steve Denton (USA)	Pat Cash (Aus)	7-6, 6-4
1984	Pat Cash (Aus)	Paul McNamee (Aus)	3-6, 6-2, 6-1
1985	Tim Mayotte (USA)	Steve Denton (USA)	7-6, 6-0
1986	Ramesh Krishnan (Ind)	Danie Visser (SA)	7-5, 6-1
1987	Scott Davis (USA)	Danie Visser (SA)	6-3, 6-7, 6-3
1988	Christian Saceanu (WG)	Leif Shiras (USA)	7-6, 6-3

1989	John McEnroe (USA)	Broderick Dyke (Aus)	6-4, 7-6
1990	Ivan Lendl (Czh)	Darren Cahill (Aus)	6-3, 7-5
1991	Ivan Lendl (Czh)	Pat Cash (Aus)	3-6, 7-6, 7-6
1992	David Wheaton (USA)	Christo van Rensburg (SA)	6-3, 1-6, 6-1
1993	David Wheaton (USA)	Chris Bailey	6-4, 3-6, 7-6
1994	Guy Forget (Fra)	Jeremy Bates	6-2, 6-3
1995	Andrew Richardson	Petr Korda (CR)	title shared
1996	Mark Petchey	Petr Korda (CR)	6-2, 6-4

Women's Singles

Year	Winner	Runner-up	Score
1888	May Jacks	Edith Gurney	1-6, 6-3, 6-0
1889	Maud Shackle	May Jacks	6-3, 7-5
1890	May Jacks	Maud Shackle	4-6, 6-0, 6-4
1891	Maud Shackle	May Jacks	6-4, 6-0
1892	Maud Shackle	May Jacks	6-3, 6-1
1893	Maud Shackle	Ruth Pennington-Legh	6-3, 6-4
1894	Edith Austin	Amy Wilson	6-4, 6-2
1895	Edith Austin	Amy Wilson	6-3, 6-1
1896	Edith Austin	Ruth Pennington-Legh	6-4, 2-6, 6-4
1897	Edith Austin	E.R. Morgan	6-2, 6-0
1898	Charlotte Cooper	Edith Austin	6-2, 4-6, 6-3
1899	Edith Austin	Charlotte Cooper	1-6, 7-5, 6-2
1900	Edith Greville	Muriel Robb	6-1, 6-3
1901	Dorothea Douglass	Edith Greville	6-1, 4-6, 6-4
1902	Dorothea Douglass	Hilda Lane	7-5, 6-4
1903	Connie Wilson	Dorothea Douglass	3-6, 6-4, 6-4
1904	Dorothea Douglass	Connie Wilson	6-2, 6-2
1905	Connie Wilson	Alice Greene	6-2, 6-4
1906	Dorothea Douglass	Connie Wilson	6-3, 2-2 retd
1907	May Sutton (USA)	Dorothea Lambert Chambers	6-2, 8-6
1908	Agnes Morton	Dora Boothby	6-2, 6-1
1909	Dora Boothby	Agnes Morton	6-4, 6-4
1910	Dorothea Lambert Chambers	Dora Boothby	6-4, 6-3
1911	Dorothea Lambert Chambers	Mildred Coles	6-3, 7-5
1912	Winifred McNair	Dora Boothby	6-1, 6-4
1913	Dorothea Lambert Chambers	Phyllis Satterthwaite	6-4, 6-4
1914	Edith Hannam	Agnes Morton	0-6, 11-9 retd

1915–18	No tournament held		
1919	Elizabeth Ryan (USA)	Dorothea Lambert Chambers	2-6, 7-5, 6-4
1920	Elizabeth Ryan (USA)	Winifred McNair	title shared
1921	Elizabeth Ryan (USA)	Geraldine Beamish	9-7, 6-4
1922	Kitty McKane	Elizabeth Ryan (USA)	6-3, 6-3
1923	Elizabeth Ryan (USA)	Phyllis Satterthwaite	6-3, 3-6, 6-3
1924	Elizabeth Ryan (USA)	Kitty McKane	6-8, 6-1, 6-1
1925	Elizabeth Ryan (USA)	Geraldine Beamish	4-6, 6-3, 6-2
1926	Lili Alvarez (Spn)	Molla Mallory (USA)	6-4, 6-2
1927	Helen Wills (USA)	Kitty Godfree	6-2, 6-4
1928	Elizabeth Ryan (USA)	Violet Chamberlain	6-2, 10-8
1929	Phyllis Covell	Peggy Saunders Michell	6-1, 6-4
1930	Jenny Sandison (Ind)	Violet Owen	6-2, 4-6, 6-4
1931	Phyllis Mudford	Dorothy Round	6-1, 6-2
1932	Mary Heeley	Freda James	1-6, 6-3, 6-0
1933	Dorothy Round	Peggy Saunders Michell	7-5, 6-2
1934	Phyllis King	Joan Hartigan (Aus)	6-2, 6-3
1935	Dorothy Round	Kay Stammers	6-2, 6-0
1936	Anita Lizana (Chl)	Betty Nuthall	3-6, 6-0, 6-1
1937	Jadwiga Jedrzejowska (Pol)	Alice Marble (USA)	6-1, 9-11, 6-1
1938	Jadwiga Jedrzejowska (Pol)	Bobbie Heiner Miller (SA)	7-5, 3-6, 6-2
1939	Alice Marble (USA)	Kay Stammers	6-3, 6-1
1940–45	No tournament held		
1946	Vera Dace	Betty Nuthall	6-4, 6-4
1947	Kay Menzies	Sheila Summers (SA)	6-2, 11-9
1948	Maria Teran de Weiss (Arg)	Patsy Rodgers	7-5, 6-1
1949	Patricia Todd (USA)	Sheila Summers (SA)	6-3, 6-0
1950	Gussie Moran (USA)	Nancy Morrison (USA)	4-6, 6-1, 6-2
1951	Betty Rosenquest (USA)	Barbara Scofield (USA)	4-6, 7-5, 6-1
1952	Hazel Redick-Smith (SA)	Vera Thomas	6-2, 6-2
1953	Maureen Connolly (USA)	Julie Hayward (USA)	6-2, 6-3
1954	Abandoned due to rain		
1955	Louise Brough (USA)	Mary Carter (Aus)	6-2, 6-4
1956	Darlene Hard (USA)	Betty Pratt (USA)	abandoned due to rain
1957	Althea Gibson (USA)	Darlene Hard (USA)	6-3, 3-6, 6-4
1958	Sandra Reynolds (SA)	Jean Forbes (SA)	6-4, 6-4
1959	Darlene Hard (USA)	Sally Moore (USA)	6-1, 7-5
1960	Christiane Mercelis (Bel)	Pauline Roberts	7-5, 4-6, 6-4

1961	Margaret Smith (Aus)	Christine Truman	6-3, 4-6, 8-6
1962	Jan Lehane (Aus)	Lesley Turner (Aus)	7-5, 6-3
1963	Margaret Smith (Aus)	Jan Lehane (Aus)	6-0, 6-1
1964	Maria Bueno (Bra)	Margaret Smith (Aus)	title shared
1965	Margaret Smith (Aus)	Maria Bueno (Bra)	4-6, 6-3, 6-3
1966	Karen Krantzcke (Aus)	Maria Bueno (Bra)	walkover
1967	Ann Jones	Virginia Wade	6-3, 1-6, 6-3
1968	Margaret Court (Aus)	Ann Jones	11-9, 6-2
1969	Denise Carter (USA)	Kerry Melville (Aus)	6-3, 7-5
1970	Patti Hogan (USA)	Olga Morozova (USSR)	6-1, 6-3
1971	Kerry Melville (Aus)	Kirsty Pigeon (USA)	6-3, 3-6, 9-7
1972	Olga Morozova (USSR)	Jill Cooper	6-4, 6-1
1973	Dianne Fromholtz (Aus)	Janet Newberry (USA)	7-5, 0-6, 6-1
1974	Paulina Pelsachov (Isr)	Kate Latham (USA)	5-7, 6-3, 6-4
1975	Greer Stevens (SA)	Patti Hogan (USA)	4-6, 6-3, 6-3
1976	Olga Morozova (USSR)	Marise Kruger (SA)	7-5, 2-6, 6-3
1977	Yvonne Vermaak (SA)	Michelle Tyler	6-4, 5-7, 6-1
1978	Evonne Cawley (Aus)	Laura DuPont (USA)	6-4, 6-2
1979	Evonne Cawley (Aus)	Pam Shriver (USA)	6-3, 6-2
1980	Andrea Jaeger (USA)	Jo Durie	6-4, 6-1
1981	Pam Shriver (USA)	Elizabeth Little (Aus)	6-2, 6-2
1982	Pam Shriver (USA)	Elizabeth Sayers (Aus)	6-3, 6-2
1983	Billie Jean King (USA)	Barbara Potter (USA)	6-4, 6-3
1984	Terry Phelps (USA)	Tina Wantanabe-Mochizuki (USA)	7-6, 6-2
1985	Barbara Potter (USA)	Annabel Croft	7-6, 4-6, 6-3
1986	Pam Shriver (USA)	Barbara Potter (USA)	6-4, 6-3
1987	Barbara Potter (USA)	Alycia Moulton (USA)	7-6, 7-5
1988	Robin White (USA)	Ann Henricksson (USA)	6-3, 6-2
1989	Ross Fairbank (SA)	Anne Minter (Aus)	6-3, 6-3
1990	Ross Fairbank (SA)	Gigi Fernandez (PR)	7-5, 6-4
1991	Andrea Strnadova (Czh)	Renae Stubbs (Aus)	6-7, 6-4, 6-3
1992	Mary Joe Fernandez (USA)	Helena Sukova (Czh)	6-4, 6-2
1993	Martina Navratilova (USA)	Kristie Boogert (Ned)	6-3, 6-3
1994	Kerry-Ann Guse (Aus)	Dianne van Rensburg (SA)	7-5, 1-6, 7-6
1995	Els Callens (Bel)	Rosalyn Niedeffer (USA)	6-2, 6-3
1996	Clare Wood	Maria Vento (Ven)	6-3, 6-2

4

Eastbourne

IN THE summer of 1924 a 14-year-old boy, on holiday from London with his family in the fashionable south-coast resort of Eastbourne, wandered into the Devonshire Park area of the town, where he noticed lots of smartly attired men and women playing lawn tennis. The teenager, who had spent his early childhood in an industrial area of northern England and not taken much notice of the sport before then, decided he liked 'the look of that setup', and went away resolved to give it a go. His father bought him an old racket for five shillings, and he started playing when he returned to Ealing.[1] The boy – Fred Perry – turned out to be supremely good. He went on to become the most successful competitor in British tennis history, winner of a combined total of 14 grand slam titles in singles and doubles.

In addition to providing a spark of inspiration to one of the nation's greatest-ever sportsmen, Devonshire Park has many other feathers in its tennis cap. As we leave outer London and head towards the Kent-Sussex coast on our travels around key locations, it's worth noting that several towns in the region have hosted high-quality competitive play. East Grinstead, Tunbridge Wells, Bexhill, Hastings, Brighton, Worthing, Chichester (where William Renshaw was champion in 1895) – they all ran tournaments that featured big-name winners at various times. But Eastbourne towers above the pack. Devonshire Park has long provided a welcoming home for a whole range of top-level domestic events, including the Inter-County Championships, the British Junior Grass Court Championships and the Professional Coaches' Championship; the last named was won on numerous occasions by Britain's famous Davis Cup coach and later BBC commentator, Dan Maskell.

It's in the context of international-level competition, however, that Eastbourne really stands out from the crowd. Unlike several of the tournaments discussed in other chapters, Devonshire Park has more or less continuously from the 1880s to the present day hosted an annual meeting on the same site, rather than at two or more different locations. The South of England Championships was for many years, if not always the most stellar (in terms of the depth and quality of its entry list), then certainly the biggest gathering of its type in the country, probably in the world. The congenial setting on the coast and the well-maintained grass courts help to explain why Devonshire Park has also been used for more home Davis Cup ties – pitting British men against teams from around the globe – than any other location, including Wimbledon. All told, Eastbourne has acquired a hard-earned reputation as one of the top three grass-court venues in the country: if not on a par with, then certainly worthy of being mentioned alongside, Wimbledon and Queen's.[2]

The South of England Championships

Devonshire Park's special place in English tennis history stems in part from its original elegance and allure. The story goes back to the 1870s when William Cavendish, the forward-thinking seventh Duke of Devonshire, set out to develop his 11-acre estate to the west of Eastbourne town centre into a focus for recreation and culture. Facilities for cricket, roller skating, athletics, cycling and lawn tennis were laid out, all in close proximity to the imposing buildings of the Winter Gardens, which soon became a well-known centre for musical concerts and entertainment. The Duke's aim was to replicate what he had earlier inspired in Buxton in Derbyshire, establishing a fashionable hotspot constructed 'by gentlemen for gentlemen'.[3] Charges to use the facilities meant it would be many a year before Devonshire Park became easily accessible to working-class residents of Eastbourne, but for well-to-do locals keen to be involved in the late-Victorian expansion of lawn tennis the new venture was a boon.

What became the highly esteemed South of England Championships started with not one, but two separate tournaments in 1881. A small-scale Devonshire Park Spring Tournament for ladies was won by Agnes Watts over Miss Hudson (although no exact record of the score appears to survive). Later in the year – in September, the month that was to become associated with the town's distinctive, season-ending slot in the grass-court calendar – 32 entrants contested a men-only event, playing for the first prize of a silver cup valued at 50 guineas. The *Eastbourne Gazette* reported that the action commenced in College Road on the opening day 'before a large and brilliant assemblage of ladies and gentlemen'.[4] The sun shone throughout proceedings, and in a field confined to local residents, Edgar Lubbock secured a comfortable straight-sets victory in the final over Robert Braddell.

Over the next three years the push to develop a single, showcase annual meeting gathered momentum. The Devonshire Parks and Baths Company – which had oversight of the Duke's estate – promoted open events in order to attract more competitors from further afield. This approach soon paid dividends. Hertfordshire's Edward 'Teddy' Williams triumphed in 1883; having not long celebrated his 17th birthday, he became (and was to remain) the youngest winner of the men's singles at any of the frontline meetings featured in this book. In September 1885 the local newspaper boasted that, despite poor weather at times, the quality of the tournament taking place 'far exceeds its predecessors in every detail'.[5] Greater numbers of visitors, it was claimed, passed through the park turnstiles to watch the tennis than at any other point during the summer, making College Road a hub of fashionable society in the resort.

The main reason for the step change in Eastbourne's fortunes was that it began to act as a magnet for some of the best amateurs of the day. The men's singles in 1885 was won by Ernest Lewis, a multiple champion indoors and outdoors at Queen's (see *Underrated Champion*, chapter 1). Devonshire Park organisers, like others at the time, allowed the victor to proceed direct to the challenge round if defending the following year, and Lewis successfully re-claimed the title for two further years. The women's event in 1885 went

LONG DRAWN-OUT

Blanche Hillyard was a strong favourite to win a fifth title at Eastbourne in 1893. Her control from the baseline enabled her to put her opponent Maud Shackle under early pressure in the South of England final, delayed for a couple of days because of rain. Mrs Hillyard took the first set 6-1 and quickly reached 4-0 in the second; a routine victory beckoned. But there then followed one of those huge momentum shifts that can occur at any level of tennis. Miss Shackle decided there was nothing to lose by throwing caution to the wind. She struck out early and aggressively in every rally, producing winner after winner; six games in a row meant the match was unexpectedly level pegging. The challenger's inspired form continued into the final set, enabling her to take the first two games. Rattled by the reversal of fortunes, Mrs Hillyard was relieved when a shower forced a short suspension of play. Having yo-yoed hitherto, upon resumption the remainder of the match was a tight affair, neither player able to force the issue as the game score mounted. At 10-9 ahead and on serve Miss Shackle had championship point, but she missed her opportunity. After enduring a marathon instead of what, at the outset, seemed more like a sprint, Mrs Hillyard took the decider 15-13.

to Blanche Bingley, whose stinging forehand was in due course to carry her to a record-setting 11 Eastbourne titles (most as Mrs Hillyard), the last coming 20 years after the first, in 1905, when she was aged 41. While Blanche, like Lewis, often benefited from the challenge round procedure, in place until the turn of the century, she did have to contend with the tournament's habit in its early years of handicapping female Wimbledon champions; this may have contributed to her also losing in a few Eastbourne finals.

Around the turn of the century the South of England Championships became a battleground between a couple of the sport's finest protagonists. Two of Sydney Smith's record-equalling five men's victories at Devonshire Park were secured at the expense of the first great superstar of lawn tennis, Laurie Doherty (albeit before Doherty began a five-year unbeaten run at Wimbledon). Smith got the better of Doherty in four sets in 1898. The tables were turned in 1900 but Smith triumphed again the following year, when after some sparkling rallies in front of a 3,000-strong crowd, the finalists shared the first four sets before Doherty retired at 1-0 in the decider. According to George Hillyard, 'Smith of Stroud', as he was often called, needed lots of practice and match play to reach peak form. With this in mind, Hillyard felt, Wimbledon (which the Gloucestershire man never won) came a little too early in the summer; to get a taste of the 'real Smith', it was best to see him in action at Eastbourne during the grass season finale.[6]

During the Edwardian period the women's roll of honour at College Road could have been mistaken for that at Wimbledon. In addition to Blanche Hillyard, the South of England title was claimed by Dorothea Douglass/Lambert Chambers five times, by Charlotte Cooper/Sterry on three occasions, by Dora Boothby in 1909, and by Ethel Larcombe three years in succession, culminating in 1913 with a fine victory over Mrs Chambers, who often went undefeated for long stretches of tournament play. The demand to watch the greats was such that in 1910 mutterings were heard among those spectators who, owing to the size of ladies' hats in front of them, found it difficult to see the action; this, despite the committee issuing notices requesting ladies not to sport hats of such magnitude.

In a further sign of the rising reputation of Eastbourne, the overseas challenge was becoming more pronounced, particularly in the men's singles. When Australia's Norman Brookes broke the stranglehold of Sydney Smith in 1905 – after a tight first set he pulled away to win comfortably – he became the first player from overseas to lift the trophy. Brookes's Australasian Davis Cup team-mate Anthony Wilding claimed victory in 1906 and 1908 (the latter after being given a walkover by George Hillyard). And 1909 saw the first men's final in which no home player featured; Otto Froitzheim defeated fellow German Friedrich Rahe in four sets. Overseas contenders did not, however, have things all their own way. In the 1911 final the young British army champion Algernon Kingscote showed great tenacity – as well as adept volleying – in coming back from two sets to love down to beat Australian Stanley Doust. The crowd got ever more involved as the match reached its climax. One onlooker claimed 'the cheering at the end of it might very well have been heard on the sea-front'.[7]

The last South of England Championships before the First World War took place in 1913 (war had been declared by the time of its scheduled date in 1914), at which point it held a unique record. For the first time in the history of lawn tennis, a frontline tournament included over 1,000 matches in its programme, a milestone initially passed in 1911. This was because organisers were keen to facilitate a variety of events – handicaps, veterans and juniors – in addition to the elite singles and doubles. The number of men's entrants in the main draw passed 100 in 1912 and continued to grow to 128 (and around 90 women) a decade later. As a result, Devonshire Park was for a while the largest tournament in England, and most likely in the world. Fortunately, some 25 courts were available to ensure matches were completed in a timely fashion, although officials did have to resort to some unorthodox measures to ensure proceedings went smoothly.

COME IN NUMBER 17

For many years, the referee at Eastbourne – trying to juggle with a huge schedule of matches, and needing to call players to and from far-flung courts around the large Devonshire Park site – resorted to using or asking helpers to use a megaphone. One competitor complained about the 'unholy din' which went on all day in the early rounds of the tournament, claiming that players were sufficiently distracted that they conceded points and even whole matches as a result. It wasn't clear if the person complaining lost (or was able to blame a loss) on this particular practice.

When the South of England resumed after the war, it looked set to continue growing in size and status. The *Eastbourne Herald* described the 1919 meeting as 'emphatically the event of the season',[8] well attended and with another bumper entry. Overseas players returned in large numbers and started to dominate. Californian ace Elizabeth Ryan became the first non-UK winner of the women's singles and proceeded to secure a hat-trick of titles. She was followed by Irene Peacock, born in India but a South African citizen, who beat rising British star Kitty McKane in the 1922 final. The men's title also went overseas every year between 1920 and 1925, with South Africa's Wimbledon finalist Brian Norton an impressive two-time champion.

But after the mid-1920s, Eastbourne's reputation dipped slightly and never quite returned to its former giddy heights. Occasional weeks of prolonged heavy rain – as in 1931 – dented the charm of a meeting traditionally associated with fine weather. The financial crash of the late 1920s also led to some scaling back. A peak of 1,400 matches on the programme earlier in the decade was never again equalled, with the popularity of the more light-hearted handicap events falling markedly. The exceptional quality of the Eastbourne entry was further affected by the expansion of, and changes to, the global circuit. The South of England's September timing clashed with the US National Championships, which meant leading contenders, especially Americans, stayed away as they prepared to compete on home soil. Many talented Europeans, meanwhile, increasingly opted to play on the continent rather than remain in England once Wimbledon was over each July.

In consequence, women's finals in particular at Devonshire Park tended to become all-British affairs. Phoebe Holcroft (later

---

UNDERRATED CHAMPION

Anita Lizana lit up the tournament scene for a short but captivating spell in the 1930s. By the time Santiago-born Senorita Lizana became the first Latin American woman to win the US Championships in 1937 she could already claim a range of achievements in Britain. In 1935 she reached the final of the Grass Court Championships at Queen's (sharing the title because of rain) and she won the first of three successive Scottish championships. The following year saw a strong across-the-board performance: she triumphed in the BCCC at Queen's, at Beckenham, and later in the season at the South of England Championships, where she beat Dorothy Round in straight sets. In 1937 she added two further titles to her portfolio: the Hard Court Championships at Bournemouth and the West of England in Bristol. Although short in stature, Miss Lizana's speed around the court and ability to mix up her game earned her comparisons with the great Suzanne Lenglen. The Chilean cut back her playing commitments after marriage in 1938, and this – together with the outbreak of war – meant she was unable to compile multiple tournament wins over several years. But for a couple of seasons she was an irrepressible force.

Mrs Watson), although she had an unorthodox style, used her domineering forehand drive to secure five victories in College Road. The last of these came in the autumn of 1928; the following year she opted to play in New York, reaching the final of the US Championships, where she lost to the all-conquering Helen Wills. Mrs Watson was followed at the South of England Championships by Phyliss Mudford King, who secured a hat-trick of titles, and by another popular home champion, Dorothy Round, who triumphed in 1934 – the same year she lifted the Wimbledon trophy. Miss Round missed out on a second Eastbourne title, however, when she was beaten in 1936 by Chile's Anita Lizana, the first non-British winner for 14 years.

On the men's side, the South of England title after the mid-1920s went to a mix of strong home aspirants and talented but not grand slam-winning overseas players. In 1931 Jiro Satoh – one of three Japanese winners in four years – beat South African Vernon Kirby in a match where the finalists sportingly agreed to carry on despite the rain and resultant slippery surface (a practice frequently seen before the Great War but by this time quite rare). The list of domestic champions through to the Second World War featured several players in or close to the British Davis Cup squad, including Charles Kingsley, Bunny Austin, Pat Hughes and Don Butler. Austin, who disliked the humidity of New York and so restricted his appearances at the US Championships, announced his emergence into the senior ranks with a striking victory at Devonshire Park in 1927.

Austin's friend and rival Fred Perry preferred to focus his autumn energies not on Devonshire Park but on the US circuit (where he won his first grand slam singles title in 1933), though that did not mean he was a stranger to Eastbourne beyond his impressionable visit as a teenager. The town's accessibility from London, its pleasant seaside ambience and the billiard table-like quality of the grass courts made it a natural choice for hosting home ties in the Davis Cup. Devonshire Park made its debut in this arena in July 1919, when temporary

YOUNG MAN IN A HURRY

Bunny Austin was the bright new hope of British men's tennis in the mid-1920s. The Surrey youngster, ahead of the emergence of Fred Perry, offered the best hope of renewed success on the world stage. Although he lost in a couple of senior finals in 1925 and 1926, Austin's breakthrough at the top level came when he took the South of England Championships by storm in 1927. At the time he was still an undergraduate at Cambridge University, but he captured the Eastbourne title without dropping a set. In the last four he beat compatriot Gordon Crole-Rees (whose tournament victories included Surbiton and Beckenham), and in the final he overcame his fellow student – and captain of the Light Blues team – William Powell. Reporters waxed lyrical about the virtues of the 21-year-old victor: he had some of the most stylish ground strokes in the game, hit with great accuracy to the corners, and he was becoming more physically robust. To underline his potential, Austin capped a good week by taking the men's doubles titles, partnered by J.J. Lezard.

stands were erected overlooking the main courts and a programme of entertainment was laid on for spectators including a grand concert in the Winter Gardens. The British Isles team (spearheaded by Algernon Kingscote, returned from military service) beat South Africa 4-1 before later losing heavily to Australasia in the final.

Eastbourne was to the fore when Austin and Perry led Britain during its Davis Cup heyday in the 1930s. En route to a first triumph in Paris in 1933 the young British team played back-to-back matches at Devonshire Park: beating Italy 4-1 (a tie that saw a rare cup defeat in singles for Perry, beaten by the ambidextrous Giorgio de Stefani) and then despatching Czechoslovakia 5-0. As four-time cup holders, the British were required to compete only once over the next few years, in the challenge round, hosted by Wimbledon, but Eastbourne still featured in the squad's preparations. Team coach Dan Maskell recalled that for three marvellous summers Austin, Perry and the others enjoyed going to the south coast to tune up for the challenge round ahead on the 'lovely' courts in College Road.[9]

Such was the suitability of Devonshire Park for Davis Cup purposes that it went on to become, in the fullness of time, the location that hosted significantly more home ties – over 30 – than anywhere else in the country. The Eastbourne leger included landmark moments such as Britain's 100th Davis Cup match (a 5-0 victory over New Zealand in 1957) and a European Zone final triumph over Czechoslovakia in 1978 – the year a British squad featuring Cox, Mottram and the Lloyd brothers progressed to the final for the first time since 1937. The last home tie at College Road came in 2010, a victory over Turkey that prevented relegation to the lowest tier of the competition and marked the start of a revival that resulted in the Andy Murray-inspired team recapturing the Davis Cup five years later.

During the Second World War, Eastbourne suffered numerous aerial bombing raids, resulting in over 150 civilian deaths. Devonshire Park was unavoidably neglected for the duration, and this influenced the decision of the Parks and Baths Company to sell the site to the borough council. In the short term the authorities were relieved simply to see the South of England Championships resume, even though the trend towards top international stars staying away became more pronounced than before. Surrey's Geoff Paish matched Sydney Smith's pre-1914 record, winning the men's title five times in succession in the 1950s, while Brighton-educated Jean Walker-Smith's four victories in the women's singles included one over the young Angela Mortimer in 1951. The Eastbourne tournament is rare among the meetings featured in these pages in that three-time grand slam champion Mortimer never captured the title; she also lost to Ann Haydon in the 1957 final.

As moves towards reform of the amateur system came closer in the 1960s, Devonshire Park's continued high standing in the tennis world rested less on the annual finale to the grass-court season in September than on the completion of long-promised regeneration of the site (which included the opening of a multi purpose conference centre, the Congress Theatre, in place of the Winter Gardens) and on its versatility in hosting a variety of other well-supported tennis events. These included, in addition to Davis Cup ties, post-war innovations such as the Slazenger Pro Championships (discussed in more detail in chapter 8) and a one-off professional exhibition in August 1963. The latter featured, in front of packed stands, no fewer than four former Wimbledon champions – Frank Sedgman, Lew Hoad, Alex Olmedo and Rod Laver.

Following the arrival of Open tennis in 1968, Eastbourne received a short-term boost in an age when sponsors' names and logos were suddenly emblazoned on marquees and on the clothing of players. The Rothmans Championships, as it was known for a few years, became part of the emerging top-tier Grand Prix circuit, and regular stalwart entrants found themselves in the same draw as some of the crème de la crème. In the first all-overseas women's final since 1921, Brazilian legend Maria Bueno beat Australia's Judy Tegart in 1968. On the men's side, grand slam champions such as Manuel Orantes (who narrowly missed out in the 1969 Eastbourne final) and Ken Rosewall (winner in 1970) could once more be seen gracing the scene in College Road. But behind the scenes all was not rosy: by the early 1970s the days of the Eastbourne tournament, in its traditional form, were numbered.

South of England Championships

Men's Singles

Year	Winner	Runner-up	Score
1881	Edgar Lubbock	Robert Braddell	6-4, 6-2, 6-0
1882	William Taylor	Teddy Williams	8-6, 2-6, 3-6, 6-3
1883	Teddy Williams	Charles Grinstead	6-1, 8-6, 6-4, 7-5
1884	Teddy Williams	William Taylor	1-6, 6-2, 6-2, 6-2

1885	Ernest Lewis	William Taylor	4-6, 7-5, 6-3, 6-3
1886	Ernest Lewis	Herbert Wilberforce	6-3, 6-4, 6-0
1887	Ernest Lewis	Herbert Wilberforce	8-6, 7-5, 6-4
1888	Andrew Ziffo	Harry Barlow	4-6, 6-2, 7-5, 6-3
1889	Andrew Ziffo	Harry Grove	4-6, 6-3, 4-6, 9-7, 6-4
1890	Andrew Ziffo	James Baldwin	7-9, 6-1, 6-2, 7-5
1891	Harry Barlow	Andrew Ziffo	6-3, 7-5, 6-0
1892	Harry Barlow	Wilberforce Eaves	7-5, 2-6, 3-6, 6-3, 6-3
1893	Wilfred Baddeley	Harry Barlow	7-5, 6-0, 6-1
1894	Wilfred Baddeley	Harry Barlow	6-3, 3-6, 6-3, 6-1
1895	Wilfred Baddeley	George Hillyard	6-3, 7-9, 7-5 retd
1896	Wilfred Baddeley	Herbert Baddeley	walkover
1897	Joshua Pim	Laurence Doherty	3-6, 6-3, 7-5, 6-3
1898	Sydney Smith	Laurence Doherty	6-3, 2-6, 8-6, 7-5
1899	Sydney Smith	Harold Mahony	6-0, 6-3, 6-4
1900	Laurence Doherty	Sydney Smith	6-4, 1-6, 6-2, 6-1
1901	Sydney Smith	Laurence Doherty	6-3, 7-9, 4-6, 6-4, 1-0 retd
1902	Sydney Smith	Clement Cazalet	6-1, 3-6, 7-5, 6-4
1903	Major Ritchie	Roy Allen	6-3, 5-7, 7-5, 6-0
1904	Sydney Smith	Major Ritchie	6-0, 6-4, 6-2
1905	Norman Brookes (Aus)	Sydney Smith	8-6, 6-4, 6-2
1906	Anthony Wilding (NZ)	Roderick McNair	6-2, 6-3, 6-2
1907	George Hillyard	Walter Crawley	6-4, 5-7, 6-4
1908	Anthony Wilding (NZ)	George Hillyard	walkover
1909	Otto Froitzheim (Ger)	Friedrich Rahe (Ger)	6-3, 6-8, 6-4, 7-5
1910	Gordon Lowe	Arthur Lowe	walkover
1911	Algernon Kingscote	Stanley Doust (Aus)	4-6, 6-8, 8-6, 6-0, 6-3
1912	Arthur Lowe	Stanley Doust (Aus)	6-4, 7-9, 6-0, 6-4
1913	James Parke	Arthur Lowe	6-3, 7-5, 2-6, 6-2
1914–18	No tournament held		
1919	Theodore Mavrogordato	Nicolae Misu (Rom)	6-3, 6-2, 6-4
1920	George Dodd (SA)	Alfred Beamish	6-4, 6-1, 6-2
1921	Brian Norton (SA)	Mohammed Sleem (Ind)	0-6, 6-4, 5-7, 6-2, 6-3
1922	Brian Norton (SA)	Gordon Lowe	6-2, 2-6, 6-4, 6-3
1923	Cotah Ramaswami (Ind)	Gordon Lowe	6-1, 8-6, 10-8
1924	Mohammed Sleem (Ind)	Gordon Lowe	6-2, 6-1, 6-1
1925	Charles Kingsley	Gordon Lowe	4-6, 6-2, 6-3, 3-6, 6-2
1926	Charles Kingsley	Bunny Austin	walkover

1927	Bunny Austin	William Powell	6-4, 6-4
1928	Yoshiro Ohta (Jpn)	Charles Kingsley	3-6, 6-1, 6-0
1929	Buster Andrews (NZ)	Keats Lester	6-4, 3-6, 6-4
1930	Ryuki Miki (Jpn)	Charles Kingsley	7-5, 6-3
1931	Jiro Satoh (Jpn)	Vernon Kirby (SA)	6-4, 6-3
1932	George Lyttleton Rogers (Ire)	Madan Atri Mohan (Ind)	6-8, 6-3, 6-4
1933	Vernon Kirby (SA)	George Lyttleton Rogers (Ire)	8-6, 6-2
1934	Nigel Sharpe	Buster Andrews (NZ)	6-3, 6-3
1935	Robert Tinkler	C.M. (Jimmy) Jones	8-6, 10-8
1936	Pat Hughes	Charles Hare	2-6, 9-7, 6-1
1937	Don Butler	Henry Billington	6-3, 6-3
1938	Don Butler	C.M. (Jimmy) Jones	6-4, 6-1
1939–45	No tournament held		
1946	Don Butler	Wai-Chuen Choy (Chn)	6-3, 6-4
1947	Ignacy Tłoczynski (Pol)	Jeff Robson (NZ)	6-2, 6-3
1948	Czesław Spychała (Pol)	Ignacy Tłoczynski (Pol)	5-7, 6-4, 8-6
1949	Heraldo Weiss (Arg)	Don Butler	6-3, 6-2
1950	Ivo Rinkel (Ned)	Geoff Paish	5-7, 7-5, 6-4
1951	Geoff Paish	Tony Mottram	6-4, 4-6, 6-1
1952	Geoff Paish	Anthony Starte	4-6, 6-2, 6-1
1953	Geoff Paish	Robert Lee	7-5, 6-0
1954	Geoff Paish	Bobby Wilson	6-2, 2-6, 7-5
1955	Geoff Paish	Mike Davies	6-4, 6-4
1956	Roger Becker	Gerald Oakley	6-3, 6-1
1957	Reg Bennett	Geoff Owen	6-3, 6-2
1958	Roger Becker	Reg Bennett	6-3, 4-6, 6-1
1959	Alan Mills	Michael Hann	8-6, 4-6, 6-3
1960	Mark Otway (NZ)	John McDonald (NZ)	6-4, 6-4
1961	Mark Otway (NZ)	Roger Becker	6-1, 4-6, 6-2
1962	Roger Becker	Mark Cox	4-6, 6-2, 6-4
1963	Mark Cox	Warren Jacques	1-6, 7-5, 6-2
1964	Geoff Bluet	Clay Iles	6-3, 6-3
1965	Gerald Battrick	Graham Stilwell	title shared
1966	Bob Maud (SA)	Brian Fairlie (NZ)	6-4, 6-2
1967	Frew McMillan (SA)	Mark Cox	6-3, 6-4
1968	Mark Cox	Owen Davidson (Aus)	6-4, 6-4
1969	Christian Kuhnke (WG)	Manuel Orantes (Spn)	6-4, 2-6, 9-7
1970	Ken Rosewall (Aus)	Bob Hewitt (SA)	6-2, 6-1

1971	Abandoned before finals due to rain		
1972	Andres Gimeno (Spn)	Pierre Barthes (Fra)	7-5, 6-3
1973	Mark Cox	Patrice Dominguez (Fra)	6-2, 2-6, 6-3

Women's Singles

Year	Winner	Runner-up	Score
1881	Agnes Watts	E. Hudson	Two sets to love
1882	E. Hudson	Minnie Congreve	6–2, 6–4
1883	M. Leslie	Minnie Congreve	10–8, 6–4
1884	Frances Burton	Nellie Burton	6–2, 6–4
1885	Blanche Bingley	Ada Strap	6-1, 6-0
1886	Margaret Bracewell	Blanche Bingley	6-1, 6-3
1887	Margaret Bracewell	Blanche Hillyard	6-4, 6-2
1888	Blanche Hillyard	Margaret Bracewell	6-1, 6-1
1889	May Langrishe	May Jacks	5-7, 6-2, 6-1
1890	May Langrishe	Edith Cole	6-2, 6-3
1891	Blanche Hillyard	May Langrishe	2-6, 7-5, 6-0
1892	Blanche Hillyard	Bertha Steedman	6-1, 6-4
1893	Blanche Hillyard	Maud Shackle	6-1, 4-6, 15-13
1894	Helen Jackson	Charlotte Cooper	6-4, 6-2
1895	Blanche Hillyard	Helen Jackson	6-4, 6-1
1896	Blanche Hillyard	Edith Austin	6-3, 4-6, 6-1
1897	Charlotte Cooper	Blanche Hillyard	6-4, 6-0
1898	Blanche Hillyard	Charlotte Cooper	7-5, 7-5
1899	Blanche Hillyard	Charlotte Cooper	6-2, 6-2
1900	Blanche Hillyard	Charlotte Cooper	7-9, 6-3, 6-3
1901	Charlotte Sterry	Blanche Hillyard	7-5, 5-7, 6-2
1902	Dorothea Douglass	Edith Austin	6-2, 6-2
1903	Connie Wilson	Dorothea Douglass	7-5, 6-2
1904	Dorothea Douglass	Charlotte Sterry	6-3, 6-4
1905	Blanche Hillyard	Agnes Morton	7-5, 4-6, 6-3
1906	Dorothea Douglass	Agnes Morton	3-6, 6-3, 6-2
1907	Dorothea Lambert Chambers	Charlotte Sterry	4-6, 6-3, 7-5
1908	Charlotte Sterry	Edith Boucher	6-4, 6-2
1909	Dora Boothby	Charlotte Sterry	6-3, 6-4
1910	Dorothea Lambert Chambers	Ethel Larcombe	7-5, 7-5
1911	Ethel Larcombe	Dora Boothby	7-5, 6-3
1912	Ethel Larcombe	Agnes Morton	6-1, 6-2

1913	Ethel Larcombe	Dorothea Lambert Chambers	6-2, 6-4
1914–18	No tournament held		
1919	Elizabeth Ryan (USA)	Phyllis Satterthwaite	6-1, 6-2
1920	Elizabeth Ryan (USA)	Geraldine Beamish	6-2, 4-6, 6-1
1921	Elizabeth Ryan (USA)	Irene Peacock (SA)	6-0, 6-3
1922	Irene Peacock (SA)	Kitty McKane	6-0, 3-6, 7-5
1923	Phoebe Holcroft	Christine Tyrrell	6-3, 6-3
1924	Ermyntrude Harvey	Phoebe Holcroft	6-0, 6-8, 6-4
1925	Phoebe Watson	Christine Tyrrell	2-6, 7-5, 6-3
1926	Phoebe Watson	Ermyntrude Harvey	6-4, 6-8, 6-2
1927	Phoebe Watson	Phyllis Covell	6-2, 6-2
1928	Phoebe Watson	Phyllis Covell	6-1, 6-2
1929	Elsie Goldsack	Jennie Sandison	8-6, 2-6, 6-3
1930	Phyllis Mudford	Mary Heeley	6-2, 7-5
1931	Freda James	Gwen Sterry	title shared
1932	Mary Heeley	Freda Ford	8-6, 6-2
1933	Phyllis King	Ermyntrude Harvey	6-3, 6-1
1934	Dorothy Round	Phyllis King	6-4, 6-1
1935	Billie Yorke	Susan Noel	3-6, 6-3, 6-2
1936	Anita Lizana (Chl)	Dorothy Round	6-4, 6-2
1937	Peggy Scriven	Jean Saunders	6-1, 6-0
1938	Phyllis King	Valerie Scott	5-7, 6-4, 6-4
1939–45	No tournament held		
1946	Joan Curry	Betty Hilton	title shared
1947	Joan Curry	Peggy Dawson-Scott	6-1, 9-7
1948	Jean Walker-Smith	Gem Hoahing	7-5, 6-4
1949	Gem Hoahing	Maria Terán de Weiss (Arg)	6-4, 6-2
1950	Jean Walker-Smith	Jean Quertier	6-2, 6-2
1951	Jean Walker-Smith	Angela Mortimer	6-2, 6-2
1952	Jean Walker-Smith	Jean Rinkel-Quertier	6-3, 6-4
1953	Shirley Bloomer	Patricia Harrison	7-5, 6-4
1954	Shirley Bloomer	Patricia Harrison	6-8, 7-5, 6-0
1955	Anne Shilcock	Jenny Middleton	6-4, 6-2
1956	Anne Shilcock	Penny Burrell	6-1, 6-2
1957	Ann Haydon	Angela Mortimer	6-3, 6-4
1958	Anne Shilcock	Sheila Waters	6-0, 6-0
1959	Sheila Armstrong	Jenny Young	6-0, 6-2
1960	Rita Bentley	Lorna Cawthorn	6-4, 6-2

1961	Lorna Cawthorn	Inga Overgaard (Den)	3-6, 6-1, 11-9
1962	Carole Rosser	Lorna Cawthorn	10-8, 6-2
1963	Vivienne Dennis	Heather Allen	6-3, 2-6, 7-5
1964	Fay Toyne (Aus)	Lorna Cawthorn	6-0, 5-7, 6-3
1965	Rita Bentley	Jill Blackman	title shared
1966	Susan Tutt	Anthea Rigby	4-6, 6-2, 6-4
1967	Lorna Greville-Collins	Margaret Harris (Aus)	6-8, 7-5, 6-1
1968	Maria Bueno (Bra)	Judy Tegart (Aus)	6-2, 6-4
1969	Karen Krantzcke (Aus)	Betty Ann Grubb (USA)	6-0, 9-7
1970	Ann Jones	Virginia Wade	8-6, 6-1
1971	Francoise Durr (Fra)	Judy Tegart-Dalton (Aus)	title shared
1972	Francoise Durr (Fra)	Judy Tegart-Dalton (Aus)	8-6, 6-3

The Eastbourne International

Devonshire Park discovered soon enough that Open tennis brought dangers as well as opportunities. Major sponsorship deals were hard to come by and usually short-term, leaving tournament committees struggling to carry on when such deals terminated – unable to cover costs, let alone offer the prize money required to attract the world's best. The Eastbourne meeting managed to stay afloat and flourish in the longer term, but only by reinventing itself. In 1970 Devonshire Park abandoned its long-standing September timing and sought out a new niche in the crowded pre-Wimbledon calendar. The authorities in College Road also decided – in line with the emerging pattern elsewhere – to provide a more focused offering, one with high-quality women's play at its heart. The South of England Championships in its old format was jettisoned, and the Eastbourne International (as it was often loosely called) was born.

The shift in scheduling to June was crucial to the success of the rebranded tournament. For many years past, Devonshire Park's clash of dates with the US Championships hampered the quality of its entry; the new date meant a host of leading stars welcomed the chance to compete on top-notch grass courts ahead of Wimbledon. Other factors also powered the development of the Eastbourne

International. The drive of club officials, with backing from the local authority in the town, ensured the venue offered the type of up-to-date facilities expected by the new breed of professional. Regular BBC television coverage began, boosting Eastbourne's profile and encouraging a string of good sponsors to come forward, including John Player (whose backing led to generous prize money being offered at the inaugural 1974 event), Colgate, BMW, Pilkington Glass, Direct Line and Hastings Direct. Some highly unusual publicity in 1975, which made front as well as back-page newspaper headlines, further helped to bring the tournament to a wider audience.

MISS GOOLAGONG'S TIME OUT

Two of the greats of the women's game, Virginia Wade and Billie Jean King, battled out an exciting final at the Eastbourne International in 1975; Wade won the deciding set 6-4. But all the attention that week was stolen by another superstar, Evonne Goolagong, who surprised fellow competitors and officials alike when she absented herself from proceedings for a day – to get married. The 23-year-old Aussie, already a Wimbledon champion, arrived late into Heathrow ahead of her first scheduled singles match at Eastbourne, which she promptly lost. It seems she had other things on her mind, for on Thursday, 19 June she wed her English boyfriend Roger Cawley in a small private ceremony held at Canterbury Registry Office. In the short term, there was no opportunity for the couple to enjoy a honeymoon. 'Miss Goolagong' (it was too late to alter her name in the tournament programme) returned to Eastbourne the following day, where she was greeted with loud cheers as she arrived on centre court for a doubles match. She and her American partner Peggy Michel got through three rounds in quick succession to reach the final on Saturday. But there was to be no fairytale ending on court; Goolagong and Michel were beaten in the final by Olga Morozova and Julie Anthony.

For the previous half-century, as we have seen, South of England women's finals at Devonshire Park had frequently been all-domestic affairs. But this changed radically in the new era of the Eastbourne International. In addition to her victory over Billie Jean King in 1975, Virginia Wade made it to finals day twice more, on both occasions losing in straight sets to America's Chris Evert. Wade's defeat in 1976 marked the last time through to the present day that a British woman has contested the final in College Road. With the number and calibre of top-ranked entrants from around the world

MEMORABLE MATCHES

Two of the greats of the modern women's game went head-to-head in the 1978 Eastbourne final – the first with TV cameras in attendance – and the spectacle did not disappoint. America's multi-grand slam champion Chris Evert faced a rising challenge from Czech exile (and later US citizen) Martina Navratilova in a match that many said was worthy of a Wimbledon final. In blustery south-coast conditions, Navratilova started strongly, racing into a 5-3 lead. Although Evert hit four consecutive winners to take the next game, Martina held on to secure the first set 6-4. Although she fell three games behind in the next set, Chrissie suddenly found her best form, playing brilliantly for a sustained period that saw her take the second 6-4 and come close to victory at 4-1 ahead in the decider. The two-time Wimbledon champion served for the title at 5-3, and later missed a match point, but she could not finish off her resolute opponent. Navratilova held her nerve, clawed her way back in and eventually, after a see-saw 16th game, she secured the win 9-7. Not only was it worthy of a Wimbledon final, it turned out to be a dress rehearsal for just that. A fortnight later, when the two met in SW19, Navratilova again came out on top, winning 7-5 in the final set to capture her first Wimbledon crown.

rising sharply, the Devonshire Park meeting thereafter featured many of the leading contenders for the Wimbledon title; indeed, the final now acted at times as a de facto warm-up for the denouement in SW19 (see *Memorable Matches* opposite).

Despite losing an even tighter Eastbourne final to her great adversary in 1979 (Evert took the third-set decider 13-11), Miss Navratilova went on to be the star of the show at Devonshire Park throughout the 1980s and beyond. A popular crowd favourite, she won the singles title six times between 1978 and 1986 (she also held, with Pam Shriver, the doubles title from 1981 to 1986). The Czechoslovak Helena Sukova inflicted a rare defeat on Martina in 1987, but the tenacious champion returned the following year to embark on another four-year unbeaten spell. Navratilova's final victory came in 1993, when she defeated Dutch opponent Miriam Oremans in three sets. In securing 11 Eastbourne titles, Martina equalled the record set long before by Blanche Bingley/Hillyard; this without having the advantage – as Blanche did in her day – of several times only having to play in one challenge round match to retain the title.

A few months after Navratilova's final victory, large parts of the north stand around Devonshire Park's main show court were destroyed by fire. This shocking setback was eventually turned into a blessing, as it paved the way for the construction of a large new stand (enabling over 7,000 spectators to watch play on the centre court), as well as a modernised media centre and enhanced hospitality areas. Before too long the International Lawn Tennis Centre, as the venue became known, was winning plaudits and helping to ensure that the Eastbourne International continued to flourish at the start of the 21st century.

The tournament brought millions of pounds into the town's coffers via extra business for hotels, shops and restaurants and many of the world's finest continued to compete on the south coast each summer. In the post-Navratilova era, the roll of honour featured an ongoing stream of grand slam champions including Monica Seles, Jana Novotna, Kim Clijsters and Justine Henin.

Not everything has gone smoothly for Devonshire Park since the turn of the century. With the LTA determined to remodel the pre-Wimbledon tournament schedule, there were rumours for a while that the Eastbourne International might be relocated to London and combined with the Queen's Championship. But ultimately it was decided the tournament should be retained and indeed extended. With fresh sponsorship from pension provider Aegon UK, and with LTA investment to fund additional seating capacity, from 2009 the International Tennis Centre took over the running of the ATP tournament previously held in Nottingham during the same pre-Wimbledon week. The return of men's competition to Eastbourne for the first time since the 1970s yielded mixed results. Hopes of instantly securing an entry to match the standard of the women were not easily realised, and the event was moved back to Nottingham for a couple of years. But with commitment and persistence Devonshire Park was again, in time, able to boast of illustrious men's champions such as Andy Roddick, Feliciano Lopez and Novak Djokovic.

Although the Eastbourne International – like the rest of the English summer season – was abandoned in 2020 due to the global coronavirus pandemic, the future for the tournament looks bright. Long-serving Devonshire Park club chairman Ken Pollock believes that Eastbourne's success results from a mixture of things: exceptional grass courts, state-of-the-art facilities, generally good weather and a glittering heritage. These factors (plus, it might be added, dedicated organisers and secure sponsorship) help to explain why a small coastal town manages to stand shoulder-to-shoulder with far larger, glamorous global cities such as Sydney and Tokyo in regularly offering world-class tennis.[10] It might be an exaggeration to imply that the weather was always fine on the south coast – a chilly sea breeze could often make itself felt, even in June – and it should not be forgotten that at various points in the past other small towns like Scarborough have hosted similarly renowned tournaments. But Mr Pollock's pride in what Eastbourne has achieved certainly stands scrutiny: over the course of the nation's tennis history from the 1880s to the present day, Devonshire Park is the venue that has most consistently punched above its weight.

RECORD BREAKERS

Most titles – Men: Sydney Smith (5), Geoff Paish (5), Wilfred Baddeley (4), Ernest Lewis (3), Andrew Ziffo (3), Don Butler (3), Roger Becker (3), Mark Cox (3)

Most titles – Women: Blanche Hillyard (11 – once as Blanche Bingley), Martina Navratilova (11), Dorothea Lambert Chambers (5 – three times as Dorothea Douglass), Phoebe Watson (5 – once as Phoebe Holcroft), Jean Walker-Smith (4)

Number of Eastbourne champions who also won Wimbledon singles

Men: 5 (1881–1973), 1 (2009–2020); Women: 8 (1881–1972) 6 (1974–2020); Total: 20

Eastbourne International

Women's Singles

Year	Winner	Runner-up	Score
1974	Chris Evert (USA)	Virginia Wade	7-5, 6-4
1975	Virginia Wade	Billie Jean King (USA)	7-5, 4-6, 6-4
1976	Chris Evert (USA)	Virginia Wade	8-6, 6-3
1977	No tournament held		
1978	Martina Navratilova (USA)	Chris Evert (USA)	6-4, 4-6, 9-7
1979	Chris Evert (USA)	Martina Navratilova (USA)	7-5, 5-7, 13-11
1980	Tracy Austin (USA)	Wendy Turnbull (Aus)	7-6, 6-2
1981	Tracy Austin (USA)	Andrea Jaeger (USA)	6-3, 6-4
1982	Martina Navratilova (USA)	Hana Mandliková (Czh)	6-4, 6-3
1983	Martina Navratilova (USA)	Wendy Turnbull (Aus)	6-1, 6-1
1984	Martina Navratilova (USA)	Kathy Jordan (USA)	6-4, 6-1
1985	Martina Navratilova (USA)	Helena Suková (Czh)	6-4, 6-3

1986	Martina Navratilova (USA)	Helena Sukova (Czh)	3-6, 6-3, 6-4
1987	Helena Sukova (Czh)	Martina Navratilova (USA)	7-6, 6-3
1988	Martina Navratilova (USA)	Natasha Zvereva (USSR)	6-2, 6-2
1989	Martina Navratilova (USA)	Raffaella Reggi (Ita)	7-6, 6-2
1990	Martina Navratilova (USA)	Gretchen Magers (USA)	6-0, 6-2
1991	Martina Navratilova (USA)	Arantxa Sanchez-Vicario (Spa)	6-4, 6-4
1992	Lori McNeil (USA)	Linda Harvey Wild (USA)	6-4, 6-4
1993	Martina Navratilova (USA)	Miriam Oremans (Ned)	2-6, 6-2, 6-3
1994	Meredith McGrath (USA)	Linda Harvey Wild (USA)	6-2, 6-4
1995	Nathalie Tauziat (Fra)	Chanda Rubin (USA)	3-6, 6-0, 7-5
1996	Monica Seles (USA)	Mary Joe Fernandez (USA)	6-0, 6-2
1997	Jana Novotna (Czh)	Arantxa Sanchez-Vicario (Spa)	title shared
1998	Jana Novotna (Czh)	Arantxa Sanchez-Vicario (Spa)	6-1, 7-5
1999	Natasha Zvereva (Blr)	Nathalie Tauziat (Fra)	0-6, 7-5, 6-3
2000	Julie Halard-Decugis (Fra)	Dominique Van Roost (Bel)	7-6, 6-4
2001	Lindsay Davenport (USA)	Magüi Serna (Spa)	6-2, 6-0
2002	Chanda Rubin (USA)	Anastasia Myskina (Rus)	6-1, 6-3
2003	Chanda Rubin (USA)	Conchita Martinez (Spa)	6-4, 3-6, 6-4
2004	Svetlana Kuznetsova (Rus)	Daniela Hantuchova (Slo)	2-6, 7-6, 6-4
2005	Kim Clijsters (Bel)	Vera Dushevina (Rus)	7-5, 6-0
2006	Justine Henin (Bel)	Anastasia Myskina (Rus)	4-6, 6-1, 7-6
2007	Justine Henin (Bel)	Amelie Mauresmo (Fra)	7-5, 6-7, 7-6
2008	Agnieszka Radwanska (Pol)	Nadia Petrova (Rus)	6-4, 6-7, 6-4
2009	Caroline Wozniacki (Den)	Virginie Razzano (Fra)	7-6, 7-5
2010	Ekaterina Makarova (Rus)	Victoria Azarenka (Blr)	7-6, 6-4
2011	Marion Bartoli (Fra)	Petra Kvitova (CR)	6-1, 4-6, 7-5
2012	Tamira Paszek (Aut)	Angelique Kerber (Ger)	5-7, 6-3, 7-5
2013	Elena Vesnina (Rus)	Jamie Hampton (USA)	6-2, 6-1
2014	Madison Keys (USA)	Angelique Kerber (Ger)	6-3, 3-6, 7-5
2015	Belinda Bencic (Swi)	Agnieszka Radwanska (Pol)	6-4, 4-6, 6-0
2016	Dominika Cibulková (Slo)	Karolina Pliskova (Slo)	7-5, 6-3
2017	Karolina Pliskova (Slo)	Caroline Wozniacki (Den)	6-4, 6-4
2018	Caroline Wozniacki (Den)	Aryna Sabalenka (Blr)	7-5, 7-6
2019	Karolina Pliskova (Slo)	Angelique Kerber (Ger)	6-1, 6-4
2020	No tournament held		

Men's Singles

Year	Winner	Runner-up	Score
2009	Dmitry Tursunov (Rus)	Frank Dancevic (Can)	6-3, 7-6
2010	Michael Llodra (Fra)	Guillermo Garcia-Lopez (Spa)	7-5, 6-2
2011	Andreas Seppi (Ita)	Janko Tipsarevic (Srb)	7-6, 3-6, 5-3 retd
2012	Andy Roddick (USA)	Andreas Seppi (Ita)	6-3, 6-2
2013	Feliciano Lopez (Spa)	Gilles Simon (Fra)	7-6, 6-7, 6-0
2014	Feliciano Lopez (Spa)	Richard Gasquet (Fra)	6-3, 6-7, 7-5
2015–16	No tournament held		
2017	Novak Djokovic (Srb)	Gael Monfils (Fra)	6-3, 6-4
2018	Mischa Zverev (Ger)	Lukas Lacko (Slo)	6-4, 6-4
2019	Taylor Fritz (USA)	Sam Querry (USA)	6-3, 6-4
2020	No tournament held		

5

Bournemouth

ON 29 April 2018 a special celebration was held at the West Hants Tennis Club in Bournemouth. A day of speeches and exhibition matches took place to mark the 50th anniversary of the first tournament in the history of world tennis to allow amateurs and professionals to compete against each other.

The British Hard Court Championships (BHCC) of 1968 marked the birth of today's ultra-competitive global tennis circuit, opening the way to the rise of a multi-million dollar industry that consigned the (officially) unpaid amateur era to the records books. Among those attending the anniversary celebration were a few players who competed in 1968 and were able to reminisce about that epoch-making week at West Hants, including some like Mark Cox who stole the headlines at the time by becoming the first amateur to beat a contract professional. Ken Rosewall and Virginia Wade, the singles champions from 1968, conveyed messages of gratitude to the authorities who finally brought the two codes together after years of agitation for reform, and Britain's Tim Henman spoke of the longer-term significance of the event; it was, he said, a 'huge game changer for players and tennis across the world'.[1]

Bournemouth is frequently – and justifiably – lauded for its unique, pivotal moment in the spotlight. But, as this chapter sets out to show, the BHCC deserves to be remembered for much more.

As we shall see, for long periods between the 1920s and 1970s West Hants was widely regarded as hosting England's most important annual tournament outside of Wimbledon.

* * *

For the first three years of its existence, the Hard Court Championships was based not in Bournemouth but 100 miles further along the south coast, at Torquay in Devon. The LTA created the event in response to the growing popularity of hard-court tennis after the First World War. Many of the new clubs springing up across the country to cater for increased demand did not have the means to maintain grass courts, and opted for surfaces that gave the potential to play all year round, rather than for a restricted period only in the warmer weather. By choosing a spring date – the inaugural meeting was held in April 1924 – the authorities hoped to provide both a focal point for the start of the English season and a counterpoint to Wimbledon. Whereas SW19 remained unchallenged at the pinnacle of lawn tennis, the BHCC was to act as the nation's premier showcase for exponents of hard-court play, both domestic and from overseas.

Torquay was firmly established by the 1920s as a holiday destination for affluent visitors and already staged a popular grass-court meeting that drew top amateurs to the resort each summer. On the basis of tradition and reputation, the municipal courts on the Torquay seafront – lined up in front of an impressive grandstand – were chosen to host the first Hard Court Championships, attended by players of six different nationalities. In reasonably mild spring weather, albeit with a stiff sea breeze blowing onshore, the Anglo-Australian Randolph Lycett took the men's title, beating Christiaan van Lennep of the Netherlands comfortably in four sets. In the women's event, all the entrants were British apart from Californian Elizabeth Ryan, a serial trophy collector in the 1920s; in addition to the inaugural singles in Torquay, Ryan also won the women's doubles and mixed doubles titles.[2]

For the next two years the tournament struggled to attract many non-UK entrants, although the standard of play in the latter stages was still high. The men's final in 1926 turned into a knife-edge encounter between the experienced favourite, Jacques 'Toto' Brugnon – one of the famed French 'Musketeers' – and the youthful Cambridge student, Bunny Austin. The rising English star led by two sets to one but squandered a lead in the fourth; after an interruption for rain, the Frenchman took control in the decider.

Another exciting home prospect, hard-hitting Joan Fry, won the women's singles, although Miss Ryan (having easily retained the title in 1925) was not in town to defend her crown. The large crowd attending for finals day was especially appreciative of the victory in the women's doubles of 14-year-old Betty Nuthall – later to become the first female British winner of the US Championships – and her partner Charlotte Sterry, now in her mid-50s but still capable of showing glimpses of the crisp volleying that helped her secure five Wimbledon titles.

A successful last day in 1926 could not disguise underlying problems facing the BHCC. With a draw made up overwhelmingly of home entrants – Brugnon was an exception to the rule and Ryan's absence was missed – the LTA felt the tournament was not fulfilling its original ambition of attracting world stars to England. A new venue was sought, closer and more accessible to London, with the result that from 1927 onwards the meeting was staged at the West Hants Lawn Tennis Club in Bournemouth. Founded just a year before in Roislin Road South, a couple of miles from the town centre and the lengthy promenade and seafront, West Hants proved to be an inspired choice. Its spacious and attractive setting in the leafy Bournemouth suburbs, its newly laid clay courts, and the adoption of a slightly later start date for the tournament than previously, all helped to ensure that the quality and international flavour of the entry rose sharply.

By the end of the 1920s the Bournemouth Championship had assumed the mantle of being the most acclaimed event in the non-Wimbledon home season. This did not mean it instantly featured all the top players of the day. American dislike of what were often dismissed as 'dirt' courts (wherever they were located) meant there was to be no winner of the men's singles from the USA until the 1950s. But the BHCC did now attract many of the star performers of European tennis, among whose number were French players who at the time were dominating the global scene both individually and in national team competition. France won the Davis Cup six times in succession in the late 1920s and 1930s, and French men and women regularly turned up in force in Bournemouth, keen, as hard-court specialists, to find top-quality opposition in the period between the ending of their own domestic winter season on the Riviera and the late-May French Championships in Paris, raised to grand slam status a few years earlier.

The first winner of the men's event at the Hard Court Championships after the switch from Torquay was René Lacoste, the acknowledged leader of the 'Musketeers' in the golden age of French tennis. A masterful baseline tactician, Lacoste arrived in Bournemouth as a three-time grand slam champion, including victory at Wimbledon in 1925. He easily beat South African Patrick Spence in the 1927 BHCC final, a feat he repeated by an almost identical score the following year. French players did not generally target English grass-court meetings outside of Wimbledon, but on the hard courts at Torquay and West Hants they illustrated their prowess by taking the men's title in four out of six years. Lacoste's two victories were sandwiched between those of Brugnon in 1926 and Christian Boussus, another skilful exponent of clay-court tennis, in 1931. In the women's singles, Simonne Mathieu – later to be a two-time winner of her home grand slam at Roland Garros – claimed the BHCC title without dropping a set in the finals of 1931 and 1932.

SOGGY FEET

Fleet Street journalist Laurie Pignon recalled that in his early days reporting on the amateur tour, there was still a place for the occasional eccentric. A particular favourite 'character' of the journalist was Howard Walton, an accomplished player (he once represented Britain in the Davis Cup) but one whose retrieving style, looping slow returns to the baseline, frustrated many an opponent on the slow clay at Bournemouth. Poor weather was a regular hazard on the south coast in spring, and on one rain-interrupted day Walton, finding it difficult to keep his feet on the slippery surface, bemused onlookers when he called for a bowl of washing-up water. At the change of ends, he proceeded to step into the bowl wearing his shoes and socks. Whether he was acclimatising to the elements or adopting an unusual tactical ploy was not clear. 'I never knew what effect it had on his feet,' Pignon wrote, 'but it certainly did not help his opponent's concentration.'[3]

It was a measure of the status rapidly acquired by Bournemouth that it was integral to the ambitions of the two men who restored British fortunes on the global stage in the 1930s. From the time when they were emerging young hopefuls through to experienced Davis Cup champions, Bunny Austin and Fred Perry both regarded the BHCC as a key part of their annual schedule. Austin, having narrowly missed out in the 1926 final in Torquay, took the title for the first time in 1929, beating Louis Raymond of South Africa. The following year he narrowly survived a second-round fright against the younger, inexperienced but fast-improving Perry. The defending champion was thoroughly rattled by his opponent's aggressive demeanour and tactics; with a little extra calmness at decisive moments, Perry would likely have won. Fred's immense frustration at missing out – he held a match point in the fifth-set decider – is usually mentioned in the context of his off-the-scale hatred of losing, though it also reflected what he felt was at stake: the hard-court title was a big deal, and he wanted to win it. By contrast, in his years of world ascendancy Perry rarely appeared in singles at the pre-Wimbledon grass-court tournaments in his homeland, preferring to get ready for SW19 with his own practice and warm-up routines.

Perry went out early at Bournemouth in 1931; he suffered an injury in a Davis Cup tie the previous week and was not fully fit. But in 1932 he fulfilled his ambition to lift the trophy when he came back from two sets to love down in the final to beat the towering Irishman George Lyttleton Rogers. This was the first of what would be an unequalled record of five successive BHCC triumphs. Perry's straight-sets victory over Australia's Jack Crawford in 1934 was confirmation of a trend seen on the wider, grand slam stage: Fred had by then eclipsed 'Gentleman Jack' to become the best player in the world. Perry's other three triumphs were all secured at the expense of Austin, exacting ample revenge for the defeat in 1930. He was described by one reporter as a 'crushing machine' as he battled his way to victory year after year at West Hants through all kinds of matches, long and short, and in all extremes of weather. In 1935 it was so cold on finals day that Fred turned up attired in a scarf, gloves and a buttoned-up full-length overcoat.[4]

Perry's association with Bournemouth was to end with a curious twist. As an eight-time grand slam singles champion, he decided in 1936 to leave amateur ranks and tour North America and Europe with Bill Tilden's professional troop. This decision meant he was barred from amateur competition and unable to defend any of his existing titles, including the BHCC. He did, however, return to the south-coast resort in the summer of 1937 – not to Roislin Road – but to Dean Court, home of the Bournemouth and Boscombe Athletic football club, where he played one of a series of exhibition matches against fellow pro Ellie Vines in front of a 4,000-strong crowd. Vines won in four sets. Perry and Vines were entitled, as touring professionals, to be paid from the receipts of paying spectators, though some commentators reflected on the irony that the British and world number one was now cold-shouldered by tennis officialdom in his own country, barred from playing at any LTA-affiliated club and forced to appear on a makeshift wooden court specially constructed and transported around the country.[5]

Fred's departure allowed his old friend and rival, Bunny Austin, to regain the BHCC spotlight. Austin claimed his second West Hants title in 1937, although the following year he suffered a surprise four-set defeat in the final to China's Kho Sin-Kie. Unfazed by a strong wind blowing across the court, the Chinese player – unseeded in the draw – outwitted the champion to become the first man from his country to win a national singles title in England. The absence of Perry, though regretted, did not dent the continued popularity of the tournament, with record crowds streaming to Roislin Road to see not only Davis Cup stars such as Austin, but also fine-quality women's play.

Worcestershire's Dorothy Round became a two-time champion, beating Helen Jacobs of the USA in 1933 and scraping to victory over fellow Brit Peggy Scriven a year later. Round's success in 1934 (the year she went on to claim her first Wimbledon title) was described by *Lawn Tennis and Badminton* as one of the 'luckiest wins of a major championship ever recorded'; she benefited from a string of net cords at vital moments that helped her come through 8-6 in the deciding set.[6]

When elite competition resumed after the Second World War, the reputation of the Bournemouth Championship was quickly restored and, if anything, enhanced. The heyday of triumphant home favourites – Perry, Austin, Round and Stammers – may have passed, but the BHCC still featured the talents of numerous champions, both from Europe and now also from further-flung parts of the globe, benefiting from the improved air travel that allowed top stars to more easily compete all year round. In the decade after resumption in 1946, the men's singles title at West Hants was claimed by players of seven different nationalities, including two Wimbledon champions – Czech exile Jaroslav Drobny and Budge Patty of the United States. The increased willingness of leading Americans to start their European season in Bournemouth was underlined by the prominence of another Wimbledon champion, Doris Hart, who won the women's title four times in succession after 1951.

UNDERRATED CHAMPION

Careers of British players are often judged in relation to performance at Wimbledon, and in this regard Kay Stammers was a 'nearly woman'; she reached the final in 1939 but was comprehensively beaten by America's Alice Marble. Yet Stammers was a highly accomplished competitor with a fine overall record, including several singles titles on home soil in the mid to late 1930s. Despite her attacking style favouring faster grass courts, the left-hander secured a creditable hat-trick on the clay at Bournemouth. In 1935 she dispatched Yorkshire's Peggy Scriven (a two-time winner at Roland Garros) in straight sets, and she twice subsequently got the better of the talented Anita Lizana. Stammers also had a respectable record at other home events: she won the North of England Championships in Scarborough and was runner-up at Beckenham and at the Covered Court Championships at Queen's. Nor should it be forgotten that Miss Stammers, still only in her mid-20s in 1939, may well have gone on to greater things but for the suspension of competition that followed the outbreak of war. Support for this view can be found in the fact that, despite losing several years of prime playing time, she was still good enough after the war – married as Mrs Menzies – to claim further frontline titles, at Surbiton and Beckenham.

LONG DRAWN-OUT

South Africa's Eric Sturgess dominated proceedings at West Hants in 1947 and 1948. On both occasions he secured three titles, although in 1948 his success was hard earned; indeed, he set up something of an endurance record. In generally fine weather the lithe, sun-tanned Sturgess advanced steadily during the week to the latter stages of the singles, men's doubles and mixed doubles. But when rain forced a lengthy suspension of play on the Friday he was faced with a heavy schedule on finals day. Going on court at 10.30am, he came through a five-set men's doubles semi-final, and without taking a break, then won the singles by beating Polish opponent Tloczynski in straight sets. Although rain interrupted proceedings for a couple of hours, when play resumed Sturgess completed three further matches: the men's doubles final, with his Dutch partner van Meegeren, followed by the semi-final and final of the mixed, which he won, partnered by Jean Quertier. He came off court, having retained his triple crown of titles, shortly before 7pm. By any reckoning his stamina was impressive. Across a period of over eight hours he had played 15 sets and a total of 127 games; all carried off, Lawn Tennis magazine reported, without 'fuss or flurry'.[7]

The post-war BHCC proved to be a particularly happy hunting ground for the swelling ranks of Australian contenders, who significantly reinforced the international flavour of the entry. Jack Harper was the first winner of the men's singles after the war, and the subsequent roll of honour included many of the Aussie legends of the modern game, both men and women: the likes of Roy Emerson, Rod Laver, Ken Rosewall, John Newcombe, Margaret Court and Evonne Goolagong. Two further Australian Wimbledon champions, Frank Sedgman and Lew Hoad, both failed, however, to capture the Bournemouth title. In the finals of 1952 and 1957 respectively, neither was able to neutralise the clay-court adroitness of Drobny, a four-time winner at West Hants. The great Hoad was considered, by some, to have reserved his very best efforts for the grand slams and the Davis Cup.

HOAD'S BIG NIGHT OUT

More so than in recent times, the amateurs of the pre-Open era travelled and socialised together, and often enjoyed a good night out when the opportunity arose. At Bournemouth in 1956, the press spoke of 'gasps of astonishment' when reigning Australian national champion Lew Hoad was beaten in straight sets in the last four by Ham Richardson, a young American student studying at Oxford University. There was much speculation as to the cause of this sensational result. Some suggested that the Arctic-like conditions, cold and windy, were not to the blond Aussie's liking. A contributory factor was later revealed by British Davis Cup player Mike Davies, who in his memoirs said that the night before the semi-final Hoad was among a group of players who visited a night club – 'yes, they ... have such things in Bournemouth', he wrote – before continuing their 'riotous party' at a luxurious flat in the town. In view of all this, it was small wonder that Hoad appeared to be playing, as one journalist put it, in 'a most casual manner'.[8]

From the mid-1950s onwards, the new post-war generation of rising Brits did not allow overseas stars to have it all their own way at West Hants. In 1958 home-based players claimed each of the five main titles, singles and doubles, for the first time in over 20 years. The winner of the men's singles was Billy Knight, whose patient tactics on the slow clay saw him claim two further victories in the 1960s. On the women's side, Britain's trio of post-war Wimbledon champions all built up enviable records at the Hard Court Championships. Devon's Angela Mortimer triumphed four times, as did Ann Jones, the latter with four successive wins from 1963 to 1966. Ann missed out setting a record of five straight victories when she lost in 1967 to up-and-coming youngster Virginia Wade, who in time herself claimed the BHCC title four times.

YOUNG WOMAN IN A HURRY

Virginia Wade was born in Bournemouth (although raised mostly in South Africa) and it was therefore a fitting venue for her first main senior success. The young Miss Wade's attacking style had already brought her prominence as a junior, but after combining tennis with undergraduate study at Sussex University a real breakthrough in her career came at West Hants in 1967. Pitted in the final against the more experienced British number one Ann Jones – one of the finest exponents of clay-court tennis in the world, two-time champion at Roland Garros – Wade's hard-hitting but disciplined shot-making saw her take the first set 6-1 in only 19 minutes. At 3-2 ahead in the second, the local girl looked on course for a swift triumph. Jones called on all her grit and tactical acumen to prolong the contest, but at 9-8 down she dropped her serve and Wade stepped up with another strong service game to clinch victory in little over an hour. Press onlookers gushed about Wade's performance and its significance. She had laid down a marker to be a contender for top honours, it was said, and British tennis was bound to be richer for the emergence of a rival to 'Queen Ann'. Before the year's end, the protagonists were to meet in two more domestic finals: Ann won at Beckenham, while Virginia edged it at the Palace Hotel in Torquay.

A year on from the Wade-Jones clash, in April 1968, West Hants found itself making tennis history. The choice of Bournemouth for such a breakthrough moment – pitting amateurs against professionals in tournament play for the first time – should not come as a surprise. The BHCC were of comparable renown to prominent European meetings such as Monte Carlo and Rome, and British administrators had (belatedly, since the late 1950s) been at the forefront of efforts to abolish differences in playing status. But there was no guarantee of success when proceedings got under way in Bournemouth.

The sport's governing authority, the ILTF, sanctioned only a limited number of experimental Open tournaments in 1968, and there was much nervousness in the air. Having left the amateur game to show they had outgrown it, the contract professionals such as Laver and Rosewall who travelled to the south coast were under pressure to prove they really were the best in the world. For their part, amateurs feared being heavily outgunned on court, even

---

MEMORABLE MATCH

Britain's Mark Cox secured a unique place in tennis history at the Hard Court Championships in 1968: he famously became the first amateur, a player still under the jurisdiction of his national association, to beat a contracted professional. Onlookers were engrossed as Cox, looking in the words of American journalist Bud Collins 'like an athletic Harpo Marx in his blond curls', wrote himself into the record books in the second round. Nerves played a part as he failed to register a game in the opening set against the veteran (approaching his 40th birthday) but still dangerous American pro Pancho Gonzales. The Leicestershire left-hander steadied himself and seized the second 6-4. The virtues of open play were suddenly on full display: a strong amateur was giving a top pro a run for his money. Gonzales took the third set, but thereafter ran out of steam against a younger, sharper opponent. The American's confident demeanour of the early exchanges was replaced by a hounded look and Cox went for the kill, taking the last two sets 6-3 each to claim victory in three and a half hours. The British man found his photo plastered across front as well as back pages the following day. The Guardian's David Gray wrote that it was a hugely significant moment; the world had just witnessed a 'lawn tennis earthquake'.[9]

---

humiliated. If this latter scenario played out, organisers feared the new venture would lack credibility and that restructuring the whole calendar around Open tournaments might prove impossible. As it turned out, aside from typically inclement English weather, the week could not have gone better, thanks in no small part to Mark Cox (see *Memorable Match* on previous page).

Mark Cox received further plaudits after he beat another professional, Australian Roy Emerson, in the last eight. Cox finally came down to earth when he lost in straight sets in the semi-finals to Rod Laver. The Leicestershire man's personal place in the annals of the sport was assured, but more importantly, he played a key role in ensuring the Bournemouth experiment was considered a huge success, having attracted over 30,000 spectators to the venue in addition to mostly positive worldwide media attention. Cox showed unequivocally that amateurs were capable of competing with the top pros, whose dignity was in turn preserved by two of their number contesting the men's final (indeed, seven of the eight men's quarter-finalists at West Hants were pros, who in due course won all but two of the ten Open tournaments that took place in 1968).

In a superb advert for the game, enjoyed by TV audiences as well as those present, Laver was pipped over four sets by fellow Aussie Ken Rosewall, who pocketed the BHCC winner's cheque of £1,000. Virginia Wade retained the women's crown with victory over Scotland's Winnie Shaw, although she declined the first prize of £300 – partly in protest at the money being so much lower than the men's and also because of uncertainty over her playing status (had she accepted, she might have been barred from remaining amateur events on the 1968 tournament schedule).[10] Although there were bumps in the road ahead – skirmishes between amateur officialdom and pro tour organisers continued for several more years – Bournemouth was a genuine milestone, pushing tennis firmly in the direction of its modern-day international circuit. From the administrator's point of view, LTA chairman Derek Hardwick was able to hail a transformative week. 'Tell them in America,' Hardwick said to journalist Bud Collins, 'what a success open tennis is …There's no going back after this.'[11]

In the medium term, the fact that everything unfolded so well in 1968 bolstered Bournemouth's reputation and its place in the tennis calendar. Sponsorship deals with Wills, Rothmans and Coca-Cola ensured that elite stars continued to travel to West Hants each spring in pursuit of lucrative prize money. Whereas the pot available in 1968 was around £3,500, by 1972 the total on offer had reached £15,000. Australia's record-breaking grand slam champion Margaret Court was irresistible in the women's singles. She took the title three years in succession, although not without difficulty in 1969, when she had to come back from 4-1 down in the deciding set to defeat Winnie Shaw. Despite Shaw being a two-time losing finalist, home supporters had some cause for cheer in the early years of the Open era. Mark Cox returned to win the men's singles in 1970, and he was followed a year later by the unseeded Welshman Gerald Battrick. Virginia Wade beat Evonne Goolagong and Julie Heldman of the USA in 1973 and 1974 respectively to add to her previous two titles.

Ironically, however, the changes ushered in by the week that gave the Hard Court Championships its cherished place in history helped, in the longer run, to cause its demise. As the global calendar became ever more crowded and commercialised, Bournemouth found it hard to attract year after year the type of world-leading entry necessary to ensure stellar sponsorship deals. British television coverage of tennis became consolidated into the prime summer months (favouring the likes of Queen's and Eastbourne), leaving West Hants struggling to compete against hard-court rivals such as Hamburg, which switched its annual date from autumn to spring in the Open era. On the men's side in particular, the Australians and Americans who graced the BHCC in earlier times now mostly stayed, preferring to compete elsewhere at venues able to offer more generous prize money (not to mention, in many cases, warmer weather than found in Bournemouth).

By the late 1970s the writing was on the wall. Despite the best efforts of club officials, the tournament was not held in either 1977 or 1979 owing to the absence of suitable sponsorship. The men's event ran four more times between 1980 and 1983, dominated in the main by European and South American clay-court specialists. It produced some memorable highlights, notably when Spaniard Angel Gimenez reached the final in 1982 after saving match points in three successive rounds. His efforts left him drained, however: he won only two games in the final against his skilful compatriot, Manuel Orantes. The women's singles operated only once in this four-year period, the title going in 1981 to Britain's Jo Durie.

The reality by the early 1980s was that the BHCC in its erstwhile format was no longer part of the frontline international schedule. Short-lived revivals did take place over a decade later. The Rover-sponsored British Clay Court Championships, part of the lower tier of the women's tour, was held at West Hants in 1995, but was not considered sufficiently successful to continue. Repackaging efforts lasted longer in the case of the so-called Bournemouth International, featuring men's singles and doubles in the second half of the 1990s. This once more attracted good European clay-court specialists to Roislin Road; the 1996 champion Albert Costa later went on to win the French Open. Even so, after four years the tournament was relocated to hard courts in Brighton, where only one further edition was held, won by Britain's Tim Henman.

Following extensive renovation and expansion of its facilities, the West Hants Club continued to thrive as an important regional tennis centre into the 21st century, hosting a range of junior and senior domestic tournaments every season. But the days of the game's superstars arriving to battle for honours were a thing of the past. As distinguished as it was in the half-century from the 1920s to the 1970s, the Hard Court Championships is likely to be remembered primarily as a catalyst for the tennis revolution in 1968. The tension in the air that spring as players from different codes gathered in

Bournemouth was palpable, as underlined by the story of a young British amateur, Clay Iles, being teased in the dressing room about the prospect of going on court for his first-round match against the intimidating veteran professional, Pancho Gonzales. Amid the jesting from fellow amateurs, Iles heard the distinctive drawl of his opponent coming from behind the adjacent lockers. 'Don't worry, kid,' Gonzales interjected. 'When that ball comes over the net, there ain't nobody's name on it.'[12] In the event, Iles was only able to garner a couple of games against the legendary pro, but in the next round the Gonzales-Cox encounter changed everything and pointed towards a new, radically different future for the sport. The rest, as they say, is history.

RECORD BREAKERS

Most titles – Men: Fred Perry (5), Jaroslav Drobny (4), Billy Knight (3)

Most titles – Women: Doris Hart (4), Angela Mortimer (4), Ann Jones (4), Virginia Wade (4), Kay Stammers (3), Margaret Court (3)

Number of British Hard Court champions who also won Wimbledon singles

Men: 7; Women: 7; Total: 14

British Hard Court Championships

Men's Singles

Year	Winner	Runner-up	Score
1924	Randolph Lycett (Aus)	Christiaan van Lennep (Ned)	6-1, 3-6, 6-4, 6-3
1925	Patrick Spence (SA)	Charles Kingsley	6-1, 6-4, 9-7
1926	Jacques Brugnon (Fra)	Bunny Austin	7-5, 4-6, 3-6, 8-6, 6-3
1927	Rene Lacoste (Fra)	Patrick Spence (SA)	6-1, 6-2, 6-2
1928	Rene Lacoste (Fra)	Patrick Spence (SA)	6-2, 6-2, 6-2
1929	Bunny Austin	Louis Raymond (SA)	6-3, 6-2, 1-6, 6-4
1930	Harry Lee	Eric Peters	6-3, 2-6, 6-4, 6-4
1931	Christian Boussus (Fra)	Pat Hughes	8-6, 6-4, 4-6, 6-2

1932	Fred Perry	George Lyttleton Rogers (Ire)	4-6, 7-9, 6-3, 6-0, 6-2
1933	Fred Perry	Bunny Austin	2-6, 7-5, 7-5, 6-2
1934	Fred Perry	Jack Crawford (Aus)	8-6, 7-5, 6-1
1935	Fred Perry	Bunny Austin	0-6, 6-4, 3-6, 6-2, 6-0
1936	Fred Perry	Bunny Austin	6-2, 8-6, 6-3
1937	Bunny Austin	Harry Lee	6-2, 6-2, 6-0
1938	Kho Sin-Kie (Chn)	Bunny Austin	6-4, 6-4, 3-6, 6-3
1939	Kho Sin-Kie (Chn)	Wai-Chuen Choy (Chn)	7-5, 6-1, 6-4
1940–45	No tournament held		
1946	Jack Harper (Aus)	Derrick Barton	7-5, 6-2, 6-1
1947	Eric Sturgess (SA)	Ignacy Tloczynski (Pol)	11-9, 6-1, 6-4
1948	Eric Sturgess (SA)	Ignacy Tloczynski (Pol)	6-2, 6-3, 6-1
1949	Pedro Masip (Spn)	Henri Cochet (Fra)	6-3, 4-6, 6-2, 9-7
1950	Jaroslav Drobny (Egy)	Geoff Brown (Aus)	7-5, 6-0, 6-4
1951	Jaroslav Drobny (Egy)	Felicisimo Ampon (Chl)	6-4, 6-2, 6-0
1952	Jaroslav Drobny (Egy)	Frank Sedgman (Aus)	6-2, 6-4, 1-6, 6-4
1953	Enrique Morea (Arg)	Felicisimo Ampon (Chl)	6-3, 6-2, 6-1
1954	Tony Mottram	Geoff Paish	6-4, 6-3, 7-5
1955	Sven Davidson (Swe)	Roger Becker	11-9, 6-3, 6-1
1956	Budge Patty (USA)	Ham Richardson (USA)	1-6, 6-3, 6-3, 6-3
1957	Jaroslav Drobny (Egy)	Lew Hoad (Aus)	6-4, 6-4, 6-4
1958	Billy Knight	Guiseppe Merlo (Ita)	5-7, 6-0, 6-2, 6-3
1959	Lew Gerrard (NZ)	Billy Knight	3-6, 2-6, 6-2, 7-5, 9-7
1960	Mike Davies	Billy Knight	6-2, 4-6, 6-2, 6-1
1961	Roy Emerson (Aus)	Rod Laver (Aus)	8-6, 6-4, 6-0
1962	Rod Laver (Aus)	Ian Crookenden (NZ)	6-3, 6-3, 6-3
1963	Billy Knight	Marty Mulligan (Aus)	5-7, 6-3, 6-1, 6-3
1964	Billy Knight	Cliff Drysdale (SA)	6-3, 1-6, 6-1, 5-7, 7-5
1965	Jan-Erik Lundqvist (Swe)	Cliff Drysdale (SA)	3-6, 6-4, 8-6, 6-1
1966	Ken Fletcher (Aus)	Tom Okker (Ned)	7-5, 6-4
1967	Jan-Erik Lundqvist (Swe)	Bob Hewitt (SA)	6-1, 6-8, 6-3, 6-2
1968	Ken Rosewall (Aus)	Rod Laver (Aus)	3-6, 6-2, 6-0, 6-3
1969	John Newcombe (Aus)	Bob Hewitt (SA)	6-8, 6-3, 5-7, 6-4, 6-4
1970	Mark Cox	Bob Hewitt (SA)	6-1, 6-2, 6-3
1971	Gerald Battrick	Zeljko Franulovic (Yug)	6-3, 6-2, 5-7, 6-0
1972	Bob Hewitt (SA)	Pierre Barthes (Fra)	6-2, 6-4, 6-3
1973	Adriano Panatta (Ita)	Ilie Nastase (Rom)	6-8, 7-5, 6-3
1974	Ilie Nastase (Rom)	Paolo Bertolucci (Ita)	6-1, 6-3, 6-0

1975	Manuel Orantes (Spn)	Patrick Proisy (Fra)	6-3, 4-6, 6-2, 7-5
1976	Wojciech Fibak (Pol)	Ilie Nastase (Rom)	6-2, 7-9, 6-2, 6-2
1977	No tournament held		
1978	Jose Higueras (Spn)	Paolo Bertolucci (Ita)	6-2, 6-1, 6-3
1979	No tournament held		
1980	Angel Gimenez (Spn)	Shlomo Glickstein (Isr)	3-6, 6-3, 6-3
1981	Victor Pecci (Par)	Balazs Taroczy (Hun)	6-3, 6-4
1982	Manuel Orantes (Spn)	Angel Gimenez (Spn)	6-2, 6-0
1983	Jose Higueras (Spn)	Tomas Smid (Czh)	2-6, 7-6, 7-5
1984–95	No tournament held		
1996	Albert Costa (Spn)	Marc-Kevin Goellner (Ger)	6-7, 6-2, 6-2
1997	Felix Mantilla (Spn)	Carlos Moya (Spn)	6-2, 6-2
1998	Felix Mantilla (Spn)	Albert Costa (Spn)	6-3, 7-5
1999	Adrian Voinea (Rom)	Stefan Koubek (Aut)	1-6, 7-5, 7-6

Women's Singles

Year	Winner	Runner-up	Score
1924	Elizabeth Ryan (USA)	Geraldine Beamish	6-2, 6-2
1925	Elizabeth Ryan (USA)	Joan Fry	6-2, 6-2
1926	Joan Fry	Phoebe Watson	6-1, 7-9, 6-1
1927	Betty Nuthall	Edith Clarke	8-6, 6-2
1928	Elsie Goldsack	Joan Ridley	8-6, 6-4
1929	Bobbie Heine (SA)	Joan Ridley	6-4, 3-6, 8-6
1930	Joan Fry	Madge List	6-1, 2-6, 6-2
1931	Simonne Mathieu (Fra)	Mary Heeley	6-4, 6-4
1932	Simonne Mathieu (Fra)	Dorothy Round	6-1, 6-2
1933	Dorothy Round	Helen Jacobs (USA)	3-6, 6-2, 6-3
1934	Dorothy Round	Peggy Scriven	6-2, 2-6, 8-6
1935	Kay Stammers	Peggy Scriven	6-2, 6-2
1936	Kay Stammers	Anita Lizana (Chl)	7-5, 7-5
1937	Anita Lizana (Chl)	Peggy Scriven	7-5, 6-3
1938	Peggy Scriven	Nancye Wynne (Aus)	7-5, 6-2
1939	Kay Stammers	Anita Ellis (Chl)	6-3, 6-3
1940–45	No Tournament held		
1946	Jean Bostock	Kay Menzies	6-3, 6-4
1947	Nancye Bolton (Aus)	Joan Curry	7-5, 6-3
1948	Betty Hilton	Pamela Bocquet	6-1, 6-4
1949	Joan Curry	Jean Quertier	3-6, 7-5, 7-5

1950	Joan Curry	Maria Teran de Weiss (Arg)	8-6, 8-6
1951	Doris Hart (USA)	Jean Walker-Smith	6-4, 8-6
1952	Doris Hart (USA)	Shirley Fry (USA)	6-4, 6-3
1953	Doris Hart (USA)	Shirley Fry (USA)	6-3, 4-6, 6-4
1954	Doris Hart (USA)	Joy Mottram	6-1, 6-3
1955	Angela Mortimer	Angela Buxton	6-1, 6-1
1956	Angela Mortimer	Shirley Bloomer	7-5, 5-7, 6-1
1957	Shirley Bloomer	Patricia Ward	3-6, 6-2, 6-3
1958	Shirley Bloomer	Ann Haydon	6-4, 6-4
1959	Angela Mortimer	Christine Truman	6-4, 2-6, 6-4
1960	Christine Truman	Ann Haydon	6-2, 6-2
1961	Angela Mortimer	Deidre Catt	6-2, 6-3
1962	Renee Schuurman (SA)	Angela Mortimer	5-7, 6-2, 6-4
1963	Ann Jones	Norma Baylon (Arg)	6-0, 1-6, 9-7
1964	Ann Jones	Jan Lehane (Aus)	6-2, 12-10
1965	Ann Jones	Annette Van Zyl (SA)	7-5, 6-1
1966	Ann Jones	Virginia Wade	6-3, 6-1
1967	Virginia Wade	Ann Jones	6-1, 10-8
1968	Virginia Wade	Winnie Shaw	6-4, 6-1
1969	Margaret Court (Aus)	Winnie Shaw	5-7, 6-4, 6-4
1970	Margaret Court (Aus)	Virginia Wade	6-2, 6-4
1971	Margaret Court (Aus)	Evonne Goolagong (Aus)	7-5, 6-1
1972	Evonne Goolagong (Aus)	Helga Masthoff (WG)	6-0, 6-4
1973	Virginia Wade	Evonne Goolagong (Aus)	6-4, 6-4
1974	Virginia Wade	Julie Heldman (USA)	6-1, 3-6, 6-1
1975	Janet Newberry (USA)	Terry Holladay (USA)	7-9, 7-5, 6-3
1976	Helga Masthoff (WG)	Sue Barker	5-7, 6-3, 6-3
1977	No tournament held		
1978	Iris Riedel (WG)	Belinda Thompson	6-2, 6-1
1979–80	No tournament held		
1981	Jo Durie	Sophie Amiach (Fra)	7-5, 1-6, 6-3
1982–94	No tournament held		
1995	Ludmilla Richterova (CR)	Patricia Hy-Boulais (Can)	6-7, 6-4, 6-3

6

The West of England

THE WEST Country is one of the surprise packages of English tennis history. It's unable today to boast of any regular international-standard play or of any iconic venues comparable to the likes of Queen's or Devonshire Park. And yet, when we continue our nationwide journey, travelling westwards and northwards from Bournemouth, we find – in Devon, Somerset and Avon – a strikingly wide range of places that have hosted top-level tournaments in the past. Two of these in particular are featured in this chapter, attracting famous domestic and overseas stars alike. As far as home competitors are concerned, almost every major British player in the history of lawn tennis, from its inception in the Victorian era, has at some point in their career plied their trade on courts in the western counties.

In the 1880s and 90s, leading English 'cracks' of the day such as the Renshaw and Doherty brothers, Maud Watson and Blanche Hillyard turned out frequently at gatherings such as those held in well-heeled Cheltenham and in Exmouth. Fred Burrow, who became referee at Exmouth in south Devon shortly before the First World War, observed that the late summer meeting in the seaside resort 'used to attract an entry second to none in the provinces'.[1] Although their fortunes fluctuated, reverting at times to mostly local entries, the tournaments in Cheltenham and Exmouth continued until well into the 20th century, with distinguished winners that later included Wimbledon champions Angela Mortimer and Ann Jones.

Britain's most successful player of all time, Fred Perry, notched up some notable victories in the West Country. He made his Davis Cup debut (later helping the team to four successive triumphs in that competition) at the Carhullen Club in Plymouth in April 1931. The British team ran out easy 5-0 winners in a rain-interrupted tie against Monaco, whose players, Perry admitted, were badly affected by the 'depressing' south-west drizzle.[2] The following year, Perry was part of the squad that enjoyed a similarly emphatic victory over Romania on the Abbey Park courts in Torquay. If not hard-fought, that tie at least provided some amusement for spectators in the shape of eccentric Romanian veteran Nicolae Misu, who threw in occasional underarm serves in an effort to catch his young opponent off guard. Perry was not to be distracted; he won with the loss of just two games.

Torquay was one of a string of fashionable Devon resorts that hosted annual summer holiday tournaments, most at various times won by leading British players. The honours boards at now-defunct events in Budleigh Salterton and Sidmouth contain the names of SW19 champions such as Ethel Larcombe and Dorothy Round. Torquay's main outdoor meeting, held at Belgrave Road, was the largest and most enduring in the county (its indoor tournament is the focus of the second half of this chapter). The Torbay Open, still running today, began in its initial form in the 1880s, and before the Great War featured well-known stars including Miss Watson, Mrs Hillyard and Ernest Lewis, three-time winner of the men's singles. In more recent years, Torbay became a magnet for attracting the best of the nation's aspiring juniors. Tim Henman won the under-12 singles in 1986, and Andy and Jamie Murray both competed in that category a decade later, when their mother Judy travelled to the south-west for a break after the horror of the Dunblane school massacre in the family's hometown. Andy, aged only nine, was beaten at the semi-final stage and his older brother Jamie lost in the final.[3]

Closer still to the present day, in February 2019, the multi-million pound Sports Training Village at Bath University (one of the LTA's high-performance academies for promising youngsters) hosted a week of Federation Cup group ties; the British women's team spearheaded by Johanna Konta progressed to the next stage of the competition after coming through successfully against opponents including Slovenia, Hungary and Serbia. It was entirely fitting that Bath should be chosen to stage the first Fed Cup event on home shores in a quarter of a century. For the city of Bath has a long pedigree and wider significance in the nation's tennis history. It was there that the most celebrated annual gathering held in western England – one that for many decades was very strongly international in flavour – started life back in the 1880s.

The West of England Championships

In common with several of the tournaments featured in other chapters, the West of England Championships had more than one home. The meeting first took place at the Lansdowne Cricket Club, in Weston, near to Bath city centre, in the early summer of 1881. Noting the rapid spread of competitive play elsewhere, the two clubs in the city, Bath Lawn Tennis Club and Sydney Lawn Tennis Club, set up a joint committee to host the new venture and secured agreement to use eight grass courts laid out at the cricket ground. As was usual at the time, the inaugural gathering featured a range of singles and doubles events that were either 'closed' – for which entrants had to belong to either of the two clubs – or 'open', available to members of all recognised tennis clubs or to persons vouched for by a patron or member of the tournament committee.

As it turned out, the 1881 entrants across all categories were from the immediate locality. But this soon started to change. By 1883 a local newspaper declared that the third annual tournament, under way at Weston, was an 'established event in the list of outdoor amusements for Bath and vicinity'.[4] The elegant Georgian spa had long been popular with wealthy visitors, and some of the most renowned gentlemen and lady amateurs from across the kingdom welcomed the opportunity to combine tennis with a few days at leisure in the city.

The winners of the main singles titles in 1883 were Irishman Ernest Browne (the first of three successive victories) and Midlands-based Maud Watson, who was on a long unbeaten streak that included victory in the first women's singles at Wimbledon the following year.

Such was the appeal of fashionable Bath that within a few years the West of England Championships featured some of the best players in world tennis (albeit that international rivalry was limited in the early days of lawn tennis). In 1886, large crowds hemmed in close to the main show court to watch two historic finals. Miss Watson lost her first significant match since 1881, going down 7-5, 6-4 to the teenage sensation Lottie Dod, while the men's singles trophy was claimed by Bostonian James Dwight, a former runner-up in the American National Championships. Extensive global travel to play competitively was not yet the norm, and this was one of the first times a player from outside the United Kingdom had triumphed at a top-level English tournament.

Dwight was president of the United States Tennis Association, and he frequently reached the latter stages of singles and doubles during his trips to Europe in the mid-1880s. Mixed doubles was popular at Bath as at many tournaments around this time, and in one final that featured leading stars of the game, Dwight and his partner Blanche Bingley fought hard before losing in three sets to seven-time Wimbledon champion William Renshaw, playing with Margaret Bracewell. The American had a habit (controversial then, as now) of crossing at the net – poaching – to take volleys on shots where the ball was travelling towards his partner at the back of the court. Dwight was short in stature and not always able to intervene effectively, and at one point he apologised to Miss Bingley, saying he hoped he hadn't blocked her view. To the amusement of spectators, Blanche replied briskly, 'Oh no, thank you. I can see right over your head.'[5]

In 1896 the Bath tournament shifted venue a few miles further west, to the county cricket ground at Clifton in Bristol. The move helped to ensure that, rare among English meetings before the end of the century, a genuine international flavour was maintained. The men's final in 1896 was between the Scottish-born Irishman Harold Mahony (who went on to win Wimbledon shortly afterwards) and William Larned of the USA. Larned was described as the best American to have appeared on English shores thus far, and he was later to win the US Championships seven times. But at Bristol he showed youthful nerves (and dislike of the windy conditions) and was beaten in straight sets by his more seasoned opponent. The women's title went to Charlotte Cooper, who like Mahony claimed the Wimbledon crown a few weeks later.

The debut of the West of England Championships at Clifton was not an altogether unvarnished success. Much of the week was disrupted by cold and wet weather, spectator numbers were disappointing and some of the finals scheduled for the last day had to be abandoned owing to heavy rain. The organisational oversight required to host a repeat gathering in 1897 was not forthcoming, the meeting lapsed, and it was to remain in abeyance for over 20 years.

When the West of England eventually revived after the First World War – at a time when tennis was re-energised and growing rapidly across the country – it did so at a third separate location, Bristol Lawn Tennis Club. This had been formed in 1912 in the imposing residential suburb of Redlands, a couple of miles north of Bristol city centre, and was to become the home of the tournament for the remainder of its existence.

GIN AND ITALIAN

A well-known presence at the West of England Championships for many years was the redoubtable Mrs Perrett, whose zest for the game was such that even in her 70s she could be seen playing all day in the hottest of temperatures. She was once drawn against an 18-year-old in singles and came off after three hours saying that the match was unfinished, but that as her young opponent had fainted on court the umpire had declared her the winner. Mrs Perrett was particularly associated with two hard and fast personal rules. If she happened to be on court at 6pm she would always stop to imbibe her one drink of the day – a strong gin and Italian. She also refused to ever knock up ahead of a match. This was her right under the rules, although it tended to baffle opponents looking to warm up, not least in 1923 when she applied the policy on Centre Court at Wimbledon. She and her partner were drawn in the first round of the doubles against the strongest combination in world tennis: none other than Suzanne Lenglen and Elizabeth Ryan.

During the inter-war years the revitalised West of England meeting developed into a popular, high-quality event in the annual pre-Wimbledon schedule. In 1937 local journalists waxed lyrical about the 'finest tournament held in Bristol' since the Great War, with one report reading, 'Brilliant tennis in brilliant weather, with foreign and British stars battling hard to win the West of England Championships.'[6] The women's final that summer was an all-overseas affair – Senorita Lizana wrestling the crown from the holder, Fraulein Spurling – although the most successful player on the women's side between the wars was London-born Phyllis Covell, a three-time champion. The men's singles during this period was increasingly dominated by overseas contenders, with winners from the likes of South Africa, New Zealand, India and Eire; the towering

Irish leftie George Lyttleton Rogers claimed three titles in succession between 1929 and 1931.

The standard of competition was not quite as exalted as in the early years in Bath – there were no Wimbledon champions on the roll of honour in this era – but some of the game's finest exponents nevertheless graced the courts at Redlands Green. Record crowds were at the Bristol club on finals day in 1939 to see British Davis Cup player Don Butler confound the strong favourite, three-time SW19 runner-up Gottfried von Cramm. Skilfully deploying his high-kick serve on a skiddy surface, Butler seized a two-set lead. The German then claimed the third easily, at which point rain forced the players off court for a short interlude. When they returned, von Cramm called upon all his experience to win a thrilling fourth set 7-5. But the Englishman, who previously won the West of England title in 1935, was not about to fold. The decider was a long and nervy affair, going with serve until, at 6-7 down, von Cramm double-faulted, allowing his opponent to get across the line. For Butler, it was the finest performance of his career, and his best day in tournament play. On court for over five hours, he also won the men's doubles and the mixed doubles title.

After the Second World War, the West of England re-established itself as an ideal mid-June warm-up for Wimbledon. The balance between domestic and international winners tilted more decisively in favour of the latter, although more slowly in the case of the women's singles. Devon's Joan Curry took the title three years running in the late 1940s, but during the 1950s America's powerful post-war generation came to the fore, triumphing six times in that decade. Victors at Redlands from across the Atlantic included Wimbledon champions Doris Hart and Althea Gibson; Brazilian star Maria Bueno also claimed the honours in 1958 and 59.

In the men's event, the eclipse of home contenders was more rapid and stark. No British man reached the final until 1957, and

MEMORABLE MATCHES

The overwhelming majority of tournament play in Britain was suspended during the Second World War, as during the 1914–18 war. But Bristol was unique among the venues featured in this book in that in 1940 it hosted an event which bore similarities with its usual annual meeting. In mid-June, as France collapsed across the Channel and the threat of Nazi invasion loomed large, two finals were contested at Redland Green featuring some of the nation's best players. Kay Menzies (formerly Miss Stammers) won an entertaining duel with Peggy Scriven, losing a long first set but then finding her rhythm off the ground to take the next two, each by the same score of 6-3. In the men's final, the young Warwickshire hopeful Tony Mottram made a name for himself by unleashing a cannonball service that carried him to victory over his more seasoned compatriot Eric Peters. Menzies and Mottram thereby made their way into the record books (as recorded in the list of results that follows). Although proceedings took place at the same time of year as normal, and in front of a typically good Redland Green crowd, this was not, however, the West of England Championships of peacetime. It was, in reality, a much-shortened charity tournament and exhibition in aid of the Lord Mayor's Red Cross Fund and the Daily Sketch War Relief Lawn Tennis Fund. Even so, it was the last time high-level competitive tennis would be glimpsed on home shores for several years.

the following year Mike Davies became the only such player to win at Bristol in the entire period between resumption in 1946 and the demise of the tournament in the 1980s. As with the women, a string of Wimbledon champions now arrived from overseas to taste success: Drobny, Seixas, Hoad and McKinley.

UNDERRATED CHAMPION

Jaroslav Drobny's accomplishments have long been well known. The left-hander with the swinging serve and penetrating forehand became a three-time grand slam champion in the 1950s, winning the French Championships twice and Wimbledon in 1954. What's less recognised is the scale of Drobny's success on English soil during the years in which the Czech exile played as an Egyptian citizen. He won seven of the tournaments featured in this book, most of them more than once. His versatility was such that he claimed titles on all types of surfaces. On grass, he won the West of England Championships and the Midland Counties three times each. His grass-court triumphs also included the North of England Championships (1949) and the Northern (1956). On clay, arguably his strongest surface, Drobny was a four-time champion at Bournemouth, his vanquished opponents there including Sedgman and Hoad. He also adapted his game well to fast indoor courts. He won the Covered Court Championships at Queen's four times and the Palace Hotel tournament on three occasions. His last victory in Torquay came shortly after his 40th birthday in 1961 (against an opponent, Mike Sangster, about half his age), by which time Drobny had been granted British citizenship.

Underlining the extent to which Bristol had consolidated its place as home to one of the prime meetings of the English grass-court season, the Redlands club was chosen to host several home ties in the Davis Cup after the mid-1950s. Starting with Britain's 3-2 victory over Chile in 1956, Bristol was to be the venue for seven such encounters spread over the course of 30 years. This total has only been bettered through to the present day by three other regional locations (i.e. excluding Wimbledon): Eastbourne, Birmingham and Glasgow. Feeding off usually vociferous home support in the packed stands, British victories at Redlands Green included a 5-0 win over

Austria in 1978, the year in which the team went on to reach the Davis Cup for the first time since the 1930s. By some distance the most controversial tie, however, took place almost a decade earlier, in 1969.

YOUNG LIBERALS ARRESTED ON CENTRE COURT

In July 1969, anti-apartheid protests against sporting links with South Africa were brought into sharp focus at Redlands Green. Britain prepared for its European Zone A final of the Davis Cup against a backdrop of protestors complaining it was wrong to compete against a regime which banned open selection of its sports teams. On the first day of the tie the city attracted huge media attention after four Young Liberals, led by young activist Peter Hain, were arrested for staging an on-court protest. The following afternoon – with the tie in the balance – some 20 protestors were chased by police after trying to breach the club's tight security. Trouble continued into the last day. Two Bristol University students, having secured plum seats for the decisive singles rubbers, rushed on to the court and were dragged off amid jeers by the crowd. Britain's youthful team remained calm despite the distractions. Mark Cox and Peter Curtis inflicted a first defeat in Davis Cup doubles on the former Wimbledon champions Bob Hewitt and Frew McMillan, and Graham Stilwell took the first of the reverse singles to ensure British victory. This meant that for only the second time since the war, Britain reached the inter-zone finals of the Davis Cup (where they narrowly lost to Romania); the previous time they did so, in 1963, Bristol had also hosted one of the ties, a comfortable win over Spain.

With the arrival of Open tennis, the tournament at Redlands enjoyed a short-lived final flourish. It benefited from a generous sponsorship deal with Wills, the Bristol-based tobacco company, taking on the name the Wills Open Championships in 1969. In echoes of the early years of the West of England at Bath, some of the world's top stars turned up in force, now vying for one of the largest prize pots (totalling in excess of £20,000) offered outside of Wimbledon. Winners of the men's singles over the next few years included legends of the modern game such as Arthur Ashe, Ken Rosewall and Rod Laver. Record-breaking grand slam champion Margaret Court claimed the women's title twice, and when Billie Jean King beat Australia's Kerry Melville to triumph in 1972 her winner's cheque – for £2,000 – was Europe's richest prize for women at that time.

But the tide quickly turned. At a time of ferment in the sport, with tournament schedules constantly under review to meet the demands of sponsors and different interest groups, many leading competitors were lured elsewhere to find pre-Wimbledon grass-court practice. No women's meeting was held at Bristol in 1971 and Mrs King's victory the following year proved to be the last time elite women's play featured. To make matters worse, atrocious weather made an untimely intervention. Ticket sales were good ahead of a men-only World Championship Tennis meeting scheduled for 1971, due to feature 32 WCT contract professionals. Incessant heavy rain, however, permitted barely 15 minutes of play in three days, leaving all concerned hugely frustrated. Wills decided to abandon its involvement in tennis sponsorship altogether in 1973, and without such backing Redlands was deprived of men's as well as women's top-level competition for the remainder of the decade.

The story was not quite at an end. With sponsorship from Lambert & Butler and others, the Bristol Open was revived during the 1980s as part of the men's Grand Prix circuit. Prize money was sufficient to attract good world-ranked players, even if this did not mean a return to the glories of yesteryear. Attendances were often thin apart from finals, although big crowds did turn out in 1989 to see Nick Brown narrowly fail to become the first British man to take the title since Mike Davies over 30 years earlier. The 27-year-old from Warrington lost 7-5 in the decider to West Germany's Eric Jelen. This proved to be the tournament's swansong. When the Grand Prix circuit, in place since the 1970s, was replaced on the men's side by a reconstituted ATP Tour, Bristol was squeezed from the pre-Wimbledon schedule at the expense of more high-profile meetings such as Queen's, although a lower-tier event continued for several more years. The West of England was left to become one of the least acknowledged of England's top-level tournaments, despite Redlands having witnessed more than its fair share of world-class tennis in the past. The club today justifiably reflects with pride on its '100 years of heritage'.[7]

RECORD BREAKERS

Most titles – Men: Ernest Browne (3), Harry Barlow (3), George Lyttleton Rogers (3), Jaroslav Drobny (3)

Most titles – Women: Lottie Dod (3), Phyllis Covell (3 – once as Phyllis Howkins), Joan Curry (3), Margaret Court (3 – once as Margaret Smith)

Number of West of England champions who also won Wimbledon singles

Men: 7; Women: 10; Total: 17

West of England Championships

Men's Singles

Year	Winner	Runner-up	Score
1881	P.G. von Donop	John Kay	5-6, 6-5, 6-3
1882	George Butterworth	Alexander Butterworth	6-4, 6-4
1883	Ernest Browne	Wilfred Milne	6-3, 6-2, 6-3
1884	Ernest Browne	C.K. Wood	6-4, 6-2, 6-4
1885	Ernest Browne	James Dwight (USA)	6-3, 6-1, 6-4
1886	James Dwight (USA)	Harry Grove	6-4, 6-3, 6-4
1887	Harry Grove	James Dwight (USA)	3-6, 6-4, 6-4, 6-2
1888	Harry Barlow	James Baldwin	6-4, 6-3, 8-10, 3-6, 8-6
1889	James Baldwin	Wilfred Milne	7-5, 6-3, 6-2

1890	Harry Barlow	James Baldwin	7-5, 6-3, 6-2
1891	Harry Barlow	James Baldwin	2-6, 6-3, 6-4, 6-4
1892–94	No tournament held		
1895	Edward Allen	George Greene	14-12, 6-4, 7-5
1896	Harold Mahony	William Larned (USA)	6-3, 6-3, 6-2
1897–1919	No tournament held		
1920	Frank Fisher (NZ)	Frank Riseley	5-7, 6-4, 6-2, 6-2
1921	Sydney Jacob	Frank Fisher (NZ)	9-7, 6-2, 4-6, 6-0
1922	Brian Norton (SA)	Theodore Mavrogordato	6-3, 6-3 retd
1923	Patrick Wheatley	Leighton Crawford	6-4, 6-3, 6-2
1924	Jack Condon (SA)	Frank Riseley	7-5, 6-2, 8-6
1925	Frank Riseley	J.P. Hogan	6-3, 6-4
1926	No tournament held		
1927	Sydney Jacob	A.E. Browne (Ire)	6-3, 6-2
1928	Denis O'Callaghan (Ire)	Sydney Jacob	9-7, 5-7, 6-3
1929	George Lyttleton Rogers (Ire)	Norman Taylor	6-1, 6-2
1930	George Lyttleton Rogers (Ire)	George Godsell	6-3, 3-6, 6-4
1931	George Lyttleton Rogers (Ire)	Nigel Sharpe	6-2, 6-1, 7-5
1932	No tournament held		
1933	Daniel Prenn (Ger)	Hendrik Timmer (Ned)	6-2, 7-9, 6-4, 6-4
1934	George Godsell	Brian Sturgeon	6-4, 0-6, 6-3, 6-4
1935	Don Butler	George Lyttleton Rogers (Ire)	8-6, 11-9, 9-7
1936	Cam Malfroy (NZ)	Robert Tinkler	4-6, 6-0, 6-4, 6-4
1937	Alan Stedman (NZ)	Kho Sin-Kie (Chn)	6-1, 1-6, 6-4
1938	Jimmy Mehta (Ind)	Cam Malfroy (NZ)	6-2, 6-3
1939	Don Butler	Gottfried von Cramm (Ger)	6-4, 6-3, 1-6, 5-7, 8-6
1940	Tony Mottram	Eric Peters	7-5, 6-3
1941–45	No tournament held		
1946	Kho Sin-Kie (Chn)	Ignacy Tloczynski (Pol)	6-4, 6-4
1947	Sumant Misra (Ind)	Madan Atri Mohan (Ind)	6-4, 4-6, 6-2
1948	Eric Sturgess (SA)	Sumant Misra (Ind)	6-4, 2-6, 6-2, 6-4
1949	Felicisimo Ampon (Phi)	Syd Levy (SA)	6-1, 6-2, 6-3
1950	Jaroslav Drobny (Egy)	Vladimir Cernik (Czh)	6-3, 10-8
1951	L. Straight Clark (USA)	Hal Burrows (USA)	9-7, 3-6, 5-7, 6-1, 7-5
1952	Jaroslav Drobny (Egy)	Armando Vieira (Bra)	7-5, 6-1
1953	Vic Seixas (USA)	Enrique Morea (Arg)	6-3, 6-1, 8-6
1954	Jaroslav Drobny (Egy)	Jack Arkinstall (Aus)	walkover
1955	Enrique Morea (Arg)	Sid Schwartz (USA)	2-6, 10-8, 6-2, 6-2

1956	Luis Ayala (Chl)	Gordon Forbes (SA)	6-2, 8-10, 6-4
1957	Lew Hoad (Aus)	Roger Becker	6-2, 6-3, 6-0
1958	Mike Davies	Ramanathan Krishnan (Ind)	6-1, 6-4, 7-9, 6-4
1959	Ramanathan Krishnan (Ind)	Jaroslav Drobny	11-9, 6-0
1960	Ronnie Holmberg (USA)	Tony Palafox (Mex)	6-3, 6-4
1961	Chuck McKinley (USA)	Bob Mark (Aus)	6-3, 6-2, 6-4
1962	Fred Stolle (Aus)	Tony Palafox (Mex)	6-3, 6-4
1963	Fred Stolle (Aus)	Chuck McKinley (USA)	6-3, 6-4
1964	Chuck McKinley (USA)	Frew McMillan (SA)	6-4, 6-4, 6-2
1965	Dennis Ralston (USA)	Clark Graebner (USA)	6-2, 6-2
1966	Cliff Richey (USA)	Mike Belkin (Can)	6-1, 6-3
1967	Tom Okker (Ned)	Cliff Drysdale (SA)	6-2, 5-7, 8-6
1968	Arthur Ashe (USA)	Clark Graebner (USA)	6-4, 6-3
1969	Ken Rosewall (Aus)	Pierre Barthes (Fra)	8-10, 6-3, 6-1
1970	Nikki Pilic (Yug)	Rod Laver (Aus)	6-3, 1-6, 6-3
1971	Rod Laver (Aus)	Cliff Drysdale (SA)	walkover
1972	Bob Hewitt (SA)	Alex Olmedo (USA)	6-4, 6-3
1973–80	No tournament held		
1981	Mark Edmondson (Aus)	Roscoe Tanner (USA)	6-3, 5-7, 6-4
1982	John Alexander (Aus)	Tim Mayotte (USA)	6-3, 6-4
1983	Johan Kriek (USA)	Tom Gullikson (USA)	7-6, 7-5
1984	Johan Kriek (USA)	Brian Teacher (USA)	6-7, 7-6, 6-4
1985	Marty Davis (USA)	Glenn Layendecker (USA)	4-6, 6-3, 7-5
1986	Vijay Amritraj (Ind)	Henri Leconte (Fra)	7-6, 1-6, 8-6
1987	Kelly Evernden (NZ)	Tim Wilkison (USA)	6-4, 7-6
1988	Christian Saceanu (WG)	Ramesh Krishnan (Ind)	6-4, 2-6, 6-2
1989	Eric Jelen (WG)	Nick Brown	6-4, 3-6, 7-5

Women's Singles

Year	Winner	Runner-up	Score
1881	Gertrude Gibbs	Annie Layard	6-0, 7-5
1882	Frances Morris	Gertrude Gibbs	6-4, 6-4
1883	Maud Watson	Miss Pope	6-2, 6-1
1884	Edith Davies	Lilian Cole	6-4, 6-4
1885	Gertrude Gibbs	Edith Davies	2-6, 6-4, 6-0
1886	Lottie Dod	Maud Watson	7-5, 6-4
1887	Lottie Dod	Maud Watson	7-5, 6-4
1888	Lottie Dod	N. Pope	6-3, 6-0

1889	Louisa Martin	Florence Stanuell	4-6, 6-1, 6-2
1890	Louisa Martin	Miss Pope	6-3, 8-6
1891	Miss Pope	Mary Agg	6-0, 7-5
1892–94	No tournament held		
1895	Helen Jackson	Madeline O'Neill	6-1, 6-1
1896	Charlotte Cooper	Ruth Dyas	4-6, 7-5, 6-3
1897–1919	No tournament held		
1920	Mabel Parton	Doris Craddock	9-7, 6-8, 6-4
1921	Phyllis Howkins	Doris Craddock	10-8, 6-2
1922	Doris Craddock	Edith Hannam	6-1, 6-1
1923	Elizabeth Ryan (USA)	Doris Craddock	8-6, 6-3
1924	Phyllis Covell	Joan Austin	6-4, 6-3
1925	Kathleen Bridge	Doris Craddock	6-4, 1-6, 6-3
1926	No tournament held		
1927	Mary McIlquham	Margaret Stocks	6-1, 6-1
1928	Phyllis Covell	Betty Dix	7-5, 6-1
1929	Gethyn Harry	Helen Boucher	4-6, 6-1, 6-1
1930	Kathleen Bridge	Freda Scott	6-1, 8-6
1931	Doris Eastley	Vera Montgomery	3-6, 7-5, 6-3
1932	No tournament held		
1933	Kay Stammers	Andree Lucas	6-2, 6-2
1934	Andree Lucas	Gethyn Harry	6-2, 6-2
1935	Gethyn Harry	Mona Riddell	6-4, 4-6, 6-3
1936	Hilde Sperling (Ger/Den)	Daphne Birch	6-2, 6-2
1937	Anita Lizana (Chl)	Hilde Sperling (Ger/Den)	6-2, 9-7
1938	Mona Riddell	Gem Hoahing	1-6, 6-3, 6-4
1939	Diana Wood	Joan Curry	6-2, 8-10, 6-2
1940	Kay Menzies	Peggy Scriven	8-10, 6-3, 6-3
1941–45	No tournament held		
1946	Joy Hibbert	Madie Moss	3-6, 6-3, 6-2
1947	Joan Curry	Pam Bocquet	6-4, 6-0
1948	Joan Curry	Pam Bocquet	6-2, 6-3
1949	Joan Curry	Peggy McCorkindale	3-6, 6-3, 9-7
1950	Dorothy Head (USA)	Helena Straubeova (Czh)	6-3, 6-1
1951	Beverly Baker (USA)	Beryl Bartlett (SA)	6-3, 6-3
1952	Patricia Todd (USA)	Beryl Bartlett (SA)	7-5, 6-2
1953	Doris Hart (USA)	Angela Mortimer	7-5, 6-3
1954	Pat Ward	Heather Brewer (Ber)	title shared

1955	Doris Hart (USA)	Dorothy Head (USA)	6-1, 6-3
1956	Althea Gibson (USA)	Daphne Seeney (Aus)	6-2, 10-8
1957	Angela Mortimer	Edda Buding (WG)	7-5, 6-0
1958	Maria Bueno (Bra)	Angela Mortimer	6-0, 6-3
1959	Maria Bueno (Bra)	Sandra Reynolds (SA)	6-4, 6-3
1960	Deidre Catt	Renee Schuurman (SA)	7-5, 7-5
1961	Sandra Reynolds (SA)	Deidre Catt	7-5, 10-8
1962	Margaret Smith (Aus)	Maria Bueno (Bra)	6-1, 3-6, 6-2
1963	Edda Buding (WG)	Elizabeth Starkie	9-7, 6-3
1964	Karen Susman (USA)	Francoise Durr (Fra)	6-8, 6-3, 6-3
1965	Nancy Richie (USA)	Elizabeth Starkie	7-5, 6-2
1966	Betty Stove (Ned)	Norma Baylon (Arg)	6-3, 7-5
1967	Pat Walken (Rho)	Edda Buding (WG)	0-6, 6-4, 6-3
1968	Kerry Melville (Aus)	Karen Krantzcke (Aus)	6-0, 6-1
1969	Margaret Court (Aus)	Billie Jean King (USA)	6-3, 6-3
1970	Margaret Court (Aus)	Francoise Durr (Fra)	6-1, 6-1
1971	No tournament held		
1972	Billie Jean King (USA)	Kerry Melville (Aus)	6-3, 6-2

The Palace Hotel Tournament, Torquay

At the time of writing, the Palace Hotel in the Babbacombe area of Torquay stood largely deserted and derelict. In 2017 the four-star, 140-bed hotel was purchased by a Singapore-based development company with ambitious plans to reconfigure the site. Demolition of the old buildings, prior to the construction of a new contemporary-style hotel and housing units, began in 2020. The demise of the Palace was lamented by many in the town, for it had enjoyed a prolonged golden age in the mid-20th century before tourist tastes changed. It was visited by a host of famous people over the years, including royalty (Princess Anne) and prime ministers (Margaret Thatcher). It also – for 40 years – occupied an unusual, intriguing place in the English tennis calendar. For in addition to hosting a long-standing outdoor summer tournament, Torquay was also the setting for a much-admired indoor meeting that took place each autumn.

The origins of the Palace Hotel tournament go back to the construction in the 1840s of a grand residential home in Babbacombe for the Bishop of Exeter, Henry Philpotts. After his death, the house passed through various owners until it was converted and expanded into a luxury hotel in the early 1920s. Set in some 25 acres of carefully landscaped gardens and facing the sea, the grounds and the gilded ballroom of the Palace thronged for many years with well-heeled visitors, waited upon by staff wearing dinner jackets. The hotel's range of facilities – including an indoor swimming pool, a mini-golf course and bowling greens – also attracted international clientele. Two 'covered' tennis courts (to use the parlance of the day) were opened in a functional side building in 1936, the year in which Britain secured its fourth consecutive Davis Cup triumph, and a decision was made to use these courts for a novel end-of-season open tournament.

Only three editions of the new venture were possible before the Second World War (the meeting scheduled for November 1939 came a couple of months after war was declared), but the inaugural women's singles final in 1936 produced a match of rare quality. Chile's Anita Lizana won a raft of titles in Britain during the mid-1930s (see *Underrated Champion*, chapter 4) and her full repertoire of shot-making was on display in what journalists described as the finest encounter of the week at the Palace, enthralling spectators in the packed gallery seats above the courts. After losing a see-saw first set 10-8, Lizana volleyed with precision and ruthlessly employed the drop shot against her tiring opponent, Dorothy Round, Britain's Wimbledon heroine of 1934. Miss Lizana performed, wrote Wallis Myers of the *Daily Telegraph*, as she usually did, 'serene in her confidence and exquisite in her touch'.[8]

During the 1939–45 conflict the Palace Hotel was requisitioned as an RAF hospital and it suffered serious bomb damage during Luftwaffe air raids, leading to several deaths and injuries. The hotel was unable to open until the spring of 1948 – the first post-war tournament followed at the end of the year – but with upgrades carried out including new multipurpose rooms to replace the ballroom it quickly returned to its former glory as tourism boomed in the 1950s.[9] More so than before the war (when a sprinkling of European contenders took part), Australians and Americans entered the ranks, and in 1956 both main singles titles went simultaneously for the first time to overseas players: Jaroslav Drobny, the 1954 Wimbledon champion, hit a purple patch in beating British Davis Cup player Gerry Oakley, while Thelma Long of Australia overcame Angela Buxton 7-5 in the deciding set of a tense three-set women's final.

The event increasingly became a go-to gathering for top British players as much as for larger numbers of overseas competitors. French, Australian and Wimbledon grand slam champion Angela Mortimer was Devon-born and her formative training years were under the watchful eye of the resident professional coach at the Palace, Arthur Roberts (whose son Paddy won the tournament in 1949). Unlike many of her compatriots at the time, Mortimer had access to all-year-round indoor training facilities at the hotel, and she made best

---

IN A HURRY

Devon star Angela Mortimer numbered several easy wins in her eight triumphs at the Palace Hotel; she was only once taken to three sets in the final. In 1958 she enjoyed her most emphatic victory when she beat compatriot Ann Haydon for the loss of just one game. The local Herald Express reported that although Mortimer – on familiar territory – was the favourite, few expected such a one-sided final. Angela and Ann (later Ann Jones) had several long and hard-fought meetings in their careers, but this was not one of them. Haydon never really got started, the Express concluded, and Mortimer, exploiting her know-how on the wooden surface, 'looked a class above her opponent'.[10] The match was over in 34 minutes.

---

use of 'home advantage' by amassing eight titles between 1952 and 1962. On the men's side, the fast wooden courts particularly suited the game of Bobby Wilson, who described Torquay as his favourite meeting on the circuit; he won four times in succession starting in 1957, and later added two further victories.

Why, we might ask, was the Palace tournament so appealing to leading players, home and overseas alike? Aside from providing a distinctive end point to the English season (superseding Eastbourne, the last of the main outdoor meetings, in this regard), the hotel itself was a major attraction. In contrast to the modest digs players would often find themselves in when travelling on tour, the Palace provided them, at specially discounted rates, with upmarket rooms and much more besides. When competitors were not on court, there were plenty of distractions readily at hand, including the swimming pool, squash, a pitch-and-putt course, table tennis and snooker. As Bobby Wilson reflected, the Torquay meeting was 'always great fun, being played in wonderful surroundings, with first-class food, no travel problems, and luxurious accommodation'.[11]

More so than was the norm elsewhere, Torquay also offered scope for top amateurs (operating in a world where they were not accompanied by the large entourages of the modern-day ultra-professional) to let their hair down a little. Many of the players were friends as well as rivals and not afraid to indulge in what Wilson called some 'high jinks'. As the tournament often took place around Guy Fawkes Night, it was not unknown for small fireworks to be thrown on to the court late at night, providing amusement for all concerned apart from the hotel management, who feared the prospect of fires being started. The 1954 men's champion, Mike Davies, certainly felt it was possible to combine hard-fought tennis with serious fun. Davies recollected that, unknown to spectators who rose to acclaim his victory over Gerry Oakley that year, he played the final with a hangover, having been out late in town the previous night.[12]

The unique appeal of the Palace meeting was such that *The Guardian's* tennis correspondent David Gray referred to it as offering 'halcyon days (and nights) for tennis enthusiasts'.[13] Whereas the occasional completion of grand slam matches late at night usually attracts adverse comment today, this was a regular occurrence at Torquay and yet tended to enhance rather than diminish the tournament's reputation. With only a couple of indoor courts available, it became regular practice – especially in the first few days of the week, with a heavy schedule to get through – that play would continue well into the early hours. Far from complaining, however, those involved mostly embraced the summons to leave their beds whenever called upon. Winners enjoyed being able to boast in the locker room, 'Oh yes, I beat so-and-so at two o'clock in the morning.'[14]

The good times continued into the 1960s. The Palace, fittingly in view of her Devon background, in 1962 witnessed the fond farewell to frontline competition of Angela Mortimer. After securing an eighth triumph with a 7-5, 6-3 victory over Ann Jones, Angela told her local newspaper that – while she would still appear in doubles – she would henceforth step back from top-level singles, having fulfilled her overriding goal of winning Wimbledon.[15] There was no such graceful swansong for another local stalwart, Torquay-born Mike Sangster, a three-time grand slam semi-finalist. Coached like Mortimer by Arthur Roberts, Sangster's youthful promise saw him win the junior title at the Palace twice in the mid-1950s. But despite having a game suited to the lightning-fast courts, based around a penetrating serve, Sangster subsequently lost in the senior final on four occasions, twice to Bobby Wilson and once each to Jaroslav Drobny and Roger Taylor.

As a highly reputable (as well as fun) event, the Palace meeting was a natural choice after the introduction of Open tennis for inclusion in the Dewar Cup circuit, a new late-season indoor competition that culminated in finals held in London. Between 1968 and 1972 the international flavour of the gathering was notably

ROGER'S UPS AND DOWNS

Yorkshire's up-and-coming star Roger Taylor had a mixed week at the Palace Hotel in 1964. The left-hander progressed well in the singles and booked his place in the final after beating Aussie veteran Bob Howe in less than an hour. But later the same evening he got into trouble when failing to turn up on time for a doubles match with his partner Bobby Wilson. When he did put in an appearance, two hours late (having been out to dinner), he faced the wrath of tournament referee Colonel John Legg. The long-time Wimbledon referee was known for treating players without fear or favour, and he decreed that there was no option but to scratch Taylor and Wilson. The Colonel said that if he failed to take strong action the result would be chaos, with players feeling at liberty to turn up when they wished. Taylor did manage to have the last laugh. Returning to court the next day for the singles final, the Yorkshireman took the title by beating Mike Sangster. In a protracted battle, Taylor served well and volleyed beautifully to come out on top 11-9, 16-14.

reinvigorated, with winners from the United States, South Africa and Australia (Margaret Court and Evonne Goolagong in the case of the latter). But when the Dewar Cup schedule was reshaped, the Palace Hotel was omitted and left on the sidelines; the difficulty of securing fresh sponsorship meant no tournament took place in 1973. In the evolving world of professionalism – where the main priority for elite players was to earn their living by seeking out the best prize money wherever available – the idea of a pleasant but financially unrewarding week at the seaside fell inexorably out of fashion, particularly among overseas aspirants.

Mirroring the pre-Second World War formative years, the last three editions of the Palace tournament in the mid-1970s were dominated by good home-based players. David Lloyd and Mark Cox took the honours in the men's singles, while Ann Jones –

whose fortunes improved after Mortimer was no longer on the scene (though she did get the better of her Devon rival in 1960) – recorded her fifth and sixth victories in 1974 and 1975. It seemed appropriate that the final women's singles title should be claimed by Sue Barker, born just a few miles from the venue in Paignton. She was the third world-class player, following in the footsteps of Mortimer and Sangster, to have been coached by Arthur Roberts at the Palace. Already at the age of 20 a grand slam champion, winner of the French Open, Barker found time between lengthy trips to the USA and the Far East in the autumn of 1976 to compete in Torquay, where she took away the modest first prize: just £50.[16]

RECORD BREAKERS

Most titles – Men: Bobby Wilson (6), Jaroslav Drobny (3)
Most titles – Women: Angela Mortimer (8), Ann Jones (6 – once as Ann Haydon), Joan Curry (4)
Number of Palace Hotel champions who also won Wimbledon singles
Men: 1; Women: 5; Total: 6

Palace Hotel Tournament

Men's Singles

Year	Winner	Runner-up	Score
1936	Harry Lee	Frank Wilde	6-4, 6-0
1937	Ronald Shayes	Frank Wilde	6-2, 6-4
1938	Ronald Shayes	Murray Deloford	6-3, 8-6
1939–47	No tournament held		
1948	Howard Walton	Don Butler	6-2, 6-3
1949	Paddy Roberts	Czeslaw Spychala (Pol)	6-3, 2-6, 6-2
1950	Ignacy Tloczynski	George Godsell	6-4, 2-6, 6-4
1951	Jaroslav Drobny (Egy)	Paddy Roberts	6-2, 6-4
1952	Tony Mottram	John Horn	3-6, 6-1, 6-0
1953	Gerry Oakley	Geoff Paish	2-6, 7-5, 10-8
1954	Mike Davies	Gerry Oakley	6-4, 6-2
1955	Bob Howe (Aus)	Roger Becker	6-3, 2-6, 6-4

1956	Jaroslav Drobny (Egy)	Gerry Oakley	6-4, 6-2
1957	Bobby Wilson	Gerry Oakley	6-4, 6-3
1958	Bobby Wilson	Alan Mills	6-4, 6-4
1959	Bobby Wilson	Mike Sangster	6-3, 6-4
1960	Bobby Wilson	Roger Becker	6-4, 6-2
1961	Jaroslav Drobny	Mike Sangster	6-2, 3-6, 6-4
1962	Bobby Wilson	Tony Pickard	6-3, 6-2
1963	Keith Diepraam (SA)	Bobby Wilson	6-3, 6-4
1964	Roger Taylor	Mike Sangster	11-9, 16-14
1965	Keith Wooldridge	Bobby Wilson	4-6, 6-3 retd
1966	Keith Wooldridge	John Clifton	5-7, 6-2, 6-1
1967	Bobby Wilson	Mike Sangster	8-6, 6-2
1968	Bob Hewitt (SA)	Owen Davidson (Aus)	6-3, 6-4
1969	Mark Cox	John Clifton	8-6, 6-3
1970	Vladimir Zednik (Czh)	Paul Hutchins	6-3, 6-3
1971	Bob Hewitt (SA)	Gerald Battrick	3-6, 6-1, 6-2
1972	Ray Moore (SA)	Pat Cramer (SA)	6-3, 6-3
1973	No tournament held		
1974	David Lloyd	Mark Farrell	6-7, 6-4, 6-2
1975	Mark Cox	Richard Lewis	6-3, 6-3
1976	David Lloyd	Martin Robinson	7-6, 6-3

Women's Singles

Year	Winner	Runner-up	Score
1936	Anita Lizana (Chl)	Dorothy Round	8-10, 6-1, 6-1
1937	Freda James	Billie Yorke	4-6, 6-1, 6-3
1938	Mary Hardwick	Nina Brown	6-2, 6-4
1939–47	No tournament held		
1948	Joan Curry	Betty Hilton	6-1, 6-3
1949	Joan Curry	Jean Walker-Smith	6-2, 3-6, 6-2
1950	Joan Curry	Jean Walker-Smith	walkover
1951	Susan Partridge	Jean Walker-Smith	6-4, 6-3
1952	Angela Mortimer	Joan Curry	6-3, 6-1
1953	Angela Mortimer	Georgie Woodgate	6-1, 6-1
1954	Angela Mortimer	Shirley Bloomer	6-2, 6-1
1955	Angela Mortimer	Angela Buxton	6-2, 6-2
1956	Thelma Long (Aus)	Angela Buxton	6-4, 4-6, 7-5
1957	Joan Curry	Rita Bentley	6-2, 10-8

1958	Angela Mortimer	Ann Haydon	6-1, 6-0
1959	Angela Mortimer	Ann Haydon	7-5, 6-3
1960	Ann Haydon	Angela Mortimer	6-4, 6-2
1961	Angela Mortimer	Deidre Catt	6-1, 6-2
1962	Angela Mortimer	Ann Jones	7-5, 6-3
1963	Deidre Catt	Ann Jones	6-3, 8-6
1964	Ann Jones	Deidre Catt	6-3, 7-5
1965	Ann Jones	Pat Faulkner (Aus)	6-1, 6-1
1966	Joyce Williams	Ann Jones	6-4, 5-5 retd
1967	Virginia Wade	Ann Jones	6-2, 12-14, 6-2
1968	Margaret Court (Aus)	Virginia Wade	12-10, 8-6
1969	Julie Heldman (USA)	Virginia Wade	4-6, 8-6, 6-3
1970	Ann Jones	Virginia Wade	6-4, 7-5
1971	Evonne Goolagong (Aus)	Francoise Durr (Fra)	6-1, 6-0
1972	Margaret Court (Aus)	Virginia Wade	2-6, 6-3, 6-1
1973	No tournament held		
1974	Ann Jones	Janet Newberry (USA)	7-5, 7-6
1975	Ann Jones	Winnie Wooldridge	4-6, 6-1, 6-3
1976	Sue Barker	Michele Tyler	6-4, 6-2

7

The Northern

RESUMING OUR clockwise journey around the country, we head north from Bristol – broadly following the route of today's M5 motorway past Birmingham (discussed in chapter 9) – and we come across several locations that have in the past hosted what the LTA calls 'world-class tennis'. The list of tournaments in north-west England that have featured competitors from overseas is extensive: it includes Sheffield and Hallamshire, Hoylake, Harrogate (where Australian Wimbledon champion Frank Sedgman claimed the men's singles title in 1952), Ilkley, Carlisle and Buxton, the last-named the picturesque Peak District setting for several years of the official All England Ladies Doubles Championships. These various gatherings each warrant more attention than space allows in this volume (although Hoylake is considered further in the next chapter). But one tournament in the north-west deserves detailed scrutiny in its own right on the basis of a sparkling history dating back to the dawn of lawn tennis in the 1870s. This meeting, particularly before the First World War, was among the most eminent in the annual tennis calendar, rapidly evolving into – indeed, originating with the intention of becoming – the so-called 'Wimbledon of the North'.

* * *

In 1879 a group of local dignitaries and enthusiasts in Lancashire formed the Northern Lawn Tennis Association. Its core aims included the promotion of a tournament similar to that 'successfully held by the All England Club at Wimbledon' over the previous couple of years.[1] Action soon followed in the form of the laying out of grass courts at the Broughton Cricket Club in Manchester, which in July 1880 hosted the first Northern Association Lawn Tennis Championships. This was a men-only competition at the outset, won in poor light by Richard Richardson of Chester.

When repeated the following summer, the meeting just about managed to cover expenses, and in 1882 the Association – under pressure from players on Merseyside – agreed to run the event at Liverpool Cricket Club in Aigburth, where it was reported that the grass 'is always in the most splendid condition'. This inspired choice saw a strong field of attendees, play of a 'very high class' and a third successive victory for Mr Richardson, this time defeating none other than the great Ernest Renshaw in front of hundreds of spectators in a thrilling five-set final.[2] The 'Northern', as it was often referred to for shorthand, was on the map.

In 1883 the tournament alighted upon a home that was to figure prominently in its rise over the following decades. In late 1881 the Northern Association supported the creation of the Northern Lawn Tennis Club, developed over the next couple of years in an affluent residential area around Seymour Grove in Old Trafford. Close by to Manchester city centre, Trafford Park was largely within the boundaries of the private estate owned for centuries by the de Trafford family, and in the late-Victorian period it became a hub for several different sports. Sir Humphrey de Trafford regarded tennis as one of his main sporting interests, and he became the first president of the club, which when completed boasted over 20 grass courts and a handsome half-timbered pavilion, built at a cost of £375. In 1884 the Northern Association, content that its original ambition of creating a top-level meeting had been met, relinquished management of the tournament on the condition that the two clubs concerned – at Old Trafford in Manchester and at Aigburth in Liverpool – would each host the event in alternate years.

Harry Scrivener, active at many tournaments in the 1890s (a two-time winner of the men's doubles at Queen's), and later a prominent journalist and referee, said that he and his contemporaries regarded the Northern as 'the third most important event of the year', outshone in the domestic schedule only by Wimbledon and the Irish Championships.[3] Underpinning this exalted status was the ability of organisers from early on to attract the crème de la crème of amateur competitors. The multiple Wimbledon-winning Renshaw brothers, William and Ernest, won the men's doubles title six times between 1882 and 1888. The willingness of players to travel from far and wide to challenge for honours in Manchester and Liverpool was indicated by the victory of American James Dwight in the men's singles in 1885; he thereby became the first man from outside the UK to win one of the main English tournaments beyond SW19. In the women's singles, introduced at the Northern in 1882, the first decade was similarly dominated by leading stars of the day, including Maud Watson – winner of the inaugural women's championship at Wimbledon (which only came two years later) – and the incomparable Cheshire-born Lottie Dod, 'the greatest sportswoman of her time', in the view of her biographer.[4]

Another reason why the Northern acquired such high renown in the late-Victorian era was that it commonly featured scores of fine players from Ireland, for whom travel to Liverpool and Manchester was quicker and more convenient than attending meetings elsewhere in England. At a time when the Irish Championships was at the height of its prestige, Anglo-Irish rivalries added further spice to proceedings at the Northern, helping to draw in enthusiastic crowds and so ensuring steady profits for the organising committee. Irish success became a hallmark of the event for many years. May Langrishe (winner of the Irish Championships when aged just

MEMORABLE MATCHES

Three of Lottie Dod's five victories at the Northern were secured at the expense of Blanche Hillyard, but each encounter was no pushover for the teenage sensation. In 1888 Miss Dod, three months short of her 16th birthday, won 6-3, 9-7; her more experienced opponent missed four opportunities to take the match into a final set. Mrs Hillyard at least had the compensation of winning the Northern mixed title, which from 1888 until 1912 was branded as the All England Mixed Doubles competition. In what The Field newspaper called the best final of its type ever seen, Hillyard and Ernest Renshaw beat the Merseyside pairing of Dod and J.C. Kay. In the 1889 women's final, record crowds at Old Trafford saw Hillyard, deploying her stinging forehand to good effect, win the first set before Lottie took charge. And four years later Miss Dod completed her trio of Northern triumphs over her great adversary, this time by the slimmest of margins, 7-5 in the deciding set. On this occasion Mrs Hillyard had match points, but according to Pastime magazine, she played too safe at the vital moment, 'had she gone for her shot, she might have won'.[5]

14) came through a field of 14 entrants to claim the women's title when it was first held in Liverpool in 1882, and Louisa Martin established what would be an unequalled women's record of seven victories. Some 3,000 spectators were in Liverpool to see Willoughby Hamilton from Kildare take the first of two men's singles titles in 1888, and he was followed by Joshua Pim, four-time champion in the 1890s.

It was therefore with pride, and without exaggeration, that local newspapers boasted of 'the best exponents from all parts of the kingdom' regularly competing at the Northern.[6] While SW19 experienced a temporary dip in popularity in the mid-1890s, the opposite was the case at the 'Wimbledon of the North'. *The Field* reported in 1894 that the stands were 'filled to overflowing' to see a tight five-setter which resulted in Wilfred Baddeley's steady baseline game ending the stranglehold of Joshua Pim on the men's title.[7] Baddeley went on to secure three more victories, including in 1897 over Reginald Doherty, who weeks later won the first of four successive titles at Wimbledon. Doherty's younger brother, Laurie, showed the potential that led to him sweeping all before him after the turn of the century by winning the Northern in 1898. The Dohertys also teamed up to claim the men's doubles title three times and their charismatic presence did much to ensure spectators continued to flock to Manchester and Liverpool in healthy numbers.

In the Edwardian period it was not only the 'best exponents from all parts of the kingdom' who appeared at the Northern; it was, increasingly, some of the best from elsewhere in the world. May Sutton arrived in Manchester from the USA in 1905 to take the English season by storm, remaining undefeated throughout, including victory at Wimbledon. She became the first overseas winner of the women's singles at the Northern (and, aged 17, the youngest champion since Lottie Dod) when she unveiled her crunching forehand to beat Hilda Lane in straight sets. Anglo-American rivalry sharpened the intensity of the women's event for the next couple of years. In 1906 Dorothea Douglass was in fine form at Liverpool and inflicted a first singles defeat on Miss Sutton outside of North America. Douglass found the best tactic to pierce the American's armoury was to pepper her opponent's backhand and remain patient until the chance came to deploy her own strongest weapon: the angled cross-court forehand winner. Charlotte Sterry took note of this masterclass; she also got the better of May Sutton in the 1907 Old Trafford final.

On the men's side, although the run of Wimbledon champions triumphing in the north-west was temporarily interrupted, the excellent standard on display was hardly diminished. Gloucestershire's Sydney Smith – undoubtedly one of the finest players never to taste victory in SW19 – benefited from the continuance of the challenge round until 1905 to establish a record of seven successive men's singles titles, starting with victory over Wilberforce Eaves in 1899. In the 1907 final Old Trafford crowds watched with a mixture of awe and distress as Australia's Norman Brookes thrashed the Lancashire and England junior champion, Xenophon Casdagli, for the loss of two games. 'The Wizard' from Melbourne, as he was dubbed, confounded opponents with a swinging left-hand serve that many found unreturnable. He underlined his reputation as one of the best on the global stage following the retirement of Laurie Doherty by proceeding – a couple of weeks after the Northern – to become the first man from outside the UK to claim the Wimbledon crown.

The Manchester leg of the tournament switched venue in the run-up to the First World War. After Sir Humphrey de Trafford sold his estate in the mid-1890s, the semi-rural character of the area was transformed by industrial growth and its supporting infrastructure: densely packed housing, railways and busy new roads. Club members at the Northern were heard to complain – no doubt exaggerating for effect – that new balls would turn black with dirt and grime after just a few games. In 1908 a decision was made to relocate to the more suburban, leafier surroundings of West Didsbury, five miles from the city centre, where the club's wooden pavilion was transported and re-erected the following year. Old Trafford was left to become associated primarily with cricket and football (the famous Manchester United stadium was built in 1914), but Northern officials were happy enough with the move. The spacious new grounds in Palatine Road allowed for an expansion in membership, and although it took a while for the grass courts to reach the same standard as those left behind, top players continued to turn up in large numbers for the biennial tournament, first hosted at Didsbury in 1911.

It was indicative of the ongoing strength in depth of the Northern entry that some of the game's very best did not always walk away with the honours. In 1913 both of the losing singles finalists at Didsbury went on to win Wimbledon that summer. In windy conditions the great Mrs Lambert Chambers found the holder, Ethel Larcombe, in obdurate form and lost in straight sets; she reversed the scoreline against the same opponent in SW19. In the men's final, reigning Wimbledon champion Anthony Wilding was a strong favourite, but met his match in the talented athlete James Parke, sometime captain of Ireland's rugby team. Parke had won the Irish Championships eight times and his aggressive tactics pinned Wilding behind the baseline as he stormed through the first two sets. The Wimbledon champion fought back to level the match, but Parke then gained a second wind and his fierce driving carried him over the line, 7-5 in the decider.

The glittering Edwardian period proved a hard act to follow. The inter-war years brought mixed fortunes for the Northern, bright moments interspersed with difficult times. After the wartime hiatus, large crowds came out from Manchester to see some entertaining finals at Didsbury in 1919. James Parke, wounded on active service during the war, moved to the locality and became a club member, and despite being almost 40 he added to his pre-1914 hat-trick of wins by beating South Africa's George Dodd in the men's final. The tournament resumed its tradition of attracting highly accomplished (if not now always world-beating) entrants, and it had never been in better shape financially, making a healthy profit of over £1,000 in 1921. Another significant landmark came in 1923, when Didsbury hosted its first Davis Cup tie, a second-round European Zone match against Spain. Although the British team suffered a narrow defeat, Manchester was regarded as a suitable base for such encounters; it was chosen five more times in the decades to come.

The Northern's success in the first half of the 1920s owed much to a pair of star attractions: in the women's draw, Californian 'Bunny' Ryan (see below), and in the men's event, local sporting legend Max Woosnam. Despite working full-time as a businessman, the famed Corinthian – who in addition to winning Olympic tennis medals in 1920 had played football for Manchester City and England – regularly found time to compete at the Northern. With his energetic style and cheerful persona, Woosnam was a huge draw. The *Manchester Evening News* wrote in 1921 that crowds at his matches were 'completely absorbed'.[8] Although only recently recovered from a broken leg, Max reached three finals at Didsbury in 1923. He narrowly lost a five-set singles final full of twists and turns, but proved fit enough to win the men's doubles with Leslie

---

UNDERRATED CHAMPION

Ted Tinling, dress designer and confidant to scores of top players, had strong views on Elizabeth Ryan. The American, who resided in Britain for much of her life, was, Tinling said, a pioneer of genuinely aggressive volleying in the women's game. But, on the other hand, he felt she was too slow around the court to be a really effective singles player. It was clear that Miss Ryan's volleying skills underpinned her record-breaking feats in doubles, which included 26 grand slam titles, 19 of them at Wimbledon alone. Although she fell short in singles at the grand slams (losing in three finals), the Californian's record elsewhere was astonishing. Tinling, it seems, paid little heed to the impressive scale and variety of tournament successes Ryan notched up in England, including five titles at the Northern between 1920 and 1925. Each of these wins came in straight sets, and two were at the expense of future Wimbledon champion Kitty McKane. Those on the receiving end of a beating from Miss Ryan would most likely have readily testified to her proficiency as she amassed a greater number of singles titles (34 in total) than any other man or woman featured in this book: seven at Beckenham, six at Surbiton, five at Queen's as well as at the Northern, four in Scarborough, three at Eastbourne, two in the Hard Court Championships, one at Bristol and one at the Midland Counties.

Godfree and the mixed with Miss Ryan. Although Woosnam lost some of his trademark speed around the court as the years went by, he was still adept enough to capture the singles title in 1926.[9]

The thrills and spills enjoyed at Didsbury after the Great War were not always replicated when the Northern was held, as remained the custom, at the Liverpool Cricket Club in alternate years. A sunny (and again profitable) week in Manchester in 1923 was followed by a washout in Aigburth the following summer; rain curtailed the completion of all but a couple of events. After lengthy and acrimonious negotiations with the cricket club, Didsbury officials secured the right to exclusively stage the official Northern Championships every June. This painful parting of the ways had some adverse consequences. The 1928 tournament, the first after the split, made a financial loss, partly owing to the cost of purchasing new trophies, and compared with the pre-1914 heyday, organisers had difficulty in attracting well-known crowd-pullers. The Northern roll of honour between the wars contained the name of only one Wimbledon champion – the veteran Mrs Lambert Chambers – plus one SW19 finalist – Bunny Austin, victorious in Manchester in 1930.

The tournament may have found a more settled, single base, but its fortunes only partially improved in the 1930s. An increasingly congested international calendar – and in particular a clash with the French Championships – compounded the problem of bringing in star attractions. The 1933 meeting featured many county-level players (both men's finalists were club members) and persuaded officials to switch date from June to mid-July, post-Wimbledon, as from 1934 onwards. This decision quickly yielded benefit. The men's title was claimed twice in the following years by 6ft 7in Irishman George Lyttleton Rogers, whose career highlights elsewhere included victories over Wimbledon champions Jack Crawford and Henri Cochet. Even so, as club historian David Allaby notes, 'the spark was no longer quite so obvious', circumstances having conspired to lower somewhat the Northern's high reputation.[10] Crowds at Didsbury hoping to see legends of the game, as of old, had to make do with rare fleeting glimpses, notably when Bill Tilden came to town.

IN A HURRY

Tilden appeared in an international friendly match between the USA and Britain, held at the Northern Club in June 1927, and gave spectators a brief insight as to why many regarded him as the finest player in the history of the sport thus far. Big Bill was due to play Colin Gregory, but the young Yorkshire champion withdrew at the last moment owing to – as one newspaper put it – 'indisposition'.[11] Gregory was a robust character. He went on to be a doctor by profession (and to win the Australian Championships), but the effect of him standing down was to leave Surrey county player D.N. Greig in the firing line. Tilden, looking to tune up for Wimbledon the following week, was in majestic form. He won the first two sets to love, each in about ten minutes. He continued to unleash the full range of his unrivalled shot-making in the third set, taking a 4-0 lead. Having won the first 16 games, he then slackened off slightly. The Surrey man, who played some good individual points and never gave up the ghost, took the next game, at which point the crowd erupted into tumultuous applause. But the end came soon enough. Tilden took the set 6-2, wrapping up the whole match in just 46 minutes.

The post-Second World War years witnessed, not a return to the pre-1914 golden age – global competition had grown too substantially since the Edwardian era to allow for that – but at least a welcome upturn in the fortunes of the Northern. Links forged across the Atlantic during the conflict by club stalwart and business owner Brian Finnigan (who competed in the US Championships) helped to ensure an unprecedented influx of strong American women when the meeting resumed in 1946, restored to its more familiar and popular early June slot. Sell-out crowds flocked to see members of

French ace Jean Borotra, 11-time winner of the British Covered Court Championships, does a trademark leap over the net to celebrate a victory at Queen's Club in 1947

The main outdoor showcase at Queen's, the Stella Artois Championships, witnesses a familiar outburst in the 1984 final from eventual champion, John McEnroe

Multi-grand slam winning American star Helen Wills, seen here in action at the Surrey Grass Court Championships, Surbiton, where she took the title in 1938

Australia's Margaret Smith (later Margaret Court) demonstrates her volleying skills in the 1961 final at Beckenham; Smith beat Christine Truman in a tight three-setter

A recent, 2018, view of the main courts at Devonshire Park, Eastbourne, one of England's premier tennis venues throughout its long history

Mark Cox (left) with Australian Roy Emerson ahead of their quarter-final at Bournemouth in 1968. The British left-hander captured the headlines at the world's first-ever open tournament as an amateur who beat two professionals: Gonzales and Emerson

Ann Jones, pictured at the Palace Hotel tournament, Torquay, in 1969; she won the event six times

The legendary Lottie Dod, shown here en route to victory over arch-rival Blanche Hillyard in the final of the Northern tournament, Manchester, in 1889

A pre-First World War view of the scenic costal setting for the North of England Championships in Scarborough

Pam Shriver of the USA receives the trophy after securing the first of four consecutive titles at Edgbaston in 1984

The final of the women's singles at Nottingham in 2019, won by Caroline Garcia of France (nearest to camera)

The Royal Albert Hall, home since the 1970s to a range of high-level tournaments including the Rothmans International and the Dewar Cup

Wembley's Empire Pool was the top location in London for indoor professional play in the pre-Open era. Pancho Segura (in the dimly-lit foreground) is pictured playing Dinny Pails in 1949

Aussie great Rod Laver is introduced to Prince Philip, the Duke of Edinburgh, at the Empire Pool in 1964; Laver went on to win the Wembley Pro six times

The lighting and technology found at indoor venues improved considerably compared with the early days at Wembley. Here Roger Federer and Novak Djokovic await the on-screen outcome of a line call challenge in the 2012 ATP World Finals at the O2 Arena

Britain's Andy Murray shows off the ATP trophy (left) and the World Number One trophy after defeating Djokovic at the O2 in November 2016

America's Wightman Cup squad; they arrived in Manchester via direct flight from New York to show off marvels such as stylish outfits and nylon stockings largely unavailable in war-ravaged Britain. Margaret Osborne deployed a polished serve-and-volley game to beat the young Louise Brough in the women's singles; both finalists were later to go on to be Wimbledon champions.

The increase in tempo, with overseas contenders arriving in greater force, was also noticeable on the men's side. Apart from Tony Mottram, winner in 1949, no British man triumphed at the Northern for 15 years after the war. Australia's Davis Cup squad, travelling together and seeking grass-court practice ahead of Wimbledon, developed a special liking for the fast grass at Didsbury. The men's singles title was won seven times in a decade by Australians, on each occasion by a different individual. The first of those, in 1946, was the debonair Jack Harper, who en route to the final got ticked off when warming up at the start of one of his matches. After ignoring requests to get ready to play, he was warned by the umpire, 'If you can just take your eyes off that girl in the stand, Jack, we can start.' The umpire, much to the amusement of spectators, hadn't realised his microphone was switched on.[12] He was not the only courtside official who wrestled with etiquette concerns at the Northern.

SPARING THE UMPIRE'S BLUSHES

Ahead of a first-round encounter at Didsbury in the mid-1930s, the duty umpire was known to be fretting about how to refer to one of the players, Lord Pollington. Should he, the umpire asked colleagues, call out 'game to Pollington', or 'game to Lord Pollington'? Whatever his decision, it was never revealed or put to the test. The noble Lord was crushed 6-0, 6-0.

A marker of how far the good times had returned to Didsbury came in 1956, when all four singles finalists were Wimbledon champions. At the age of 34, Jaroslav Drobny mixed power and subtlety to get the better of Lew Hoad in a tight three-setter (though the Aussie star returned to take the men's title the following year), while Althea Gibson used her trademark heavy hitting from the baseline to claim the first of three successive Northern victories in beating compatriot Louise Brough. It was not, however, all plain sailing for the tournament. Changes to the timing of French Championships meant the meeting again clashed with the second week in Paris, limiting the availability of some of the top players. And clouds on the horizon were literal as well as metaphorical. Wallis Myers of *The Telegraph* once said he would never go to Manchester without an umbrella, and the heavens opened to blight finals day in 1961 and again in 1964, the 75th anniversary of the tournament.

FEELING THE HEAT

Devon's Mike Sangster had to share the title when heavy rain struck in 1961, but he faced a meteorological challenge of a different sort – sweltering heat – when he came through a trio of epic battles to take the Northern title in 1963. After three hours he managed to beat South African Frew Macmillan 6-4, 15-17, 6-4 in the quarter-finals. The following day, in a semi-final decided by the odd winner or error here and there, Sangster defeated Roger Taylor 10-8, 3-6, 7-5. In the final, the Torquay star then got past young Aussie newcomer Tony Roche, this time by another narrow margin, 19-17, 6-4. These feats of endurance suggested a player at the peak of fitness. And yet in the semi-final encounter with Taylor, Sangster astonished those watching when, in the second set, he suddenly put on a cardigan – this, despite the intensity of the match and the scorching temperature of 85°F. He explained afterwards that he ricked his back in the first set and wanted to prevent it from becoming too stiff.[13] The injury can't have been too serious. He not only beat Roche the following day; for good measure he won the men's doubles, partnered by Billy Knight.

Despite its ups and downs, the Northern looked better set than many English meetings to cope with the momentous changes that shook up the sport in the late 1960s. In the years ahead of the arrival of Open tennis the stands were often packed, the TV cameras attended to show match highlights, and the arena was graced by a string of the world's elite, including Billie Jean King, who beat Britain's Winnie Shaw in just half an hour in the 1966 final, and Maria Bueno, who secured a maiden Northern title the following year at her fifth attempt. With a handsome sponsorship deal in place, Didsbury moved from one era to another in seamless fashion. The 1968 women's final turned into an intriguing three-set nail-biter between two of the best-known figures of the day: Margaret Court squeezed through 6-4 in the decider against Virginia Wade.

In 1969 America's Clark Graebner brought novelty as well as some glamour to proceedings when he blazed his way to victory using a gold-plated, steel-framed racket. But the outlook for the tournament suddenly darkened after Rothmans withdrew sponsorship at the start of the 1970s. Weeks of negotiations produced a short-term fix in the form of an agreement between the club, the LTA and local sponsors, allowing the 1971 meeting to go ahead. Looking further into the future, plans were put in place for a major upgrade – including new hard courts and a facelift for facilities such as changing rooms and bars – designed to show the club's determination to move with the times. Manchester's inclusion on the list of leading pre-Wimbledon tournaments nevertheless looked uncertain until a solid sponsorship deal was struck with the Refuge Assurance insurance company in 1972.

The ensuing three-year period did not get off to the best of starts when the 1972 women's final saw South African Esme Emanuel (who lost to American Patti Hogan) angrily mounting the umpire's chair as the official tried to calm rising tempers. The following June, in 1973, Glynis Coles became the first British woman to lift the trophy since Betty Hilton in 1948. The best of the Refuge Assurance years was also the last. The main crowd-puller in 1974 was the emerging 21-year-old megastar Jimmy Connors, unable to compete at the French Open that summer for contractual reasons. The American duly secured the Northern title, though not before being given a harder workout than anticipated in the first set of the final (coming through 13-11) by Mike Collins of Surrey. Connors pocketed the £500 first prize before moving on to claim the Wimbledon crown a few weeks later.

In the absence of fresh sponsorship arrangements, Didsbury went without a frontline tournament in 1975 for the first time in 30 years. With elite player schedules constantly shifting, the Northern was now threatened with extinction. Once again local businesses rallied round strongly, and the completion of improvements to the club's infrastructure also helped to ensure that top-drawer tennis resumed in 1976 and continued on the women's side until restructuring of the tour saw the curtain come down in the early 1980s. During this period British women took the title five times, three of those victories notched up by local favourite Anne Hobbs, who in 1978 became the first Northern club member to win the women's singles. Anne, who reached a world-high ranking of 33, secured her most memorable triumph a couple of years later when she gained her first tour win over title-holder Sue Barker, edging through 9-7 in the decider.

In the case of the men's event, the Northern – or the Greater Manchester Grass Court Tennis Championships as it was known after being rebranded – enjoyed something of a flourish in its final years. It remained part of the Grand Prix circuit and attracted some of sport's leading names, including a couple of Wimbledon champions who in the 1980s followed in the footsteps of Jimmy Connors: John McEnroe lifted the trophy in 1982 and Stefan Edberg triumphed in successive years later in the decade. Another Wimbledon champion, Stan Smith, missed out in the 1980 Manchester final when he was unable to contain the high-velocity serving of fellow American Roscoe Tanner, which whistled off the parched surface that summer. For a further five years after the reorganisation of the men's tour at the end of the 1980s, the tournament was an integral part of the elite ATP circuit. This resulted in a roll of honour during the twilight years that was almost as distinguished as in the pre-1914 heyday. Those who took the men's title in this time-frame included Pat Rafter, Goran Ivanisevic and American teenager Pete Sampras, who in 1990 secured his first grass-court title as a professional, in Manchester.[14]

With the LTA seeking to streamline the pre-Wimbledon grass-court schedule, Didsbury found itself sidelined after 1994, although international-standard play has revived in various guises in recent times, attracting world-class if not world-leading players. Contemporary versions of the Manchester Trophy have included a men's Challenger competition in 2015 and 2016 (won in those years by Sam Groth and Dustin Brown respectively) and a women's event, part of the ITF women's circuit since 2017. The Northern club, with its stylish multipurpose sports facilities, remains confident of a bright future. As for its past, the fortunes of its showcase grass-court meeting waxed and waned, but its peak periods – prior to 1914, the early post-1945 years and (in the case of the men) the 1980s–90s – ensured that, overall, the number of Northern winners who were also Wimbledon champions ended up being higher than at most English tournaments taking place much closer to the southern heartlands of lawn tennis.

RECORD BREAKERS

Most titles – Men: Sydney Smith (7), Joshua Pim (4), Wilfred Baddeley (4), James Parke (4), Richard Richardson (3), John Olliff (3), Mike Sangster (3 – one shared)

Most titles – Women: Louisa Martin (7), Lottie Dod (5), Dorothea Lambert Chambers (5 – twice as Dorothea Douglass), Elizabeth Ryan (5)

Number of Northern champions who also won Wimbledon singles Men: 13; Women: 15; Total: 28

Northern Tournament

Men's Singles

Year	Winner	Runner-up	Score
1880	Richard Richardson	Walter Fairlie	6-0, 6-3, 6-0
1881	Richard Richardson	John Comber	6-1, 6-1, 6-0
1882	Richard Richardson	Ernest Renshaw	6-1, 3-6, 5-7, 6-4, 11-9
1883	Herbert Wilberforce	Champion Russell	6-1, 3-6, 6-1, 6-0
1884	Donald Stewart	Herbert Wilberforce	5-7, 6-4, 6-4, 6-0
1885	James Dwight (USA)	Donald Stewart	6-2, 6-2, 6-4
1886	Harry Grove	James Dwight (USA)	6-4, 6-3, 6-1
1887	Harry Grove	David Chaytor	4-6, 6-2, 8-10, 6-4, 6-2
1888	Willoughby Hamilton	Harry Grove	6-1, 8-6, 6-1
1889	Willoughby Hamilton	Harold Mahony	6-3, 3-6, 6-1, 6-2
1890	Joshua Pim	Willoughby Hamilton	2-6, 6-8, 7-5, 7-5, 6-3
1891	Joshua Pim	Wilfred Baddeley	4-6, 8-6, 6-4, 7-5
1892	Joshua Pim	Harry Barlow	4-6, 6-1, 6-4, 6-4
1893	Joshua Pim	Harold Mahony	4-6, 6-3, 7-5, 6-2
1894	Wilfred Baddeley	Joshua Pim	4-6, 11-9, 4-6, 6-3, 6-4
1895	Wilfred Baddeley	Herbert Baddeley	6-8, 6-2, 6-4, 1-0 retd
1896	Wilfred Baddeley	Harold Mahony	6-1, 10-12, 7-5, 6-4
1897	Wilfred Baddeley	Reginald Doherty	6-2, 7-5, 2-6, 6-0
1898	Laurence Doherty	Clarence Hobart (USA)	6-1, 6-1, 8-6
1899	Sydney Smith	Wilberforce Eaves	7-9, 6-3, 6-3, 8-6
1900	Sydney Smith	Edward Allen	6-3, 6-8, 6-4, 4-6, 6-2
1901	Sydney Smith	Wilberforce Eaves	10-12, 7-5, 6-2, 6-4
1902	Sydney Smith	Harold Mahony	7-5, 7-5, 3-6, 10-8
1903	Sydney Smith	Xenophon Casdagli	6-1, 6-3, 6-2
1904	Sydney Smith	Frank Riseley	6-2, 7-9, 2-6, 6-2, 6-2
1905	Sydney Smith	Frank Riseley	walkover
1906	Frank Riseley	Sydney Smith	4-6, 7-5, 6-1, 6-3
1907	Norman Brookes (Aus)	Xenophon Casdagli	6-0, 6-2
1908	Arthur Gore	James Parke	6-3, 4-6, 6-1, 6-8, 6-4
1909	Robert Powell (Can)	Theodore Mavrogordato	6-4, 6-1, 6-4
1910	Beals Wright (USA)	James Parke	divided – trophy to Wright
1911	James Parke	Stanley Doust (Aus)	7-5, 5-7, 6-1, 8-6
1912	James Parke	Theodore Mavrogordato	6-3, 1-6, 6-3, 6-4
1913	James Parke	Anthony Wilding (NZ)	6-2, 7-5, 6-8, 2-6, 7-5

1914	Theodore Mavrogordato	Alfred Dunlop (Aus)	9-7, 8-6, 6-2
1915–18	No tournament held		
1919	James Parke	George Dodd (SA)	0-6, 6-3, 9-7, 6-0
1920	Theodore Mavrogordato	Randolph Lycett (Aus)	8-6, 6-2, 5-7, 3-0 retd
1921	Randolph Lycett (Aus)	Theodore Mavrogordato	8-6, 2-6, 6-4, 1-6, 6-4
1922	Ali-Hassan Fyzee (Ind)	Louis Meldon	9-7, 6-4, 11-9
1923	Patrick Wheatley	Max Woosnam	6-3, 4-6, 9-7, 9-11, 6-2
1924	Ernest Charlton	Bunny Ireland (Ire)	10-8, 6-4, 4-6, 7-5
1925	Norman Dicks	Gerard Sherwell (SA)	6-1, 7-5, 2-6, 6-3
1926	Max Woosnam	Douglas Hodges	7-9, 6-2, 6-2, 8-6
1927	Edward McCrea (Ire)	Douglas Hodges	4-6, 4-6, 6-2, 6-2, 7-5
1928	John Olliff	Edward McCrea (Ire)	6-2, 3-6, 6-4, 6-4
1929	John Olliff	Charles Kingsley	2-6, 6-3, 6-4, 2-6, 14-12
1930	Bunny Austin	John Olliff	8-6, 6-2, 6-4
1931	John Olliff	Nigel Sharpe	6-3, 3-6, 7-9, 6-3 retd
1932	Buster Andrews (NZ)	Martin Wedd	6-2, 6-3
1933	Herby Aldred	Lionel Antrobus	3-6, 6-3, 6-1
1934	George Lyttleton Rogers (Ire)	Cam Malfroy (NZ)	6-4, 4-6, 6-4
1935	Jiro Yamagishi (Jpn)	George Lyttleton Rogers (Ire)	6-3, 8-6
1936	Charles Hare	David Jones (USA)	6-4, 5-7, 6-4
1937	George Lyttleton Rogers (Ire)	Eric Filby	6-4, 2-6, 6-4
1938	Jack Piercy	Clifford Hovell	6-4, 10-8
1939	Eric Filby	R.E. Burton	6-4, 6-3
1940–45	No tournament held		
1946	Jack Harper (Aus)	Derrick Barton	6-4, 6-1
1947	Bill Sidwell (Aus)	Torsten Johansson (Swe)	6-2, 6-3
1948	John Bromwich (Aus)	Eric Sturgess (SA)	2-6, 6-2, 8-6
1949	Tony Mottram	Naresh Kumar (Ind)	6-2, 6-2
1950	Geoff Brown (Aus)	Sumant Misra (Ind)	6-0, 6-2
1951	Gardnar Mulloy (USA)	Don Candy (Aus)	6-4, 6-2
1952	Frank Sedgman (Aus)	Don Candy (Aus)	6-2, 4-6, 6-3, 6-2
1953	Mervyn Rose (Aus)	Clive Wilderspin (Aus)	4-6, 6-3, 6-0
1954	Ken Rosewall (Aus)	Rex Hartwig (Aus)	6-2, 6-1
1955	Hugh Stewart (USA)	Roger Becker	6-4, 3-6, 6-1
1956	Jaroslav Drobny (Egy)	Lew Hoad (Aus)	2-6, 6-3, 7-5
1957	Lew Hoad (Aus)	Ramanathan Krishnan (Ind)	6-2, 6-1
1958	Ramanathan Krishnan (Ind)	Naresh Kumar (Ind)	5-7, 6-3, 6-2
1959	Kurt Nielsen (Den)	Torben Ulrich (Den)	4-6, 6-3, 6-4

1960	Mark Otway (NZ)	Marty Mulligan (Aus)	3-6, 6-2, 7-5
1961	Mike Sangster	Luis Ayala (Chl)	title shared
1962	Mike Sangster	Billy Knight	10-12, 6-3, 6-4
1963	Mike Sangster	Tony Roche (Aus)	19-17, 6-4
1964	Roger Taylor	Billy Knight	title shared
1965	Tom Okker (Ned)	Roger Taylor	7-5, 6-3
1966	John Barrett	Lew Gerrard (NZ)	6-3, 6-3
1967	Owen Davidson (Aus)	Ray Ruffels (Aus)	6-1, 6-8, 6-4
1968	Ken Fletcher (Aus)	Luis Ayala (Chl)	6-3, 6-2
1969	Clark Graebner (USA)	Graham Stilwell	9-7, 3-6, 6-4
1970	Robert Lutz (USA)	Tom Gorman (USA)	6-2, 9-7
1971	Colin Dibley (Aus)	Bob Hewitt (SA)	6-1, 6-4
1972	Thomas Koch (Bra)	Patrice Dominguez (Fra)	6-2, 5-7, 6-4
1973	Sherwood Stewart (USA)	Dick Crealy (Aus)	6-3, 6-4
1974	Jimmy Connors (USA)	Mike Collins	13-11, 6-2
1975	No tournament held		
1976	Roscoe Tanner (USA)	Paul McNamee (Aus)	6-3, 7-9, 12-10
1977	Billy Martin (USA)	Saeed Meer (Pak)	6-2, 6-1
1978	Billy Martin (USA)	Chris Bradnam	9-8, 7-5
1979	Colin Dibley (Aus)	Mark Cox	6-4, 6-4
1980	Roscoe Tanner (USA)	Stan Smith (USA)	6-3, 6-4
1981	Phil Dent (Aus)	Brad Drewett (Aus)	7-5, 6-1
1982	John McEnroe (USA)	Russell Simpson (NZ)	6-3, 6-7, 10-8
1983	Tim Mayotte (USA)	Pat DuPre (USA)	3-6, 6-4, 6-4
1984	Jeremy Bates	Jeff Turpin (USA)	6-4, 8-6
1985	Jeremy Bates	Dan Cassidy (USA)	6-4, 6-2
1986	Glenn Michibata (Can)	Jay Lapudis (USA)	6-3, 6-3
1987	Stefan Edberg (Swe)	Kevin Curren (SA)	6-3, 6-4
1988	Stefan Edberg (Swe)	Kevin Curren (SA)	6-3, 6-4
1989	Patrick Baur (Ger)	Andrew Castle	6-4, 6-7, 7-5
1990	Pete Sampras (USA)	Gilad Bloom (Isr)	7-6, 7-6
1991	Goran Ivanisevic (Yug)	Pete Sampras (USA)	6-4, 6-4
1992	Jacco Eltingh (Ned)	Mal Washington (USA)	6-3, 6-4
1993	Jason Stoltenberg (Aus)	Wally Masur (Aus)	6-1, 6-3
1994	Pat Rafter (Aus)	Wayne Ferreira (SA)	7-6, 7-6

Women's Singles

Year	Winner	Runner-up	Score
1882	May Langrishe	Miss Langley	6-3, 8-6
1883	Edith Coleridge	Miss Eckersley	7-5, 6-3
1884	Edith Davies	Margaret Bracewell	2-6, 6-4, 6-4
1885	Maud Watson	Edith Davies	6-3, 6-3
1886	Maud Watson	Lottie Dod	7-5, 6-3
1887	Lottie Dod	Maud Watson	6-2, 6-1
1888	Lottie Dod	Blanche Hillyard	6-3, 9-7
1889	Lottie Dod	Blanche Hillyard	6-8, 6-3, 6-3
1890	Mary Steedman	Beatrice Wood	6-2, 6-0
1891	Florence Stanuell	Beatrice Wood	6-3, 2-6, 6-4
1892	Lottie Dod	Louisa Martin	6-1, 6-0
1893	Lottie Dod	Blanche Hillyard	6-3, 3-6, 7-5
1894	Blanche Hillyard	Beatrice Draffen	7-5, 5-7, 6-3
1895	Louisa Martin	Helen Jackson	7-5, 6-3
1896	Louisa Martin	Blanche Hillyard	6-2, 7-5
1897	Charlotte Cooper	Louisa Martin	3-6, 6-3, 6-4
1898	Louisa Martin	Charlotte Cooper	10-8, 6-4
1899	Louisa Martin	Ruth Durlacher	6-8, 6-2, 6-2
1900	Blanche Hillyard	Louisa Martin	2-6, 8-6, 6-4
1901	Louisa Martin	Blanche Hillyard	6-3, 4-6, 6-3
1902	Louisa Martin	Muriel Robb	6-8, 7-5, 6-3
1903	Louisa Martin	Dorothea Douglass	4-6, 7-5, 6-4
1904	Dorothea Douglass	Ethel Thomson	6-4, 6-2
1905	May Sutton (USA)	Hilda Lane	7-5, 8-6
1906	Dorothea Douglass	May Sutton (USA)	7-5, 6-2
1907	Charlotte Sterry	May Sutton (USA)	7-5, 6-0
1908	Edith Boucher	Charlotte Sterry	7-5, 6-2
1909	Edith Johnson	Maude Garfit	6-3, 9-11, 6-0
1910	Edith Johnson	Maude Garfit	3-6, 6-4, 6-0
1911	Dorothea Lambert Chambers	Mabel Parton	6-2, 6-2
1912	Ethel Larcombe	Mabel Parton	6-4, 6-1
1913	Ethel Larcombe	Dorothea Lambert Chambers	6-2, 6-4
1914	Dorothea Lambert Chambers	Agnes Morton	6-1, 6-2
1915–18	No tournament held		
1919	Dorothea Lambert Chambers	Ethel Larcombe	7-5, 6-3
1920	Elizabeth Ryan (USA)	Aurea Edgington	6-1, 6-3

1921	Elizabeth Ryan (USA)	Kitty McKane	7-6, 6-4
1922	Elizabeth Ryan (USA)	Kitty McKane	6-2, 8-6
1923	Elizabeth Ryan (USA)	Dorothy Holman	6-3, 6-3
1924	Mary Holmes	Clare Beckingham	6-4, 0-6, 6-3
1925	Elizabeth Ryan (USA)	Miss R. Thomas	6-4, 6-3
1926	Clare Beckingham	Elsie Goldsack	6-1, 6-1
1927	Clare Beckingham	Elsie Goldsack	6-2, 8-6
1928	Gwen Sterry	Sylvia Lumley-Ellis	6-4, 6-2
1929	Joan Fry	Gwen Sterry	6-3, 4-6, 6-1
1930	Evelyn Goldsworth	N. Hunt	7-5, 6-2
1931	Evelyn Goldsworth	Ena Alexandroff (Egy)	8-10, 6-4, 6-3
1932	Joan Ingram	Molly Hargreaves	11-9, 6-1
1933	Evelyn Goldsworth	Jackie McAlpine	7-5, 6-1
1934	Jean Saunders	Doris Bullock	6-0, 6-2
1935	Mary Hardwick	Dora Beazley	6-4, 6-2
1936	Patience Thomson	Dora Beazley	7-5, 7-9, 6-4
1937	Dora Beazley	Pamela Morrison	2-6, 7-5, 6-2
1938	Peggy Saunders Michell	Dora Beazley	6-1, 5-7, 7-5
1939	Patience Thomson	Gem Hoahing	title shared
1940–45	No tournament held		
1946	Margaret Osborne (USA)	Louise Brough (USA)	6-4, 6-3
1947	Jean Bostock	Betty Hilton	11-9, 6-2
1948	Betty Hilton	Jean Bostock	6-3, 8-6
1949	Patricia Todd (USA)	Lesley Fulton	6-3, 6-2
1950	Shirley Fry (USA)	Gladys Lines	6-2, 6-3
1951	Doris Hart (USA)	Beverly Baker (USA)	8-6, 6-3
1952	Maureen Connolly (USA)	Jean Quertier Rinkel	6-3, 6-1
1953	Doris Hart (USA)	Helen Fletcher	7-5, 1-6, 9-7
1954	Maureen Connolly (USA)	Louise Brough (USA)	6-3, 6-2
1955	Doris Hart (USA)	Louise Brough (USA)	9-11, 6-2, 6-2
1956	Althea Gibson (USA)	Louise Brough (USA)	2-6, 6-4, 6-4
1957	Althea Gibson (USA)	Darlene Hard (USA)	6-3, 6-4
1958	Althea Gibson (USA)	Maria Bueno (Bra)	6-1, 8-6
1959	Sally Moore (USA)	Rosie Reyes (Mex)	6-2, 2-6, 6-2
1960	Darlene Hard (USA)	Rita Bentley	6-3, 6-3
1961	Sandra Reynolds (SA)	Lesley Turner (Aus)	6-4, 6-3
1962	Darlene Hard (USA)	Judy Tegart (Aus)	6-3, 6-2
1963	Jan Lehane (Aus)	Darlene Hard (USA)	6-4, 8-10, 6-4

1964	Abandoned due to rain		
1965	Margaret Smith (Aus)	Maria Bueno (Bra)	6-1, 7-5
1966	Billie Jean King (USA)	Winnie Shaw	6-2, 6-1
1967	Maria Bueno (Bra)	Karen Krantzcke (Aus)	6-4, 6-3
1968	Margaret Court (Aus)	Virginia Wade	6-4, 4-6, 6-4
1969	Mary-Ann Curtis (USA)	Patti Hogan (USA)	6-4, 6-4
1970	Kerry Melville (Aus)	Carole Graebner (USA)	6-3, 6-1
1971	Patti Hogan (USA)	Kristien Kemmer (USA)	6-2, 3-6, 6-3
1972	Patti Hogan (USA)	Esme Emanuel (SA)	6-2, 6-3
1973	Glynis Coles	Linky Boshoff (SA)	6-1, 3-6, 6-4
1974	Kate Latham (USA)	Lesley Charles	6-3, 6-4
1975	No tournament held		
1976	Sue Mappin	Lesley Charles	6-4, 7-5
1977	Judy Connor (NZ)	Brenda Perry (NZ)	6-2, 6-3
1978	Anne Hobbs	Corinne Molesworth	6-3, 6-4
1979	Sue Barker	Anne Hobbs	7-5, 4-6, 6-0
1980	Anne Hobbs	Sue Barker	6-4, 4-6, 9-7
1981	Sharon Walsh (USA)	Rosie Casals (USA)	4-6, 6-1, 6-4
1982	Anne Hobbs	Kate Latham (USA)	6-2, 6-0
1983	Cathy Drury	Brenda Remilton (Aus)	7-6, 7-6

8

Scarborough

MANCHESTER WAS not the only location that provided a long-term platform for world-class tennis in northern England. Travelling 100 or so miles eastward, across the Pennine Hills past Leeds and beyond York, brings us in our nationwide journeyings to the North Sea. England's eastern coastline in general, from Northumberland right down to Essex and the Thames Estuary, contains an array of settings that have witnessed top-level competition, including Davis Cup ties as well as popular grass-court tournaments. Most of the leading events that flourished at various times on or near the eastern shoreline are now defunct: they diminished in importance or disappeared altogether by the 1980s and 1990s, with the result that the North Sea coast is something of a forgotten backwater in England's tennis history.

Before focusing on Scarborough, brief mention might be made of other once high-profile tournaments that have graced eastern coastal districts in the past. The Northumberland Championships in Newcastle began in the early 1880s and continued long enough (in adapted guises) to survive for over a century. The honours list was often dominated by nationally ranked British stars, although overseas winners included Anita Lizana in the 1930s and Judy Tegart in the 1960s. Sunderland, Darlington and Hull also hosted reputable summer meetings. In the case of Sunderland, which before the First World War featured proficient home players such as the Allen twins as well as Australasian Davis Cup squad members, the referee described it as 'a jolly meeting, in spite of the fact that it almost invariably included a thunderstorm of excessive violence'.[1]

Further south, Spilsby in Lincolnshire (a little inland from Skegness) and Cromer in Norfolk regularly ran holiday-time tournaments, although these were less long-lasting than the meeting at Felixstowe in Suffolk. This started in the mid-1880s and was important enough to be designated a few years later as the East of England Championships (in the same era when Bath hosted the West of England and Eastbourne the South of England Championships). Pre-Great War winners included Reginald Doherty, Herbert Roper Barrett, Edward Allen and George Hillyard. The Felixstowe club, with good-grade grass courts and a spacious clubhouse, was also the venue for a fourth-round Davis Cup tie in 1928, Britain losing out 4-1 to an Italian side that went on to reach the inter-zone final that year. The East of England Championships as originally constituted was discontinued after the arrival of Open tennis, but more recently Felixstowe featured on the lower-tier men's Challenger tour, attracting some of the world's best emerging talents.[2]

Finally, Frinton-on-Sea in Essex also lays claim to a vibrant tournament history. Traditionally held every July, the Frinton meeting initially attracted those looking to combine good-quality tennis with sunbathing on the long beach. Enthusiasts waxed lyrical about the splendid sight of 16 grass courts in full use along the seafront, backed by imposing houses with gardens in full bloom. The size of the programme expanded steadily, up to about 700 matches by 1921, the year in which Kitty McKane claimed her third successive victory in the women's singles. After the Second World War, Frinton became the home of the Essex Championships – previously held at a variety of locations – and the international flavour of the entry became more pronounced. Australian men came to the fore, so much so that there were almost a dozen (and three New Zealander) winners including Neale Fraser, Ken Fletcher and Owen Davidson in the post-war years, prior to the event being wound up in the early 1970s. On the women's side, Frinton briefly appeared on the WTA tour in the Open era, with another famous Aussie – Margaret Court – lifting the trophy twice.

The North of England Championships

The Yorkshire County Tennis Association was created in its original form in 1884, dedicated like similar bodies elsewhere to promoting tennis across its sprawling administrative region in northern England. Among the tournaments it facilitated that summer was one at Scarborough cricket ground, offering a range of singles and doubles events, some confined to county players, others open to all amateurs without residency restrictions. Situated on the north-east coast midway between Middlesbrough and Hull, Scarborough was ideally placed to benefit from the late-Victorian discovery and growth of lawn tennis. It was an established seaside resort and had good connections that helped facilitate an influx of wealthy visitors every summer; the railway to York had opened as early as 1845. It was to become *the* North Sea coastal location most closely associated with top-notch (and varied forms of) international-standard tennis, although this did not come about overnight.

In 1885 the Yorkshire Association, encouraged by its efforts the previous year, arranged an August tournament on the newly completed, eye-catching grounds of the North of England Lawn Tennis Club at South Cliff, overlooking the sea in Scarborough. With some 20 grass courts available, a range of county-only and open events were held. The following year a decision was made to run the county-restricted meeting elsewhere, in Harrogate, but the authorities at South Cliff arranged a fixture of their own, purchasing separate prizes and thereby giving a more distinct identity to the North of England Championships. The standard of play was high from the outset, foremost figures in the early stages being four-time men's winner, Irishman Ernest Browne, and in the women's open event, Yorkshire-born Margaret Bracewell.

UNDERRATED CHAMPION

Margaret Bracewell, the daughter of a cotton manufacturer, is overshadowed in the record books by famous Wimbledon champions such as Maud Watson, Lottie Dod and Blanche Bingley, but she was a force to be reckoned with in the late 1880s. Miss Bracewell was a three-time winner at the Midland Counties, she twice triumphed at Eastbourne (both times beating Bingley in the final) and she dominated the women's singles in the early years of the North of England tournament. Her victories in the finals of 1886 and 1887 were straightforward enough; in the latter case she crushed Lottie Dod's sister, Ann, for the loss of just one game. But in 1888 the contest between Bracewell and Bertha Steedman stretched out over two days. Play was halted by bad light with the score at one set all, and when the match resumed the next afternoon, it was agreed – in the interests of fairness to the finalists and spectators alike – that it would become a five-set encounter. Hence it was that Margaret Bracewell recorded what was, for women's singles, a highly unusual three-sets-to-one victory. As it was her third successive triumph, she also took ownership of the diamond bracelet donated to the ladies event by tournament patron Lord Londesborough.

The Scarborough meeting was not free from difficulties in its formative years. On some occasions it featured 'cracks' of the highest class – seven-time Wimbledon champion William Renshaw took the men's title in 1893 – but at other times the entry lists were quite thin, with county-level players predominating. Spectator numbers also varied, making it hard for the tournament to always cover costs. Crowd fluctuations were often in accordance with whether the Yorkshire Association decided to run the North of England in tandem with the county closed championships (which bolstered attendances) or whether to rotate the latter – which happened frequently – to other locations such as Hull, Sheffield, Ilkley or Harrogate. And although not unique in this respect, South Cliff's exposed coastal setting meant it suffered more than its fair share of disruptive weather. In 1889 the club was swamped following a deluge, and two years later the *Yorkshire Evening Post* lamented that the courts were 'wet and muddy, and the wind high, playing being consequently somewhat erratic'.[3]

WIND STOPS PLAY

There were some years when rain or sea fog disrupted proceedings all week in Scarborough; this, despite the tournament taking place at the height of summer in July or August. What posed a further challenge was the manner in which North Sea breezes might suddenly spring up. Although the main courts were partially sheltered from the elements, elsewhere on the grounds the effects of high incoming winds were alarming. On one occasion an umpire's chair, with the official in situ, was blown right over. Another time the tournament referee, noticing that serving was almost impossible as the ball, when thrown in the air, veered off behind the server's head, decided enough was enough. It was the only time in 30 years of officiating – the referee conceded – that play had to be suspended purely on account of gale-force winds.

While it had its problems, the North of England Championships was well-regarded enough to attract, in 1901, two players who went on to become all-time greats. In the women's final Dorothea Douglass, after coming through a tight second set 10-8, romped home to beat the title holder Alice Pickering. *The Field* reported that Miss Douglass (later to be seven-time Wimbledon champion) was improving all the while and 'will now have to be reckoned with even in the very best of company'.[4] The men's title went to Laurence Doherty, for whom Scarborough was to be a favourite hunting ground. His 1901 victory, when he defeated Ernest Black, came in advance of his five-year undefeated spell in SW19. Later, despite retiring from most high-level competition after 1906, 'Little Do' returned to Scarborough to claim three further titles, his last coming against Gordon Lowe in 1910. The legendary champion triumphed in this twilight phase of his singles career with little prior practice, and his presence, reporters noted, 'naturally gave an extraordinary impetus to the gathering'.[5]

Rumbling concerns in the Edwardian era about the suitability of South Cliff (the Yorkshire Association held its summer open singles elsewhere at times) meant that Scarborough only fully came into its own following the creation of the Yorkshire Lawn Tennis Club in 1910. County officials backed the construction of a brand-new site in the town, more sheltered from the wind at the base of Oliver's Mount in Filey Road. The cost came in at around £3,500, much of it spent on a grand pavilion with a central octagonal turret, plus levelling costs and the laying out of a dozen grass and two hard courts (more of both types were added later). Although the newly formed club was independently run, several of its leading members were also county officials, and Scarborough thereafter became recognised as the beating heart of Yorkshire tennis, acting as an administrative base as well as hosting a range of domestic and international-standard competitions every year. Despite a railway strike, the inaugural North of England Championships at Filey Road in 1911 were considered highly successful. Good crowds ensured the tournament made a handsome profit and the winners of the main singles events were leading stars of the day: James Parke and Ethel Larcombe.

After the Great War, Scarborough continued to blossom, delivering consistently high-grade late-summer competition. Fred Burrow, taking over as referee at Filey Road in 1921, not only lauded the two show courts – cleverly shielded from the worst excesses of the wind – as among the finest he saw on his travels, but also felt the 'wonderful entry' was possibly the best that year outside of Wimbledon.[6] In spite of rain and sea fog on several days, close on 900 matches were completed in the week, and the winners of both main titles were globally known names: South Africa's Brian Norton, who took five sets to get past Irishman Edward McCrea in the men's final, and Elizabeth Ryan, who secured her fourth successive singles victory. Miss Ryan's undefeated run was broken the following year when she lost to Kitty McKane, the first of a string of home players to claim the women's title at Filey Road. Mary Heeley stood out in this regard, triumphing five times during the 1930s, including an impressive win over Chile's Anita Lizana in 1935. On the men's side, finals at Scarborough between the wars were increasingly all-overseas affairs.

IN A HURRY

In 1924 the British holder of the North of England men's title, Sydney Jacob, fell at the semi-final stage to Mohammed Sleem, an Indian Davis Cup player. Sleem was renowned for his imperturbability and his relentless baseline retrieving style; some compared his attritional tactics to playing against a brick wall. Jacob, like many, became hugely frustrated and managed to get only three games. Sleem's opponent in the final, Louis Raymond of South Africa, decided in advance of going on to the court that he would 'live or die' in short order. The lesson he drew from watching the Indian was that there was no point in trying to beat him at his own game. Instead, he resolved that he would hit Sleem off the court. The 3,000-strong crowd at the Filey Road ground was duly treated to a sustained display of all-out attacking from the South African, as point after point he served-and-volleyed or sought to harry Sleem into errors. In probably his finest performance, Raymond won handsomely 6-2, 6-3, 6-3, though some onlookers doubted that he would have been able to maintain his intense levels of concentration, energy and aggression for much longer.

Although the Yorkshire Lawn Tennis Club (LTC) suffered a decline in membership owing to the economic slump that followed the Wall Street Crash (the grounds and pavilion were taken over by the town council in 1935), the North of England tournament picked up where it left off after the Second World War. As was the case before 1939, nationally ranked British women were prominent on the roll of honour. This pattern was punctuated by only occasional triumphs for contenders from Australasia, as when New Zealander Judy Burke beat Liverpool-born Angela Buxton in 1954. By way of contrast, though again echoing the pre-war trend, no British man won at Filey Road until Bobby Wilson in 1953, the first of three titles he claimed on his visits to Scarborough. The outstanding men's final of this era came in 1952 when ex-captain of the Royal South African Air Force, Eric Sturgess, beat former Wimbledon champion Budge Patty. In a match that went the distance, the steady accuracy of Sturgess finally got the better of the more swashbuckling American, 6-3 in the fifth set. According to the *Yorkshire Post*, the packed gallery around the main show courts had been treated to an 'exhibition of world-class tennis'.[7]

With hindsight, the decade or so after 1945 marked the full (and, as it turned out, final) flowering of top-quality tennis at Filey Road. What elevated this period above others was the fact that Scarborough had numerous strings to its bow, over and above its reputable summer grass-court meeting. Since the First World War it had been the home to a spring counterpart, the North of England Hard Court Championships. Held each year around Easter, this kicked off the English outdoor season and became seen as an important warm-up for players keen to do well at the British Hard Court Championships, scheduled to follow later in Bournemouth. Eight of the first ten post-1945 men's champions at Filey Road came from overseas, starting with Australia's Jack Harper in 1946. The established status of the North of England Hard Court tournament was such that Teddy Tinling mentioned it in saying that for many decades the full-length English circuit – featuring many stars of the world game – ran from 'Scarborough at Easter to Torquay in November'.[8]

Between the mid-1920s and the start of the 1960s, Scarborough's immaculately maintained grass courts were also deemed suitable to host six Davis Cup ties, a respectable total that placed it on a par with far larger venues such as Manchester. Five of the six ties came after the Second World War, underlining Filey Road's revitalisation in this era. The most satisfying from a home perspective was a 5-0 third-round victory over Germany in 1958. This was the year when a talented British squad including Wilson, Knight, Davies and Becker went on to reach the European Zone final for the first time in a quarter of a century. The victory in Scarborough reversed a crushing defeat at the hands of the Germans by the same margin when war loomed in 1939. In a strange statistical quirk, Germany won only one set in the 1958 encounter, courtesy of youthful newcomer Wilhelm Bungert, just as the British team shorn of its cup stalwarts Perry and Austin gained only one set when the two nations met in Berlin three months before the invasion of Poland.

A further massive draw for spectators at Filey Road after the war was a newly created event for professional players, the Slazenger Pro Championships (see chapters 5 and 10 for more detail on the early history of pro tennis). This began in 1946 and was won three times by Fred Perry, including victory in July 1948 over Frenchman Yvon Petra, the first post-war men's champion at Wimbledon. Perry had connections with the Slazenger company which he maintained after leaving amateur ranks in 1936, and travelling from his new home in North America to play in Scarborough became a regular part of his summer routine for a few years. The legendary champion later admitted he was a reluctant participant in post-war pro tournaments, having suffered a fracture in 1941 from which his elbow never fully recovered, but his ferocious competitive instincts (and his immodest streak) remained with him. 'When people asked me how on earth I beat somebody like Petra with a bad arm,' he wrote in his autobiography, he responded that it was because, 'I knew a little more about the game than he did.'[9]

For several years, many of the world's leading professionals – those who left the amateur game in search of above-board financial rewards – showed off their skills in front of packed Filey Road stands. Winners of the Slazenger Pro included Jack Kramer and Pancho Gonzales, the latter becoming a two-time champion. One of the prize recruits to the pro tour, Australian Frank Sedgman (Wimbledon champion in 1952), missed out, losing 8-6 in the fifth set of the 1953 Scarborough final to Ecuadorian Pancho Segura. As time went on, changes to the annual pro calendar meant it became harder to attract the top stars from the USA and Australia, with the result that by the mid-1950s the entry list was increasingly made up of lesser-known Europeans and coaching professionals. In 1958 a decision was made to relocate the event to Eastbourne, producing immediate dividends; the first final at Devonshire Park featured two of the leading additions to pro ranks, Ken Rosewall and Tony Trabert.

By the time the Slazenger Pro left Scarborough, the showcase North of England Championships were also past their prime. All-overseas finals were becoming a rarity, one of the last being a titanic struggle in 1958 which saw Aussie Ashley Cooper beat compatriot Mervyn Rose 14-12 in the fifth-set decider (in the process setting a record for the total number of games played, 77, unmatched by any other men's final recorded in these pages). Behind the scenes, rising maintenance costs put increasing financial strain on the Yorkshire LTC. Organisers were unable to offer the generous expenses expected by leading amateurs, and without such incentives top stars absented themselves. European players increasingly gave priority to meetings on the continent post-Wimbledon, and from the early 1960s onwards the numbers arriving from elsewhere in the world also fell.

The clearest indication that the post-1945 lease of life enjoyed at Filey Road had run its course came when plans were approved by the local council in 1968 to turn the whole site into a multi-sport leisure centre. Although the redevelopment, completed in 1974, included provision for ten courts (a mix of grass and hard), Scarborough could no longer claim to be the stand-out, bespoke, tennis venue in the region.

Hoylake

The North of England Championships had an unusual sequel. Just as the Slazenger Pro departed from the town in search of fresh impetus and new audiences, so in an attempt to keep Scarborough's most long-standing meeting alive in the altered context of Open tennis its location was changed, dramatically so: right across to the other side of northern England, to Hoylake – just west of Liverpool – on the Wirral Peninsula. Hoylake had its own idiosyncratic tennis tradition. Its annual tournament (which originated before the Second World War) was unique among top-tier English gatherings in being played on public courts, at Ashton Park. With numbers of overseas entrants rising steadily, Hoylake grew in stature during the 1950s, and because it was traditionally held in the same week as Scarborough (and secured strong backing from the *Liverpool Daily Post*), it was regarded as the best choice for injecting renewed energy into the rebranded North of England Championships.

Hoylake in the early Open era certainly provided for a distinctive atmosphere. In the absence of many suitable permanent buildings in Ashton Park, tents were erected every year to accommodate players, officials and journalists. The informality of proceedings was widely admired and commented upon, with fans and autograph hunters mixing with players in a way that had become unviable at most venues. *The Guardian*'s David Gray wrote enthusiastically that, especially when the sun shone, as it often seemed to, there was 'nothing like this tournament anywhere in the world'. Gray claimed, 'You had to be there, to appreciate the unique quality of Hoylake's tennisomania.'[10]

With support from local newspapers and businesses, the North of England – sometimes now also referred to as the Rothmans Hoylake Open and briefly included as part of the evolving Grand Prix circuit – for a while featured well-known global icons such as John Newcombe, who saved two match points before beating fellow Aussie Owen Davidson in the 1970 men's final. The Hoylake meeting was particularly strong on the women's side. Every winner between 1968 and the early 1970s was a sometime Wimbledon champion: Margaret Court, Virginia Wade, Evonne Goolagong (who won in 1970 and shared the title in 1972) and Billie Jean King.

In the evolving world of serious professionalism, however, the tournament was living on borrowed time; the old-fashioned spontaneity and fun that made Hoylake so appealing could not be maintained. Without fresh and adequate ongoing sponsorship, and with Britain's post-Wimbledon calendar being squeezed by rival meetings abroad, the North of England Championships were finally consigned to the record books after 1974.

* * *

History, it's often said, is written by the winners. With this in mind, it follows that frontline tournaments still flourishing and offering world-class tennis on home shores today, the likes of Queen's and Eastbourne, are warmly praised as 'winners', their famous pasts seen as an integral part of their contemporary appeal. By contrast, Scarborough is largely overlooked. It suffers not only because the leading stars of the day who played there have long since departed the scene, but also because the actual site where the action took place is no longer associated with top-level competition. The facilities of the post-1970s sports centre have been gradually relocated to other places in the town. The adapted pavilion at Filey Road, though Grade II listed, stands unused today, and most of what remains of the once lush and well-kept club grounds have been turned into car parking or are run down and awaiting redevelopment.[11]

And yet, as we have seen, Scarborough richly deserves to be remembered and celebrated for its tennis exploits. Its golden age lasted for almost half a century and featured many of the legends of the game – amateurs and professionals, men and women alike – all striving for success in front of crowded stands on what referee Fred Burrow described as 'two of the most perfect courts to be found anywhere'.[12]

RECORD BREAKERS

Most titles – Men: Ernest Browne (4), David Chaytor (4), Laurence Doherty (4), Ernest Black (3), Charles Kingsley (3), Bobby Wilson (3)

Most titles – Women: Lucy Kendal (7), Mary Heeley (5), Elizabeth Ryan (4), Margaret Bracewell (3), Beatrice Draffen (3 – once as Beatrice Wood), Alice Pickering (3), Gem Hoahing (3)

Number of North of England champions who also won Wimbledon singles

Men: 5; Women: 8; Total: 13

North of England Championships

Men's Singles

Year	Winner	Runner-up	Score
1884	Ernest Browne	Marmaduke Constable	6-1 retd
1885	Ernest Browne	E.W. Fletcher	6-0, 6-2, 6-4
1886	Ernest Browne	Harry Grove	6-3, 4-6, 6-3, 2-6, 6-2
1887	Ernest Browne	James Baldwin	7-5, 6-1, 6-3
1888	Harry Grove	Henry Nadin	6-1, 6-1, 6-1
1889	Percy Brown	Harry Grove	6-3, 6-1, 7-5
1890	James Baldwin	Percy Brown	8-10, 6-1, 6-1, 6-4
1891	Harry Barlow	James Baldwin	6-3, 6-2, 2-6, 7-5
1892	Harry Barlow	David Chaytor	5-7, 6-1, 6-2, 6-1
1893	William Renshaw	Harry Barlow	6-3, 7-5, 6-3

1894	Roy Allen	Charles Wade	6-0, 6-4
1895	David Chaytor	Harold Nisbet	7-9, 4-6, 6-4, 9-7, 6-1
1896	Harold Nisbet	Frank Riseley	3-6, 7-5, 6-4, 5-7, 6-2
1897	David Chaytor	A.H. Riseley	6-4, 6-3, 6-2
1898	David Chaytor	Ernest Black	6-2, 6-2, 4-6, 6-3
1899	Ernest Black	David Chaytor	8-6, 3-6, 6-4, 4-6, 6-4
1900	David Chaytor	Charles Wade	6-2, 6-2, 6-3
1901	Laurence Doherty	Ernest Black	6-2, 6-1, 6-1
1902	Ernest Black	E. Watson	7-5, 8-6
1903	Walter Crawley	R. Le Roy (USA)	6-3, 6-4, 6-2
1904	Ernest Black	E. Watson	7-5, 4-6, 6-3, 6-2
1905	Edward Allen	Charles Allen	walkover
1906	Arthur Lowe	S.E. Charlton	7-5, 6-4
1907	Walter Crawley	Arthur Lowe	6-1, 6-3
1908	Laurence Doherty	George Hillyard	6-1, 6-4, 6-2
1909	Laurence Doherty	Gordon Lowe	7-5, 6-1, 6-3
1910	Laurence Doherty	Gordon Lowe	6-3, 6-2, 6-2
1911	James Parke	Alfred Dunlop (Aus)	6-4, 10-8, 6-1
1912	Arthur Lowe	James Parke	6-4, 6-4
1913	James Parke	Arthur Lowe	6-4, 3-6, 7-5, 6-2
1914–18	No tournament held		
1919	Pat O'Hara Wood (Aus)	Brian Norton (SA)	4-6, 6-2, 6-1, 10-8
1920	Thomas Sherwell (Can)	Clive Branfoot	4-6, 6-4, 7-5
1921	Brian Norton (SA)	Edward McCrea	6-4, 6-3, 1-6, 2-6, 6-4
1922	Gordon Lowe	Randolph Lycett (Aus)	6-2, 5-7, 7-9, 6-1, 6-2
1923	Sydney Jacob	Edward McCrea (Ire)	6-3, 6-0, 6-2
1924	Louis Raymond (SA)	Mohammed Sleem (Ind)	6-2, 6-3, 6-3
1925	Charles Kingsley	Gordon Crole-Rees	6-4, 3-6, 6-4, 6-3
1926	Charles Kingsley	Keats Lester	10-8, 6-0, 1-6, 8-6
1927	Colin Gregory	Randolph Lycett (Aus)	6-8, 12-10, 9-7 retd
1928	Buster Andrews (NZ)	John Olliff	7-5, 6-4, 6-1
1929	Charles Kingsley	Keats Lester	7-9, 6-1, 6-1, 6-4
1930	Buster Andrews (NZ)	Colin Gregory	6-0, 9-7
1931	Vernon Kirby (SA)	Jack Chamberlain	6-3, 6-3
1932	George Lyttleton Rogers (Ire)	Madan Atri Mohan (Ind)	6-2, 3-6, 6-1
1933	Alan Stedman (NZ)	Lester Keats	6-2, 7-5, 3-6, 6-3
1934	Harry Hopman (Aus)	Alan Stedman (NZ)	6-4, 6-2, 6-4
1935	Alan Stedman (NZ)	George Lyttleton Rogers (Ire)	6-2, 6-3

1936	Adrian Quist (Aus)	Charles Hare	6-1, 6-4, 6-2
1937	George Lyttleton Rogers (Ire)	Pat Sherwood	8-6, 6-3
1938	Don Butler	C.M. (Jimmy) Jones	6-2, 6-4
1939	Murray Deloford	Dennis Coombe	6-2, 6-2
1940–45		No tournament held	
1946	Ignacy Tloczynski (Pol)	Don Butler	10-8, 6-2
1947	Ignacy Tloczynski (Pol)	Ghaus Mohammed Khan (Ind)	7-5, 6-4, 2-6, 6-3
1948	Franjo Kukuljevic (Yug)	Gerry Oakley	3-6, 6-1, 6-3, 6-4
1949	Jaroslav Drobny (Egy)	Tony Mottram	6-1, 6-1, 6-3
1950	Bill Sidwell (Aus)	Geoff Brown (Aus)	2-6, 6-4, 6-1, 6-2
1951	Nigel Cockburn (SA)	Czeslaw Spychala (Pol)	7-5, 2-6, 6-1, 3-6, 6-1
1952	Eric Sturgess (SA)	Budge Patty (USA)	6-3, 3-6, 4-6, 6-1, 6-3
1953	Bobby Wilson	Billy Knight	6-3, 7-5
1954	Bobby Wilson	John Barry (NZ)	6-4, 6-2
1955	Sven Davidson (Swe)	Billy Knight	4-6, 6-0, 8-6, 6-0
1956	Bobby Wilson	Tony Pickard	6-3, 6-3
1957	Alan Mills	Colin Hannam	7-5, 3-6, 6-3
1958	Ashley Cooper (Aus)	Mervyn Rose (Aus)	4-6, 7-5, 10-12, 6-1, 14-12
1959	not known		
1960	Mark Otway (NZ)	John McDonald (NZ)	6-3, 6-4
1961	Lawrence Strong	R.A. Storey	6-3, 7-5
1962	Michael Waters	R.A. Storey	6-4, 6-2
1963	Colin McHugo	Harry Sheridan	7-5, 6-2
1964	Keith Wooldridge	Clay Iles	9-7, 6-3, 6-3
1965	Graham Stilwell	Keith Wooldridge	6-3, 6-3
1966	Brian Fairlie (NZ)	Jasjit Singh (Ind)	7-5, 6-3
1967	Keith Wooldridge	Haroun Rahim (Pak)	3-6, 6-4, 6-4

Hoylake

1968	Mike Sangster	Herb Fitzgibbon (USA)	2-6, 6-4, 12-10
1969	Ray Ruffels (Aus)	Brian Fairlie (NZ)	6-3, 6-3
1970	John Newcombe (Aus)	Owen Davidson (Aus)	4-6, 9-7, 6-4
1971	Andrew Pattison (Zim)	Jaidip Mukerjea (Ind)	6-2, 5-7, 6-2
1972	Hank Irvine (Rho)	Ray Keldie (Aus)	title shared
1973	Bob Giltinan (Aus)	Owen Davidson (Aus)	1-6, 6-3, 6-2
1974	Bernie Mitton (SA)	John Yuill (SA)	6-4, 6-4

Women's Singles

Year	Winner	Runner-up	Score
1884	Constance Hodgson	Beatrice Wood	7-5, 6-3
1885	Mabel Boulton	Beatrice Wood	6-2, 6-2
1886	Margaret Bracewell	Mabel Boulton	6-4, 8-6
1887	Margaret Bracewell	Ann Dod	6-0, 6-1
1888	Margaret Bracewell	Bertha Steedman	1-6, 6-4, 9-7, 6-4
1889	Edith Gurney	Beatrice Wood	6-4, 8-6
1890	Beatrice Wood	Miss Crossley	6-4, 6-4
1891	Helen Jackson	Miss Pope	6-3, 6-1
1892	Beatrice Draffen	Kate Nunneley	6-4, 7-5
1893	Miss L.C. Clark	May Arbuthnot	6-4, 2-6, 6-2
1894	Beatrice Draffen	Katherine Grey	6-3, 6-1
1895	Lucy Kendal	Marion Morton	6-2, 6-1
1896	Lucy Kendal	Beatrice Draffen	6-0, 8-6
1897	Lucy Kendal	Muriel Robb	6-3, 6-0
1898	Katherine Grey	Alice Pickering	6-4, 6-4
1899	Alice Pickering	Marion Morton	6-1, 6-2
1900	Alice Pickering	Ethel Jessop	6-0, 6-2
1901	Dorothea Douglass	Alice Pickering	4-6, 10-8, 6-1
1902	Alice Pickering	Lucy Kendal	6-3, 6-4
1903	Lucy Kendal	Alice Pickering	3-6, 6-8, 7-5
1904	Lucy Kendal	Gladys Eastlake-Smith	6-0, 4-6, 6-4
1905	Lucy Kendal	E.M. Carter	6-2, 6-1
1906	Lucy Kendal	Gladys Eastlake-Smith	6-4, 6-1
1907	Gladys Eastlake-Smith	Bertha Holder	6-0, 6-2
1908	Edith Boucher	Gladys Lamplough	6-1, 6-1
1909	Gladys Lamplough	Helen Aitchison	6-4, 6-3
1910	Katherine Clegg	Rosamund Salisbury	3-6, 6-2, 7-5
1911	Ethel Larcombe	Edith Hannam	6-2, 6-1
1912	Ethel Larcombe	Violet Pinckney	6-2, 4-6, 6-3
1913	Elizabeth Ryan (USA)	Ethel Larcombe	6-3, 6-3
1914–18	No tournament held		
1919	Elizabeth Ryan (USA)	Lesley Cadle	6-2, 6-1
1920	Elizabeth Ryan (USA)	Eleanor Rose	6-1, 6-3
1921	Elizabeth Ryan (USA)	Winifred McNair	6-3, 8-6
1922	Kitty McKane	Elizabeth Ryan (USA)	6-2, 6-2
1923	Dorothy Barron	Phyllis Satterthwaite	walkover

1924	Kitty McKane	Dorothy Holman	6-2, 6-0
1925	Geraldine Beamish	Claire Beckingham	6-3, 6-2
1926	Ruth Watson	Joan Ridley	6-3, 6-1
1927	Joan Lycett	Claire Beckingham	6-4, 3-6, 6-2
1928	Dorothy Barron	Claire Beckingham	6-2, 6-3
1929	Joan Fry	Dorothy Anderson	6-3, 6-3
1930	Mary Heeley	Joan Fry	6-4, 6-3
1931	Mary Heeley	Freda James	2-6, 6-1, 6-2
1932	Sheila Hewitt	Freda James	6-3, 5-5 retd
1933	Kay Stammers	Susan Noel	10-8, 5-7, 6-0
1934	Joan Hartigan (Aus)	Susan Noel	2-6, 6-1, 10-8
1935	Mary Heeley	Anita Lizana (Chl)	6-3, 6-8, 6-4
1936	Mary Heeley	Florence Ford	5-7, 6-4, 6-2
1937	Mary Heeley	Denise Huntbach	6-1, 6-1
1938	Valerie Scott	Florence Ford	6-2, 3-6, 6-3
1939	Jean Nicoll	Zora Nechilova (Czh)	6-3, 6-2
1940–45	No tournament held		
1946	Jean Quertier	Betty Hilton	6-3, 6-1
1947	Gem Hoahing	Valerie Cooper	6-2, 6-0
1948	Gem Hoahing	Natalia Zinovieff	6-2, 7-5
1949	Gem Hoahing	Joyce Fitch (Aus)	6-3, 6-2
1950	Thelma Long (Aus)	Jean Quertier	6-4, 7-5
1951	Billie Woodgate	Barbara Knapp	4-6, 6-2, 6-1
1952	Jean Walker-Smith	Beryl Penrose (Aus)	7-5, 6-2
1953	Georgie Woodgate	Margaret Harrison	6-1, 2-6, 6-4
1954	Judy Burke (NZ)	Angela Buxton	4-6, 6-4, 6-4
1955	Mary Carter (Aus)	Beryl Penrose (Aus)	6-3, 4-6, 6-3
1956	Ann Haydon	Elaine Watson	6-2, 7-5
1957	Georgie Woodgate	Rosemary Deloford	6-3, 4-6, 6-4
1958	Heather Segal (SA)	Mary Hawton	6-1, 6-4
1959	Elaine Shenton	C. Clark	3-6, 6-2, 6-2
1960	Susan Waters	Jenny Young	5-7, 6-2, 6-3
1961	Ann McAlpine	Vivienne Cox	6-4, 7-5
1962	J. Mcintosh	E. Smith	6-3, 6-4
1963	E. Smith	Marilyn Greenwood	7-5, 6-4
1964	Robin Lloyd	Nell Truman	6-4, 1-6, 7-5
1965	Stephanie Percival	Sally Holdsworth	6-3, 6-2

| 1966 | Elizabeth Starkie | Robin Lloyd | 6-1, 6-3 |
| 1967 | Robin Lloyd | Sally Holdsworth | 6-2, 6-2 |

Hoylake

1968	Margaret Court (Aus)	Virginia Wade	6-2, 6-4
1969	Virginia Wade	Christine Janes	0-6, 6-4, 8-6
1970	Evonne Goolagong (Aus)	Kerry Melville (Aus)	2-6, 6-2, 6-1
1971	Billie Jean King (USA)	Rosie Casals (USA)	6-3, 6-3
1972	Evonne Goolagong (Aus)	Betty Stove (Ned)	title shared
1973	Patti Hogan (USA)	Sharon Walsh (USA)	11-9, 4-6, 6-4
1974	Jackie Fayter	Patti Hogan (USA)	6-0, 7-5

9

Midland Counties

IN THEIR fine illustrated study of the history and heritage of sport in England's 'second city', Birmingham, authors Steve Beauchampé and Simon Inglis note that if ever a designation of areas of 'special sporting interest' were to be created, then Edgbaston would be a prime candidate for nomination.[1] Much of the Edgbaston district, just a short distance to the south-west of Birmingham city centre, was owned by the Calthorpe Estate, and as leisure pursuits thrived in the late-Victorian period the estate encouraged the development of a haven for the wealthy classes looking to indulge their sporting interests. From the turn of the century the Edgbaston ground of Warwickshire County Cricket Club started to host international Test matches, and elsewhere on the estate a range of other pastimes flourished. These included bowls, cycling, athletics, football and – unsurprisingly, in view of the region's prominence in founding the sport – lawn tennis.

The Midlands (to which we next travel as we head back towards the starting point of our nationwide tour of prominent venues) is often referred to as the cradle of lawn tennis. Solicitor Harry Gem was known to have played pelota, an early version of the game, at his house in Edgbaston several years before Major Walter Clopton Wingfield patented Sphairistike, the decisive moment that opened the way for tennis to become a national and global sport.

Gem was also instrumental in establishing what's believed to be the first lawn tennis club, at Royal Leamington Spa, in the early 1870s. Within a couple of decades, it was said that no respectable residence in Edgbaston, an area with numerous detached villas set in spacious gardens, was without a grass court. The district was also an ideal breeding ground for several clubs, where keen players could gather together to socialise and play. Among the earliest to be founded was the Edgbaston Archery and Lawn Tennis Society in Westbourne Road, still in existence today adjacent to the handsome Botanical Gardens, and with strong claims to be the oldest surviving tennis club in the world still based on its original site.

The Midland Counties Championships

Three Edgbaston clubs in particular were, in the fullness of time, to be instrumental in bringing world-class tennis to Birmingham. The Tally Ho club started life in the adjacent suburb of Harborne, but moved close to the county cricket ground in 1907. Winners of the Tally Ho annual tournament include men's legends such as Fred Perry and Jaroslav Drobny and on the women's side homegrown Wimbledon champions Dorothy Round and Ann Jones. The Priory Lawn Tennis Club began in 1875 with two courts in Pershore Road before relocating a few years later to a permanent home between Priory Road and Sir Harrys Road, where over 20 courts were laid out. This gave the Priory Club a base that was easily accessible to the city centre, and it increasingly attracted younger elements of the middle classes who by the time of the First World War were being drawn to tennis in larger numbers than hitherto. The Priory's steady growth was such that from the mid-1920, it too hosted a popular annual meeting (discussed further below).

The third – and for many decades the leading club in the area in offering high-quality tournament play – was the Edgbaston Cricket and Lawn Tennis Club (ECLTC), formed in 1878. This was established to the west of the Priory, on the other side of the elegant

Edgbaston Park, and was set in the grounds of a large mansion owned by an engineering magnate. The ECLTC was, at the outset, highly traditionalist and socially exclusive. In the early years, play was prohibited on Sundays and lady members were not admitted to the pavilion tea room. Many of Birmingham's leading civic and commercial families valued belonging to a high-class, secluded establishment, tree-lined and with rustic charm despite being so close to the city centre. Lord Calthorpe acted as president and the club's membership included the likes of the Lowe brothers – both adept players, successful in national and international tournaments – sons of Sir Francis Lowe, the long-standing Member of Parliament for Edgbaston.[2]

Seeking to emulate other upmarket clubs elsewhere in the country, the ECLTC decided to host an open tournament in 1881. The first winner of the women's singles was to become one of the most celebrated figures in the early history of lawn tennis. Vicar's daughter Maud Watson, aged 16, born in London but residing during her childhood in and around Birmingham, came through a field of 11 entrants, defeating her sister Lilian in the final. *The Field*, although not recording the score, reported that the play of the Watson sisters was 'very good and at times brilliant'.[3] Three years later the sisters contested the inaugural women's final at Wimbledon, also won by Maud, whose calm temperament and ability to exploit her opponents' weaknesses ensured that for a few seasons she went unbeaten in singles on the fledging women's circuit.

The success of the 1881 gathering encouraged the authorities at Edgbaston Park Road to stage, from the following year onwards, a larger tournament, held post-Wimbledon every July. Like many others, the ECLTC meeting included a range of events, singles and doubles, level and handicap, open to all comers, with the exception of what became known as the Midland Counties Cup. This was restricted to entrants who lived within a 60-mile radius of Birmingham, as well as to winners of all-comers' prizes at the All

England Club. Unfortunately, rain caused significant delays in 1882, but when the finals were eventually completed George Brewerton became the first winner of the men's Midland Counties title, beating John Deykin in four sets.[4]

For several years the Edgbaston tournament, while seen as a cherished part of Birmingham's social calendar – a chance for the local great and good to congregate in agreeable surroundings – was not always a showcase for the strongest amateurs of the day. The residency restriction for the Midland Counties Cup meant that entries for the parallel men's open singles were often larger in number and of higher quality. In 1894, for example, the open event was claimed by Wilfred Baddeley, already a two-time Wimbledon champion, whereas the Midland Counties title went to George Hillyard, a talented competitor but one who never progressed beyond the last eight in SW19. The women's singles at Edgbaston, meanwhile, although it featured some excellent winners in the early years such as Margaret Bracewell and Blanche Bingley, was operated on a handicap basis only, which may have explained some unexpected outcomes, such as Blanche's defeat in the 1893 final. Maud Watson, in the last main competition of her career, returned to take the title for a second time in 1889 despite 'owing 30', giving her opponent in the final a two-point lead in every game.

A step change in the status of the Edgbaston meeting had to wait until 1899, when club officials decided to amend the rules relating to the main prizes. In commemoration of a well-known stalwart of Midlands tennis, the John Deykin Challenge Cup was introduced; this with a residential requirement that entrants live within 50 miles of Birmingham. The Midland Counties Championship, henceforth, was thrown open to all comers for the first time[5] (and the challenge round was to be dispensed with a couple of years later). By making these changes, the ECLTC ensured the Midland Counties Cup was seen as its blue riband event, one that drew more of the leading 'cracks' of the day to Birmingham every summer. Within short order, the women's singles title at Edgbaston was claimed by four different Wimbledon champions, while on the men's side, the nascent challenge from overseas competitors was only temporarily held at bay by the skill and tenacity of one of England's finest players around the turn of the century, Sydney Smith.

MEMORABLE MATCH/UNDERRATED CHAMPION

Gloucestershire's Sydney Smith beat several tricky opponents, including Wilberforce Eaves, Frank Riseley and Major Ritchie, in claiming the Midland Counties title five times in a row between 1900 and 1904. But his sternest test came against Australian newcomer Norman Brookes in 1905. Brookes, who reached the Wimbledon final that year, brought to the court a sharp tactical brain and a swerving left-handed serve that earned him the nickname 'Terror from the Antipodes'. The intensity of the struggle was such that the first set lasted for an hour and consisted of 28 games, Smith eventually shading it 15-13. In spite of intermittent rain showers, the battle continued without interruption. Although he dropped the third set, Smith would not be denied. His devastating forehand helped him to secure a sixth Edgbaston title in four sets. He was, as one local newspaper called him, a player of 'great repute',[6] although it was his misfortune that his peak years coincided with those of the Doherty brothers, who with one exception took the Wimbledon title every year between 1897 and 1906. This should not be allowed to detract, however, from Smith's hugely impressive record, not only at the Midland Counties but elsewhere. He was a multiple winner at Surbiton, the Northern and at Eastbourne, winning over 20 top titles in all. The great Laurence Doherty was sometimes heard telling friends that the one person he didn't want to meet in any tournament was S.H. Smith; there could be few higher accolades.

In the Edwardian period, Edgbaston's steady upward trajectory saw it consolidate its position as one of the most highly regarded meetings on the post-Wimbledon English circuit. *Lawn Tennis and Badminton* reported that facilities at the ECLTC were second to none, the grounds were always in beautiful condition – a green oasis close to the city centre – and competitors agreed they rarely played on finer courts. The great Norman Brookes may not have left carrying the Midlands Counties Cup, but his Aussie compatriot Stanley Doust became the first overseas winner of the men's singles when he beat James Parke in the 1909 final. The extent to which pre-1914 Edgbaston had become a venue sought out by stars from home and abroad alike was underlined when Doust – who later became tennis correspondent of the *Daily Mail* – went on to complete a hat-trick of victories in 1912 and 1913.

Some of the finest quality tennis ever to be seen at the Midland Counties came early in the inter-war era. Fresh from bursting on to the British scene with victory at Wimbledon, the supremely talented Bill Tilden pulled in the crowds at Edgbaston Park Road in 1920 as he progressed serenely to the final. There he faced South African Charles Winslow (beaten by Doust in the 1912 final), who surprised his celebrated opponent by using a short, angled dink shot that often dropped dead. Although the American took a tight first set 6-4, Tilden was sufficiently discomfited that at one point – the local newspaper noted – he 'paused to remove his famous blue bearskin, a thing he has not done in any previous match of the tournament'.[7] Winslow refused to buckle despite losing the second set, and excitement in the gallery seats grew when he claimed the third 6-3. The legendary American then recovered his poise to secure victory in the fourth, thereby becoming the first man to claim the Edgbaston title in the same year as triumphing in SW19; a feat not to be repeated until Jaroslav Drobny did so in 1954.

In the wake of Tilden's triumph, the ECLTC invested in a striking new centre court, capable of seating 3,000 spectators, and all the outlying courts were levelled off (in the early years a few of them, critics complained, were sloping). Overseas competitors increasingly made their mark. In searing heat, the star of the show in 1921 was South Africa's Brian Norton. Just a few weeks after coming close to beating Tilden in the Wimbledon final (famously being unable to convert two match points), Norton – after a see-saw 8-6 first set – comfortably eased past veteran Frank Riseley in the Edgbaston final. In 1924 the relentless Californian trophy-gatherer Elizabeth Ryan became the first woman from outside the UK to take the Midland Counties title. As she did on many occasions elsewhere, she secured a clean sweep by also winning the women's and the mixed doubles.

LIVE AND LEARN

Bristol's Frank Riseley was a three-time runner-up at Wimbledon before the First World War, each time coming up against Laurie Doherty in his pomp. Always a keen competitor, Riseley was in his mid-40s when he reached the Midland Counties final in 1921. Although unable to keep pace with Brian Norton that day, Riseley demonstrated he was still a wily opponent as he progressed towards the final. In the second round he was drawn against Axel Gravem, a talented young American. Having never seen Riseley in action, Gravem asked the referee what to expect. Wishing to remain diplomatic and impartial, the official replied that Riseley was a great player in the past but competed less these days, adding that the youngster should at least learn something from the encounter. After Riseley came out on top, the American – on his way back to the dressing room – gave the referee a rueful grin, commenting, 'Say, I sure did learn something!'[8] Gravem at least had the consolation of winning the men's doubles that year.

For the remainder of the inter-war years, the Midland Counties meeting benefited from a consistently large and strong entry: a good balance of home and overseas contenders, many of them fresh from competing in SW19. Winners of the singles titles during this period included talents from several different nations: in the case of the men, from Japan, Australia, New Zealand, China and Yugoslavia, and in the women's event from France, Germany, Hungary (in the shape of a Countess, Gabriela Szapary), Poland and France. Poland's Jadwiga Jedrzejowska scored a particularly creditable, hard-fought win over Anita Lizana in 1935 and successfully defended the title the following year.

In the 1930s, All England Club secretary Duncan Macaulay took over as referee at Edgbaston, and he later reflected that the meeting remained one of the most reputable outside of Wimbledon. While there was strength in depth and international flavour in the singles, Macaulay noted that the biggest draw for the crowds was watching the doubles play of the charismatic veteran French Musketeer Jean Borotra, who often arrived by private aeroplane after proceedings were already under way, agreeing to play several matches back-to-back if needed in order to catch up with the daily schedule. Along with compatriot Antoine Gentien, Borotra won the men's doubles four times between 1932 and 1938. The French pair also shared the title with Gottfried von Cramm and Don Butler in 1939 when heavy rain washed out finals, the first time all the main events at Edgbaston went unfinished.[9]

In a clear sign of Birmingham's settled prominence, other forms of international-level play were also hosted between the wars. The ECLTC staged two Davis Cup ties in the 1920s, victories over Spain (when the home team was captained by illustrious all-rounder Max Woosnam) and over Germany. Nearby, the Tally Ho club, which boasted excellent show courts, was chosen for a Davis Cup encounter against Sweden in 1927; this resulted in a 4-1 success for Britain. Many overseas hopefuls entered the annual Tally Ho tournament, as they did the popular Whitsun meeting at the Priory Club, whose facilities were improving steadily to match those of its neighbours. The standard of competition at the Priory tournament was such that distinguished winners in the late 1930s included Dorothy Round (raised not far away in Dudley), who beat Chile's Lizana in the 1937 final; Kho Sin-Kie of China, men's champion in 1937 and 1939; and multiple grand slam winner Helen Jacobs of the USA.

For a decade after the Second World War, the tennis fortunes of England's second city continued to look secure. As was the case in the 1930s, some of the world's elite remained in the country each year after Wimbledon, playing a range of late-summer tournaments including the Midlands Counties. The roll of honour at the ECLTC included women as well as men who triumphed in SW19: American Doris Hart was a two-time winner at Edgbaston and Jaroslav Drobny lifted the trophy three times between 1950 and 1955. Tony Mottram, a long-standing member of the Priory Club, was the only British man to win the Midlands Counties Cup during these years (and also featured prominently in a Davis Cup tie against the Netherlands, held in Birmingham in 1948). Victory in the men's singles at Edgbaston Park Road in 1957 for another former Wimbledon champion, America's Budge Patty, suggested that the future for the tournament was bright.

But early in 1958 the ECLTC was confronted by a sudden crisis, one which jeopardised and undermined its showpiece meeting. Lance Tingay of the *Daily Telegraph* reported in February that the LTA was withholding its backing for the Midland Counties later that summer. The governing body claimed to have discovered 'serious irregularities' in the tournament committee's finances for the previous year. It had long been an open secret that top stars were often given, as an inducement to appear at certain events, far more than the standard-level expenses permitted in the amateur rulebook. The LTA, angered that an Australian international went public with claims about the generosity of his treatment by Edgbaston organisers, decided it was time to take a stand against breaches of the regulations. Defenders of the Midlands Counties responded that the meeting was being made a scapegoat. So-called 'shamateurism' was known to be rife, tennis writer Jimmy Jones argued, and club officials were simply trying to avoid charges of hypocrisy by presenting their accounts in the form they did.[10]

The Edgbaston club in consequence had little choice but to put on a greatly scaled-back tournament in 1958, a shadow of its former self and restricted to county-standard players. This came at a time when – in a further blow to Birmingham tennis – the Priory's Whitsun gathering had also been discontinued, suffering latterly because of a scheduling clash with the French Championships in Paris. In 1959 the Midlands Counties was again opened up to all-comers from home and abroad, but the organisers did not go out of their way to encourage overseas competitors and Warwickshire county players were again to the fore. The following year, the tournament committee went a step further by sanctioning the re-introduction of modest expenses, with the result that small numbers of entrants from South America and Australia returned to the fray, in addition to some top British stars. As luck would have it, however, the main finals were over so quickly that little was achieved in terms of restoring Edgbaston to its former status.

IN A HURRY

One-sided tournament finals have occurred throughout lawn tennis history. But it was unusual for a top-level event to feature overwhelmingly lopsided finals for both women and men on the same afternoon. This was the case at the Midland Counties in 1960. Australian Margaret Hellyer, best known as a doubles specialist, had no answer to the relentlessly accurate ground strokes of Angela Mortimer in the women's final. The British woman conceded only one game to her opponent; the whole match was timed at 23 minutes. Another home nation victory followed when in the men's final Bobby Wilson despatched Brazilian number three Ivo Ribiero for the loss of two games in just under half an hour. Wilson was at his fluent best and he made only one unforced error in the first set. All told, the paying customers witnessed less than an hour of singles play. They still had doubles to enjoy, though even here there were unfortunate consequences to the early completion of the singles finals, at least for one pairing. Warwickshire's K.F. Buswell, scheduled to play with partner R.W. Dixon in a men's doubles semi-final, was given permission to arrive late as he was helping out at a friend's wedding. But the tournament referee, finding himself without a game to put on Edgbaston's centre court, reluctantly decided that the absent Buswell and his partner would have to scratch. The players, it seems, were not the only ones in a hurry that day.

The Midland Counties did manage to enjoy one last hurrah when local newspapers, led by the *Birmingham Post*, provided a three-year financial package aimed at returning at least a semblance of the tournament's former glory. The push for revitalisation produced immediate dividends in the form of a fluctuating, richly entertaining men's final in 1963. Australian Wimbledon champion Roy Emerson was a strong favourite, but trailed 4-1 in the deciding set against Mexican Rafael Osuna (who shortly afterwards would win the US Championships and become world number one). Following a rain break, both men sportingly agreed to resume the contest, even though the court was damp and slippery. The Mexican must have rued the interruption as he won only one more game; Emerson stormed back to take the final set and the title 7-5.

In 1965, spectators were treated to similar high drama in the women's final when Virginia Wade, aged 20 and ranked British number five at the time, went close to defeating reigning SW19 champion Margaret Smith. Miss Wade led 4-2 in the third set, with chances to break for a 5-2 lead, before the experienced Aussie turned things round to claim victory.

The ending of the three-year support scheme, however, sounded the death knell for the tournament in the form in which it had existed – aside from the 1958 hiatus – since the start of the 20th century. Against the backdrop of major club reorganisation in Birmingham (described below), and in the absence of fresh outside assistance, the meeting struggled on intermittently for a while, its entry confined on the whole to aspiring Warwickshire-based players. Concerted efforts in 1970 to find sponsorship that would enable another full-scale revival to take place came to nothing; the Midland Counties Championship as of old was no more.

Midland Counties Championships

Men's Singles

Year	Winner	Runner-up	Score
1881	Walter Chamberlain	F.S. Goodwin	6-3, 6-1, 6-4
1882	George Brewerton	John Deykin	6-8, 6-4, 6-0, 6-2
1883	Charles Grinstead	Teddy Williams	6-3, 6-3
1884	Walter Chamberlain	John Deykin	6-3, 2-6, 10-8, 6-1
1885	Conway Morgan	Walter Chamberlain	6-4, 2-6, 2-6, 6-2, 9-7
1886	Frank Noon	Conway Morgan	6-4, 6-2, 6-4
1887	John Deykin	Frank Noon	6-4, 6-4, 6-2
1888	Harry Scrivener	John Deykin	6-2, 6-0, 9-7
1889	John Deykin	Harold Carlton	2-6, 6-1, 3-6, 6-3, 6-4
1890	John Deykin	Henry Nadin	6-3, 6-3, 4-6, 9-7
1891	James Baldwin	Harry Barlow	6-3, 7-9, 3-6, 6-2, 6-1
1892	Harry Barlow	Tom Chaytor	6-4, 6-1
1893	George Hillyard	Henry Nadin	6-3, 6-1, 6-3
1894	George Hillyard	R.A. Bennett	6-4, 6-2, 6-1
1895	George Hillyard	Sydney Smith	6-4, 8-6, 4-6, 6-1
1896	Wilberforce Eaves	Sydney Smith	4-6, 6-3, 9-7, 7-9, 6-4
1897	Sydney Smith	George Hillyard	6-2, 6-3, 8-6
1898	Sydney Smith	George Hillyard	4-6, 9-7, 6-4, 1-6, 6-2
1899	Wilberforce Eaves	Ernest Black	8-6, 6-2
1900	Sydney Smith	George Hillyard	6-2, 6-3, 7-5
1901	Sydney Smith	Wilberforce Eaves	6-3, 6-1
1902	Sydney Smith	Frank Riseley	6-4, 6-3, 6-4
1903	Sydney Smith	Major Ritchie	5-7, 7-5, 6-4, 6-2
1904	Sydney Smith	Wilberforce Eaves	6-4, 3-6, 6-2

1905	Sydney Smith	Norman Brookes (Aus)	15-13, 6-4, 4-6, 6-4
1906	John Boucher	Wilberforce Eaves	6-4, 3-6, 6-4, 6-3
1907	John Boucher	James Parke	6-2, 8-10, 6-3, 9-7
1908	John Boucher	James Parke	6-2, 6-3, 6-2
1909	Stanley Doust (Aus)	James Parke	6-2, 6-0
1910	James Parke	Stanley Doust (Aus)	9-7, 6-3, 6-2
1911	Arthur Lowe	James Parke	2-6, 6-3, 6-2
1912	Stanley Doust (Aus)	Charles Winslow (SA)	6-4, 6-0, 6-1
1913	Stanley Doust (Aus)	Erik Larsen (Den)	6-1, 6-3
1914	Alfred Beamish	William Clements	6-1, 9-7, 2-6, 6-0
1915–18	No tournament held		
1919	Stanley Doust (Aus)	Pat O'Hara Wood (Aus)	6-4, 6-4
1920	Bill Tilden (USA)	Charles Winslow (SA)	6-4, 6-2, 3-6, 6-4
1921	Brian Norton (SA)	Frank Riseley	8-6, 6-0, 6-0
1922	Gordon Lowe	Norman Gregg (Aus)	6-2, 6-2, 6-2
1923	Athar Ali Fyzee (Ind)	Donald Greig	6-2, 6-4
1924	Jack Hillyard	Gordon Crole-Rees	6-4, 7-5, 6-4
1925	Brian Gilbert	Hector Fisher (Sui)	4-6, 7-5, 6-3, 5-7, 6-3
1926	Hector Fisher (Sui)	Jack Hillyard	6-1, 9-7, 5-7, 6-1
1927	Bunny Austin	Keats Lester	6-1, 6-3
1928	Mohammed Sleem (Ind)	Keats Lester	4-6, 6-1, 6-0, 6-0
1929	William Powell	Jack Lysaght	6-1, 6-2
1930	Keats Lester	Ryuki Miki (Jpn)	6-3, 6-3
1931	Jiro Satoh (Jpn)	Herman David	7-5, 6-4
1932	John Olliff	Antoine Gentien (Fra)	1-6, 6-4, 2-0 retd
1933	Ryuki Miki (Jpn)	Keats Lester	6-4, 6-2
1934	Keats Lester	Antoine Gentien (Fra)	4-6, 6-3, 6-3
1935	Viv McGrath (Aus)	Walter Musgrove (SA)	8-6, 6-2
1936	Cam Malfroy (NZ)	Alan Stedman (NZ)	title shared
1937	Kho Sin-Kie (Chn)	Herman David	6-4, 6-3
1938	Franjo Puncec (Yug)	Kho Sin-Kie (Chn)	6-3, 2-6, 7-5
1939	Don Butler	Herman David	title shared
1940–45	No tournament held		
1946	Kho Sin-Kie (Chn)	Enrique Morea (Arg)	6-2, 1-6, 6-3
1947	Constantin Tanacescu (Rom)	Jack Crawford (Aus)	6-1, 8-6, 3-6, 1-6, 6-3
1948	Felicisimo Ampon (Phi)	Reymundo Deyro (Phi)	6-2, 6-3
1949	Tony Mottram	Ricardo Balbiers (Chl)	6-3, 9-7
1950	Jaroslav Drobny (Egy)	Koon-Hong Ip (HK)	6-2, 6-2

1951	Don Candy (Aus)	Naresh Kumar (Ind)	6-4, 6-2
1952	Owen Williams (SA)	Trevor Fancutt (SA)	6-4, 6-2
1953	Russell Seymour (SA)	Tony Mottram	8-6, 7-5
1954	Jaroslav Drobny (Egy)	Roger Becker	6-0, 6-3
1955	Jaroslav Drobny (Egy)	Arthur Larsen (USA)	7-5, 4-6, 6-4
1956	Trevor Fancutt (SA)	Mike Davies	7-5, 6-3, 6-4
1957	Budge Patty (USA)	Luis Ayala (Chl)	7-5, 3-6, 6-1
1958	No tournament held		
1959	K.F. Buswell	Bob Powell	7-5, 8-6
1960	Bobby Wilson	Ivo Ribiero (Bra)	6-0, 6-2
1961	F. Mohtadi	R.M. Harvey	6-4, 6-3
1962	Roger Becker	Ian Crookenden (NZ)	6-3, 3-6, 6-3
1963	Roy Emerson (Aus)	Rafael Osuna (Mex)	4-6, 6-3, 7-5
1964	Fred Stolle (Aus)	Billy Knight	3-6, 6-3, 6-2
1965	Billy Knight	Bobby Wilson	7-5, 6-3

Women's Singles

Year	Winner	Runner-up	Score
1881	Maud Watson	Lilian Watson	not known
1882	Constance Smith	Miss Heaton	6-2, 6-1
1883	Miss Hutton	Miss L. Sanders	6-5, 8-6
1884	Miss Noon	Miss E. Richardson	3-6, 8-6, 6-3
1885	Margaret Bracewell	Mary Steedman	6-3, 6-2
1886	Blanche Bingley	Lilian Watson	6-0, 6-2
1887	Margaret Bracewell	Florence Mardell	6-0, 4-6, 7-5
1888	Margaret Bracewell	Florence Mardell	7-5, 6-2
1889	Maud Watson	Mrs G.M. Elkington	6-1, 9-7
1890	Miss L. Johnstone	Ethel Valentin	6-2, 5-6, 6-4
1891	Alice Pickering	Mrs Wills	6-1, 6-3
1892	Winifred Longhurst	Edith Longhurst	title shared
1893	Miss D. Morgan	Blanche Hillyard	12-10 retd
1894	Miss Sweet Escott	Miss Vaudrey	title shared
1895	Winifred Longhurst	Miss C.M. Jones	4-6, 6-4, 7-5
1896	Bertha Steedman	Katherine Grey	6-4, 6-2
1897	Ruth Dyas	Alice Pickering	8-6, 3-6, 6-3
1898	Blanche Hillyard	Maud Garfit	6-3, 6-1
1899	Charlotte Cooper	Ruth Durlacher	3-6, 6-4, 8-6
1900	Muriel Robb	Constance Hill	6-3, 2-6, 6-3

1901	Ruth Durlacher	Maud Garfit	6-4, 6-4
1902	Winifred Longhurst	Muriel Robb	7-5, 7-5
1903	Ethel Thomson	Gertrude Houselander	6-4, 6-2
1904	Connie Wilson	Blanche Hillyard	6-3, 6-3
1905	Connie Wilson	Dorothea Douglass	7-5, 6-4
1906	Connie Wilson	Alice Greene	6-1, 3-6, 6-4
1907	Charlotte Sterry	Alice Greene	6-3, 9-7
1908	Charlotte Sterry	Edith Boucher	6-1, 6-0
1909	Helen Aitchison	Agnes Tuckey	6-2, 4-6, 6-3
1910	Dora Boothby	Helen Aitchison	7-5, 7-5
1911	Edith Hannam	Dora Boothby	6-4, 2-6, 7-5
1912	Edith Hannam	Ethel Larcombe	4-6, 6-2, 7-5
1913	Edith Hannam	Elizabeth Ryan (USA)	6-4, 6-0
1914	Winifred McNair	Helen Aitchison	4-6, 6-3, 9-7
1915–18	No tournament held		
1919	Ethel Larcombe	Winifred McNair	4-6, 6-2, 7-5
1920	Dorothy Shepherd	Lesley Cadle	8-6, 7-5
1921	Geraldine Beamish	Dorothy Shepherd	8-6, 6-2
1922	Geraldine Beamish	M. Fergus	6-1, 6-1
1923	Jessie Colegate	Dorothy Barron	10-8, 2-6, 6-4
1924	Elizabeth Ryan (USA)	Phyllis Satterthwaite	6-2, 6-4
1925	Phyllis Satterthwaite	Gwyneth Sterry	6-1, 6-0
1926	Ermyntrude Harvey	Joan Fry	2-6, 6-4, 6-3
1927	Jessie Colegate	Mary McIlquham	6-2, 6-1
1928	Naomi Trentham	Gwyneth Sterry	3-6, 9-7, 9-7
1929	Dorothy Round	Joan Fry	6-1, 6-4
1930	Naomi Trentham	Mary McIlquham	6-1, 1-6, 7-5
1931	Lolette Payot (Sui-Fra)	Mary Heeley	6-4, 4-6, 6-4
1932	Marie-Luise Horn (Ger)	Freda James	6-2, 6-3
1933	Olga Webb	Marie-Luise Horn (Ger)	6-4, 6-4
1934	Countess Gabriela Szapary (Hun)	E. Woodhall	6-3, 4-6, 6-1
1935	Jadwiga Jedrzejowska (Pol)	Anita Lizana (Chl)	3-6, 6-3, 6-2
1936	Jadwiga Jedrzejowska (Pol)	Irmgard Rost (Ger)	6-3, 6-3
1937	Mary Heeley	Anita Lizana (Chl)	0-6, 6-4, 6-3
1938	Mary Hardwick	Simonne Mathieu (Fra)	7-5, 6-1
1939	Simonne Mathieu (Fra)	Freda Hammersley	title shared
1940–45	No tournament held		
1946	Joan Curry	Jadwiga Jedrzejowska	7-5, 6-3

1947	Joan Curry	Elsie Phillips	6-3, 6-0
1948	Barbara Knapp	Dorothy Little	7-5, 6-0
1949	Maria Teran de Weiss (Arg)	Joy Gannon	9-7, 6-3
1950	Nancy Chaffee (USA)	Rita Anderson	6-0, 6-2
1951	Doris Hart (USA)	Shirley Fry (USA)	4-6, 6-2, 7-5
1952	Doris Hart (USA)	Shirley Fry (USA)	7-5, 3-6, 9-7
1953	Heather Brewer (Ber)	Billie Woodgate	6-4, 6-1
1954	Heather Brewer (Ber)	Joan Curry	6-3, 3-6, 6-4
1955	Hazel Redick-Smith (SA)	Beryl Penrose (Aus)	11-9, 2-6, 11-9
1956	Angela Mortimer	Jenny Hoad (Aus)	6-2, 4-6, 6-0
1957	Angela Mortimer	Maria Amorim (Bra)	6-1, 6-1
1958	No tournament held		
1959	Hazel Cheadle	Miss Bishop	6-4, 8-6
1960	Angela Mortimer	Margaret Hellyer (Aus)	6-0, 6-1
1961	Barbara Knapp	S.F. Morris	6-3, 6-1
1962	Ann Haydon	Rita Bentley	title shared
1963	Renee Schuurman (SA)	Ann Jones	8-6, 6-4
1964	Jan Lehane (Aus)	Ann Jones	7-5, 6-1
1965	Margaret Smith (Aus)	Virginia Wade	6-3, 4-6, 7-5

Edgbaston Priory and the Birmingham Classic

In spite of the demise of the Midlands Counties as a top-tier tournament, 1965 marked a new beginning as much as an end point for Edgbaston tennis. As landlord, the Calthorpe Estate became increasingly receptive to the idea of selling off the Edgbaston club site to facilitate the expansion of Birmingham University (it was eventually used for student accommodation, which was given the name 'Tennis Court Halls'). Talk of a possible merger with the Priory Club intensified after a fire destroyed the pavilion in Priory Road in 1963. The ECLTC offered the use of its facilities to Priory members while renovation work was undertaken. This gesture strengthened bonds between the two clubs, which despite being rivals for local bragging rights – and notwithstanding some powerful dissenting voices – formally agreed on 1 January 1965 to join forces. The upshot was the opening, when rebuilding was completed, of the reconstituted Edgbaston Priory Club in the expansive, tree-lined setting between Priory Road and Sir Harrys Road. Later still, in 1990, the Tally Ho club disappeared when its lease expired, after which its members also joined Edgbaston Priory, meaning that the three separate entities founded in the Victorian period had all become one.[11]

Although it came too late to save the Midland Counties meeting in its traditional form, the creation of Edgbaston Priory – which chose as its symbol a phoenix rising from the ashes – paved the way for the re-emergence of Birmingham as a hub for high-grade tennis. As the era of Open tennis unfolded, the newly-merged club was able to offer excellent facilities such as its attractively rebuilt clubhouse and multi-sport opportunities including swimming, squash and a gym. With assistance from the LTA, the number of courts, on a mix of surfaces, rose to almost 30 (including ten grass), and membership soared, making it the largest private sports club in the region. In recognition of how far the new Priory had come in a short space of time, in 1969 it hosted an important Davis Cup tie which saw a British team spearheaded by Mark Cox (who had played at the old Priory as a junior in the 1950s) achieve a stirring victory over West Germany.

LONG DRAWN-OUT

The British team laid the groundwork for a 3-2 Davis Cup victory over West Germany in the European Zone A semi-final with two singles victories on the opening day. Mark Cox beat German number two Christian Kuhnke and, more surprisingly, Graham Stilwell despatched former Wimbledon finalist William Bungert in straight sets. The most memorable, in fact record-breaking, rubber came in the doubles on the second day of the tie. Kunkhe and Bungert combined to keep German hopes alive by defeating Mark Cox and Peter Curtis 10-8, 17-19, 13-11, 3-6, 6-2. Although this fluctuating contest lasted for nearly four hours, it was not the length of the match that stood out. It was rather the number of games played, totalling 95. This beat the previous record for a Davis Cup doubles rubber by a single game. That total, in a tie between Australia and Mexico, dated from 1964, and in a curious coincidence one of those involved in that encounter, Aussie Fred Stolle, was courtside at Edgbaston acting as a coach to the West German team. With the tie on a knife-edge going into the final day, Stilwell lost to Kunkhe, but – possibly taking advantage of a five-year age gap after the exhausting exertions of the previous day – Cox beat 30-year-old Bunghert in five sets to ensure Britain went forward to the zone final.

Much later, after 1999, the National Indoor Arena on the outskirts of the city was chosen as the site for numerous Davis Cup ties, burnishing Birmingham's tennis credentials (sufficient to rank the city behind only Eastbourne and Wimbledon in terms of the total number of home cup ties hosted). As for Edgbaston Priory, it continued to enhance its reputation in the 1970s by staging some notable one-off events, including an International Lawn Tennis Club of Great Britain golden jubilee meeting in 1974. Despite chilly temperatures, the Priory also successfully ran a John Player-sponsored tournament in 1978 that saw fleets of cars whisk several of the best-known names in the men's game into the ground. Jimmy Connors came through to win in a field that included Stan Smith, Ilie Nastase, Arthur Ashe, Brian Gottfried and Roscoe Tanner.[12]

It was in the arena of women's international tennis, however, that Edgbaston Priory blossomed most fully in the Open era. Britain's 1969 Wimbledon champion, Ann Jones, born in the adjacent Kings Heath area of the city, had a long attachment to Birmingham tennis; she turned out for Warwickshire in the annual Inter-County Cup over 20 times between the 1950s and the 1980s. With assistance from the LTA (and from another famous player-organiser, Billie Jean King), Mrs Jones took the lead in bringing a new star-studded tournament to the Priory. This began life in 1982 as the Edgbaston Cup and under various names associated with its chief sponsors – Dow, DFS, Aegon, Nature Valley (and often called, for shorthand, the Birmingham Classic) – it has survived through to the present day, securing a valuable place in Britain's annual pre-Wimbledon grass-court schedule.[13]

As well as building a reputation for an informal, friendly atmosphere, the Birmingham Classic has regularly attracted many of the top 50 women in the world rankings. Billie Jean King herself claimed the singles title in 1982 and 1983, and she was followed by a string of further top-notch American champions. By the end of the century the winners list contained the likes of Pam Shriver (a record-setting four-time victor), Martina Navratilova, Zina Garrison, Lori McNeil and Lisa Raymond.

In more recent times, the roll of honour has featured many European stars, including grand slam champions such as Maria Sharapova, Anna Ivanovic, Angelique Kerber and Petra Kvitova – all proud winners of the trophy named after Maud Watson, who brought the first Wimbledon silverware for women back to her Midlands home in 1884.

Under LTA plans to shake up the pre-SW19 roster, Edgbaston had to contend with rumours and threats around 2008 and '09 that the Classic might be relocated to a more profitable site in London. But Priory officials responded by working closely with local interest groups to outline fresh redevelopment plans, agreed in 2010 and leading three years later to the unveiling of the biggest upgrades since the club mergers of the 1960s. In addition to a new indoor tennis centre and a modernised centre court, capable of seating 4,000 spectators, the Priory now boasted a refurbished clubhouse containing swish dining and conference facilities. The Birmingham Classic was, as a result, able to survive and thrive, continuing to stage one of the most esteemed grass tournaments on the women's international circuit. Fittingly, in view of her contributions both on and off court, the refashioned centre court opened in 2013 was named after the second city's most renowned player of modern times, Ann Jones.[14]

RECORD BREAKERS MIDLAND COUNTIES/BIRMINGHAM CLASSIC

Most titles – Men: Sydney Smith (8), Stanley Doust (4), John Deykin (3), George Hillyard (3), John Boucher (3), Jaroslav Drobny (3)

Most titles – Women: Pam Shriver (4), Margaret Bracewell (3), Winifred Longhurst (3 including one shared title), Connie Wilson (3), Charlotte Sterry (3 – once as Charlotte Cooper), Edith Hannam (3), Angela Mortimer (3)

Number of Midland Counties/Edgbaston champions who also won Wimbledon singles

Men: 4; Women: 11 (1881–1965), 5 (1982–2020); Total: 20

Birmingham Classic

Women's Singles

Year	Winner	Runner-up	Score
1982	Billie Jean King (USA)	Rosalyn Fairbank (SA)	6-2, 6-1
1983	Billie Jean King (USA)	Alycia Moulton (USA)	6-0, 7-5
1984	Pam Shriver (USA)	Anne White (USA)	7-6, 6-3
1985	Pam Shriver (USA)	Betsy Nagelsen (USA)	6-1, 6-0
1986	Pam Shriver (USA)	Manuela Maleeva (Bul)	6-2, 7-6
1987	Pam Shriver (USA)	Larisa Savchenko (USSR)	4-6, 6-2, 6-2
1988	Claudia Kohde-Kilsch (WG)	Pam Shriver (USA)	6-2, 6-1
1989	Martina Navratilova (USA)	Zina Garrison (USA)	7-6, 6-3
1990	Zina Garrison (USA)	Helena Sukova (Czh)	6-4, 6-1
1991	Martina Navratilova (USA)	Natasha Zvereva (USSR)	6-4, 7-6
1992	Brenda Schultz (Ned)	Jenny Bryne (Aus)	6-2, 6-2
1993	Lori McNeil (USA)	Zina Garrison (USA)	6-4, 2-6, 6-3
1994	Lori McNeil (USA)	Zina Garrison (USA)	6-2, 6-2

1995	Zina Garrison (USA)	Lori McNeil (USA)	6-3, 6-3
1996	Meredith McGrath (USA)	Nathalie Tauziat (Fra)	2-6, 6-4, 6-4
1997	Nathalie Tauziat (Fra)	Yayuk Basuki (Ins)	2-6, 6-2, 6-2
1998	Tournament abandoned due to rain		
1999	Julie Halard-Decugis (Fra)	Nathalie Tauziat (Fra)	6-2, 3-6, 6-4
2000	Lisa Raymond (USA)	Tamarine Tanasugarn (Tha)	6-2, 6-7, 6-4
2001	Nathalie Tauziat (Fra)	Miriam Oremans (Bel)	6-3, 7-5
2002	Jelena Dokic (Yug)	Anastasia Myskina (Rus)	6-2, 6-3
2003	Magdalena Maleeva (Bul)	Shinobu Asagoe (Jpn)	6-1, 6-4
2004	Maria Sharapova (Rus)	Tatiana Golovin (Fra)	4-6, 6-2, 6-1
2005	Maria Sharapova (Rus)	Jelena Jankovic (Srb)	6-2, 4-6, 6-1
2006	Vera Zvonereva (Rus)	Jamea Jackson (USA)	7-6, 7-6
2007	Jelena Jankovic (Srb)	Maria Sharapova (Rus)	4-6, 6-3, 7-5
2008	Kateryna Bondarenko (Ukr)	Yanina Wickmayer (Bel)	7-6, 3-6, 7-6
2009	Magdalena Rybarikova (Slo)	Li Na (Chn)	6-0, 7-6
2010	Li Na (Chn)	Maria Sharapova (Rus)	7-5, 6-1
2011	Sabine Lisicki (Ger)	Daniela Hantuchova (Slo)	6-3, 6-2
2012	Melanie Oudin (USA)	Jelena Jankovic (Srb)	6-4, 6-2
2013	Daniela Hantuchova (Slo)	Donna Vekic (Cro)	7-6, 6-4
2014	Anna Ivanovic (Srb)	Barbora Strycova (CR)	6-3, 6-2
2015	Angelique Kerber (Ger)	Karolina Pliskova (CR)	6-7, 6-3, 7-6
2016	Madison Keys (USA)	Barbora Strycova (CR)	6-3, 6-4
2017	Petra Kvitova (CR)	Ashleigh Barty (Aus)	4-6, 6-3, 6-2
2018	Petra Kvitova (CR)	Magdalena Rybarikova (Slo)	4-6, 6-1, 6-2
2019	Ashleigh Barty (Aus)	Julia Gorges (Ger)	6-3, 7-5
2020	No tournament held		

Nottingham

Elsewhere in the Midlands, Leamington and Leicester – starting in the early 1880s – operated well-regarded tournaments for many years, as did Malvern, where the Worcestershire Championships took place against the picturesque backcloth of the Malvern Hills. But aside from Birmingham, the regional location that most often staged world-class tennis was Nottingham, which first ran an open meeting over two days at the Trent Bridge cricket ground in the city in 1887.[15]

For lengthy periods that followed, especially ahead of the Great War, Nottingham matched Edgbaston in terms of quality and depth of entry. The 1911 meeting, for example, had as much international flavour as any other English tournament that summer, and the packed stands enjoyed two entertaining finals: Australia's Rodney Heath took the men's title (becoming the first non-UK winner) and the great Dorothea Lambert Chambers came back from a set and 6-5 down to beat Edith Hannam in the women's singles. For a while Nottingham also incorporated the official All England Married Couples Championships. George and Blanche Hillyard – owners of a large house in a nearby Leicestershire village – won the cup outright in 1912, the year of their silver wedding anniversary, and were presented with a gift by the committee as a thank you for being so influential 'in getting the best players to come to the tournament'.[16]

At other points in time, including much of the inter-war period, the entry in Nottingham (by this stage taking place at the Park Tennis Club close to the city centre) mainly consisted of home-based county or nationally ranked players. A renewed run of overseas winners after 1945 – including the likes of New Zealanders Lew Gerrard and Brian Fairlie – meant the tournament was well placed to raise its profile following the introduction of Open tennis. John Player, the tobacco company, decided to invest heavily in tennis sponsorship and prioritised the city where its headquarters were based. This meant the so-called Nottingham Open became for a while part of the men's Grand Prix circuit. American Wimbledon champion Stan Smith was a two-time winner in the 1970s and took away some of the most generous prize money available on the men's tour during that period. Billie Jean King beat Virginia Wade in a competitive 1973 final before the women's circuit was reorganised, leaving Nottingham as the preserve of the men only for the time being.

As other tournaments found, sponsorship deals came and went, leaving organisers scrabbling to cover costs, let alone continue offering the big prize money expected by the modern professional. Additionally, Nottingham could do little about the heavy rain that washed out the finals two years in succession, in 1976 and 1977; Jimmy Connors and Ilie Nastase were stranded at a set each in 1976 when the weather intervened. After that, the meeting went into abeyance for several years, returning in 1995 and subsequently featuring world-ranked winners such as Greg Rusedski, Jonas Bjorkman and Richard Gasquet.

Local officials were bitterly disappointed when the LTA, in a shake-up of the pre-Wimbledon calendar, removed the Open from the ATP Tour in 2009, especially as its base – now the Nottingham Tennis Centre, adjacent to the University of Nottingham – was undergoing extensive refurbishment. Since then, the men's event has veered between different grades of the circuit, although the city has recently succeeded in once more bringing back high-quality women's tennis. Winners since 2015 of the Nottingham WTA International, currently known as the Nature Valley Open, have included two stars who at different times ranked at world number one, Karolina Pliskova and Ashleigh Barty, the latter of whom beat Britain's Johanna Konta in a close three-set final in 2018.

Nottingham Open

Men's Singles

Year	Winner	Runner-up	Score
1970	Stan Smith (USA)	Chauncey Steele (USA)	6-3, 6-1
1971	Jaime Fillol (Chl)	Greg Perkins (USA)	6-2, 6-3
1972	Geoff Masters (Aus)	Premjit Lall (Ind)	abandoned due to rain
1973	Eric van Dillen (USA)	Frew McMillan (SA)	3-6, 6-1, 6-1
1974	Stan Smith (USA)	Alex Metreveli (USSR)	6-3, 1-6, 6-3
1975	Tom Okker (Ned)	Tony Roche (Aus)	6-1, 3-6, 6-3
1976	Jimmy Connors (USA)	Ilie Nastase (Rom)	abandoned due to rain
1977	Jaime Fillol (Chl)	Tim Gullikson (USA)	abandoned due to rain
1978–94	No tournament held		
1995	Javier Frana (Arg)	Todd Woodbridge (Aus)	7-6, 6-3

1996	Jan Siemerink (Ned)	Sandon Stolle (Aus)	6-3, 7-6
1997	Greg Rusedski	Karol Kucera (Slo)	6-4, 7-5
1998	Jonas Bjorkman (Swe)	Byron Black (Zim)	6-3, 6-2
1999	Cedric Pioline (Fra)	Kevin Ullyet (Zim)	6-3, 7-5
2000	Sebastien Grosjean (Fra)	Byron Black (Zim)	7-6, 6-3
2001	Thomas Johansson (Swe)	Harel Levy (Isr)	7-5, 6-3
2002	Jonas Bjorkman (Swe)	Wayne Arthurs (Aus)	6-2, 6-7, 6-2
2003	Greg Rusedski	Mardy Fish (USA)	6-3, 6-2
2004	Paradorn Srichaphan (Tha)	Thomas Johansson (Swe)	1-6, 7-6, 6-3
2005	Richard Gasquet (Fra)	Max Mirnyi (Blr)	6-2, 6-3
2006	Richard Gasquet (Fra)	Jonas Bjorkman (Swe)	6-4, 6-3
2007	Ivo Karlovic (Cro)	Arnaud Clement (Fra)	3-6, 6-4, 6-4
2008	Ivo Karlovic (Cro)	Fernando Verdasco (Spn)	7-5, 6-7, 7-6
2009–14	No tournament held		
2015	Denis Istomin (Uzb)	Sam Querry (USA)	7-6, 7-6
2016	Steve Johnson (USA)	Pablo Cuevas (Uru)	7-6, 7-5
2017	Dudi Sela (Isr)	Thomas Fabbiano (Ita)	4-6, 6-4, 6-3
2018	Alex de Minaur (Aus)	Dan Evans	7-6, 7-5
2019	Dan Evans	Evgeny Donskoy (Rus)	7-6, 6-3
2020	No tournament held		

Women's Singles

Year	Winner	Runner-up	Score
1971	Julie Heldman (USA)	Barbara Hawcroft (Aus)	6-4, 7-9, 6-3
1972	Billie Jean King (USA)	Evonne Goolagong (Aus) abandoned due to rain	
1973	Billie Jean King (USA)	Virginia Wade	8-6, 6-4
1974–2014	No tournament held		
2015	Ana Konjuh (Cro)	Monica Niculescu (Rom)	1-6, 6-4, 6-2
2016	Karolina Pliskova (Czh)	Alison Riske (USA)	7-6, 7-5
2017	Donna Vekic (Cro)	Johanna Konta	2-6, 7-6, 7-5
2018	Ashleigh Barty (Aus)	Johanna Konta	6-3, 3-6, 6-4
2019	Caroline Garcia (Fra)	Donna Vekic (Cro)	2-6, 7-6, 7-6
2020	No tournament held		

10

Wembley, the Albert Hall and the O2 Arena

WE END our journey around England's foremost tennis venues beyond SW19 where we began, in London. In the opening chapter we saw that in the pre-Open era, Queen's Club in West Kensington operated two frontline meetings annually, the London Grass Court Championships and the British Covered Court Championships. The latter does not, however, tell the whole story of world-class indoor provision in London. Several other locations have also witnessed key moments in tennis history.

The National Sports Centre at Crystal Palace, for example, saw high drama in 1978 when Britain's Davis Cup team secured a thrilling semi-final victory over Australia, thereby reaching the final of that competition for the first time since the 1930s. This chapter focuses on three particularly prominent indoor settings in the capital, beginning with the one that was in the spotlight over the longest period of time.

While Madison Square Garden in New York was the heart of professional tennis in the United States, its equivalent in Britain was found in the unlikely setting of Wembley, the spiritual home of English football.

The Empire Pool, Wembley

Despite the strong unpaid, amateur ethos that characterised lawn tennis globally, professional tours started to emerge in the 1920s. The new superstars of the post-First World War era, Suzanne Lenglen and Bill Tilden, strongly resented amateur regulations that prevented them from being officially rewarded for their endeavours with anything more than trophies and prize vouchers. Lenglen and Tilden, followed by a small number of like-minded players, accepted offers from entrepreneurial promoters to benefit financially by embarking on exhibition tours in the United States. This meant they could be paid above board, but they were thereafter banned from all amateur competition, including the grand slams.

An alternative – potential rival – to the traditional amateur circuit thus came into existence, though at the outset it was considered little more than an irritant, too small in scope to pose a serious threat. The international governing authorities treated the 'Tilden circus' with disdain, and in most countries, including England, touring pros when they started to venture beyond North America were barred from appearing at clubs affiliated to national associations.

With the LTA adopting a hostile stance, a high-profile, accessible venue was imperative if professional tennis was to make any inroads in the original home of the sport. Arthur Elvin – the managing director of Wembley Stadium in north-west London, which was constructed in the 1920s and home to football's famous FA Cup Final – was the brainchild behind a large new indoor arena on the same site, the Empire Pool, opened initially to host sports such as swimming, ice hockey and boxing. As a businessman, Elvin was receptive to the idea of trialling a top-level professional tennis event, and this duly took place in November 1934. On wooden boards temporarily laid over the skating rink and swimming pool, a round-robin tournament featuring six leading men (no corresponding women's event was organised) was won by American star Ellsworth Vines, who joined the Tilden group having achieved his aims in the amateur game by winning both the US Championships and Wimbledon.

The Wembley Championships did not, to begin with, warrant the same media attention afforded to frontline amateur tournaments taking place in London or elsewhere in the country. This neglect reflected a common perception of pro tennis in its infancy as thin in numbers and largely exhibition in nature, lacking genuine competitiveness and possibly even fixed in advance: an accusation strenuously denied by those who took part. But the 1934 experiment was considered sufficiently successful in commercial terms – proving spectators would pay to watch well-known stars, whatever their playing status – that it was repeated the following year. A more conventional knockout format was adopted and crowd numbers were respectable, especially towards the end of the tournament, which culminated in strong-serving Ellie Vines retaining his title with a five-set victory over Tilden.

Many of the great names of men's tennis in due course followed Vines on to the roll of honour at Wembley, although one notable exception was Fred Perry, Britain's most successful grand slam champion of the past 100 years. After Perry's decision to leave amateur ranks in 1936, most of his numerous professional encounters against Vines over the following few years were held in the USA, where Fred went to live and where crowds and gate receipts could be maximised.

Despite his recruitment to the pro ranks being much lauded by Tilden, Perry in his prime never competed in the Wembley Championships, although he did fleetingly appear at the Empire Pool in 1937. During the spring of that year Vines and Perry conducted a European leg of their season-long tour, starting with a one-off mini-series over three nights in front of some 8,000 spectators at Wembley. Perry came out on top to claim the King George VI Coronation Cup.

UNDERRATED CHAMPION

Although overshadowed in terms of renown and crowd-pulling power by Vines, Perry and Donald Budge, Hans Nüsslein – winner of the Wembley Championships in 1937 – was a mainstay of the professional circuit as it sought to establish itself before the Second World War. As a teenager Nüsslein took small payments for giving lessons to fellow club members in his hometown of Nuremburg, for which he received a lifetime ban from amateur competition by the German Tennis Federation. He turned to coaching and in the early 1930s, after almost winning an exhibition against a startled Bill Tilden ('Who is Nüsslein?' Tilden asked), he was invited to join the pro tour in the USA. With a classical style and no major weaknesses in his all-court game, Nüsslein continued to catch his more illustrious peers off guard. He pushed Vines hard in the first Wembley final of 1934, beat Tilden to take the title in 1937, and gave a serious fright in 1939 to Californian Don Budge, widely acclaimed as the best player of the time. After Budge edged a long first set 13-11 it was thought he would ease to victory, but the German struck back to take the second, and the American encountered further dogged resistance in the third-set decider before squeezing through 6-4. Onlookers described some of the tennis as electrifying, providing one of the most exciting matches yet seen in the pro arena.[1]

The professional scene was slow to re-emerge in Britain after the Second World War. Tilden was arrested and imprisoned on indecency charges, and revival only occurred when American Jack Kramer – Wimbledon and US champion in 1947 and a fierce critic of amateur officials and governance – emerged to replace Tilden in the dual role of player-promoter. Kramer won the first post-war Empire Pool tournament in the spring of 1949, using his power and precision to defeat Bobby Riggs in a four-set final. Amateur governing bodies in

Europe reluctantly accepted that pro tours had become an enduring feature of the tennis landscape, worthy of acknowledgement at least, rather than constant frosty opposition. In 1951 the LTA gave official recognition to the Wembley meeting, after which it was renamed the London Indoor Professional Championships. It subsequently became a major highlight in the increasingly global pro calendar, drawing in ever-larger crowds and attracting much greater media attention than hitherto, including BBC television coverage.

In its 1950s and 60s heyday, the London Pro was regarded by informed observers as producing the highest-quality men's tennis seen in England at that time, surpassing what was generally on offer in the amateur arena.[2] Three men in particular dominated this era, the first of whom was Mexican-American Pancho Gonzales, a key defector from amateur ranks after winning the US Championships in 1949. He claimed the title at the Empire Pool four times, including a stirring five-set victory over Jack Kramer in 1952. The charismatic, abrasive Gonzales pulled back from 4-2 down in the decider and then, after several deuces, broke his opponent at 5-5 before serving out for victory. Lance Tingay of *The Telegraph* (which now provided detailed insights into the pro game, unlike prior to 1939) wrote that as the final set unfolded the capacity crowd was in a 'delirium of excitement' on a scale rarely seen even at Wimbledon.[3] Although the leading force at Wembley in the first half of the 1950s, Gonzales did not, however, have things all his own way.

One perennial issue facing pro tennis – given the invariably small number of players involved, compared with amateur meetings – was the need for new blood to infuse fresh life into tours that could easily become stale. By 1954 there was a sense of drift and hence it was important for promoters that in late 1955 they were able to sign up American Tony Trabert, winner of three of the grand slams (and of 18 titles in all) that year. Pro tennis more than regained its momentum when it became clear as new tours got under way in North America that Trabert did not get on well with Gonzales.

IN A HURRY...

The final at Wembley in 1953 was billed as the heavyweight championship of professional tennis. It pitted Pancho Gonzales, the mercurial victor at the Empire Pool for the previous three years, against the new kid on the block, Frank Sedgman. The Australian had recently joined the pro circuit after scaling the heights in the amateur game: he won Wimbledon in 1952 and later in the year helped his national team to secure another Davis Cup triumph. The Wembley final was much anticipated, but like many hyped-up boxing contests, it turned out to be a damp squib. Many amateurs-turned-pro in the past were desperate to prove their worth when they switched codes, and Sedgman was no exception. He harried and hustled Gonzales from the start, giving his opponent no chance to settle; the Aussie challenger dropped only two points in taking the first four games. As the match unfolded, Sedgman's level never dipped for a moment. He served beautifully, volleyed crisply and remained almost error-free off the ground. As a straight-sets defeat loomed, the disgruntled Gonzales was seen and heard – by a large television audience – wailing in frustration at his inability to stem the tide. The match was over in 49 minutes. Sedgman told journalists afterwards that he played better than when he triumphed at Wimbledon; he described it as his most complete performance.

The personal animosity between the two men was obvious on court and helped to bring crowds flocking to watch them spar, as well as dispelling any lingering doubts about the seriousness of pro competition.[4] The British tennis public was denied a first opportunity to witness the bitterness close up for themselves at Wembley in 1956 when Trabert lost to Sedgman in the semi-finals. They were, though, treated to one of the longest and most sparkling men's finals of the period.

... AND LONG DRAWN-OUT

Pancho Gonzales had a long memory. The Wembley tournament was not held in 1954 or 55 owing to scheduling problems, but when it resumed in 1956 Gonzales was determined to avenge the thrashing he received at the hands of Frank Sedgman three years earlier. In contrast to the 1953 meeting, both men were in tip-top form in the 1956 final. Over the course of a titanic four-set struggle, barely a single unforced error was recorded in what some observers described as the best match seen on English shores since the Second World War. Sedgman was stronger at the outset and took the first set before surging to 4-1 ahead in the second. At this point a repeat of 1953 was not out of the question. But Gonzales was playing well himself; he pegged the Aussie back and after a long struggle levelled things up by taking the set 11-9. Another high-quality display of attack and counter-attack followed in the third. The 4,000-strong crowd was left gasping at the quality of the winners and retrieving from both men, and loud cheering ensued when 'Big Pancho' edged the set, again by 11-9. Sedgman never relented or lost focus, but by forcing at just the right moment Gonzales was able to claim the fourth set, and the title, nine games to seven. Words like 'epic' and 'thrilling' were not just hyperbole. The BBC, unusually in this era, stayed on air until after midnight to cover the end of the match. Most spectators also remained in their seats, even at the cost of finding that public transport was thin on the ground when they left Wembley looking to get home in the early hours of Sunday morning.

Another excellent final in 1957 saw the classical Aussie stylist Ken Rosewall secure his first major pro title with a five-set win over Pancho Segura, entitling him to prize money of £425. Rosewall was the second outstanding champion at Wembley during the 1950s and 60s, going on to win a record-equalling six titles, as well as triumphing in the doubles on nine occasions. Three of his four successive singles victories in the early 1960s came at the expense of compatriot and two-time Wimbledon champion Lew Hoad, who pulled out all the stops in the 1962 final – a marathon that lasted three and a half hours – but was unable to find a way past Rosewall. The London Pro was by now frequently talked about as providing a higher standard of men's play than seen at Wimbledon. Crowd numbers at 'the Pool' increased, boosting gate receipts and ensuring that for a decade after 1958 the winner received £1,000: the same figure that was to be offered at the groundbreaking Bournemouth Open meeting in 1968.

The third kingpin at Wembley prior to the advent of Open tennis was another Australian legend, Rod Laver. His win over Rosewall after five pulsating sets in 1964 marked a changing of the guard; the first of four consecutive triumphs for Laver (he too eventually claimed six titles). Rosewall served at 5-4 in the decider, but 'the Rocket' adopted all-out attack to break back and went on to squeeze through 8-6 in a final that finished well after midnight. Peter Wilson of the *Daily Mirror* wrote that in his long years of covering top-level tennis he could not recall seeing a finer match. Every set was fiercely contested, Wilson noted, and he had no idea who would prevail until a lucky net cord broke the holder's rhythm at the decisive moment; this was all that divided the two protagonists in their 'superlative, sporting combat'.[5]

The exceptional talent on display year in, year out on the fast wooden courts at Wembley was one of the factors that influenced the British tennis authorities – fearful of the effects of excluding the world's best men from Wimbledon – in throwing their weight behind moves to abolish the amateur-professional divide in the mid-1960s. Seen in this context, the London Pro ultimately became a victim of its own success. The arrival of Open tennis gradually undermined Wembley's special status, in that it no longer uniquely showcased the talents of the crème de la crème. The Lavers and

Rosewalls could once more compete legitimately in SW19 and at other erstwhile amateur tournaments (where they silenced any remaining cynics about pro tours by claiming many further titles).

In the medium term, the standard of play at the Empire Pool, and the rewards on offer, remained high and heady. With £5,000 at stake, all the top contract pros turned up for the re-designated Jack Kramer Tournament of Champions at Wembley in the autumn of 1968. Another fine two-hour final saw the subtle skills of Rosewall overcome the combative instincts of fellow Aussie John Newcombe in four sets. But upheaval and change were the order of the day. Carpet courts replaced the wood surface at Wembley, and in 1969 the tournament was incorporated into the British Covered Court Championships. The event's identity was more difficult to maintain when it subsequently became known as the Wills Championships and as the Embassy British Indoor Championships, and a contractual dispute between different organisational and player groups (a common feature of the early Open era) meant no meeting was held in 1972.

Revival had to wait until 1976, after which substantial sponsorship for the Benson & Hedges Championships ensured that many top world-ranked men again featured at Wembley. Bjorn Borg took the title in 1977 and in later years the Empire Pool became one of several locations in England where the see-saw rivalry between John McEnroe and Jimmy Connors unfolded. Connors won the 1981 final in five sets; McEnroe gained revenge when he took his fifth and last Wembley title a couple of years later. The tournament remained part of the Grand Prix circuit throughout the 1980s but – like many in the elite calendar – it was downgraded after the new ATP Tour came into force at the end of the decade. The so-called Diet Pepsi Challenge was moved to Birmingham in 1991, although the previous year the curtain had already come down on Wembley's sparkling, albeit patchy, history – taking into account the number of times no meeting was held – when in the last final held at the Pool defending champion Michael Chang was beaten by Jakob Hlasek of Switzerland.

RECORD BREAKERS

Most titles: Ken Rosewall (6), Rod Laver (6), John McEnroe (5), Pancho Gonzales (4), Ivan Lendl (3)

Number of Wembley Professional champions who also won Wimbledon singles

Total: 8

Wembley Professional Championships

Men's Singles

Year	Winner	Runner-up	Score
1934	Ellsworth Vines (USA)	Hans Nüsslein (Ger)	4-6, 7-5, 6-3, 8-6
1935	Ellsworth Vines (USA)	Bill Tilden (USA)	6-1, 6-3, 5-7, 3-6, 6-3
1936	No tournament held		
1937	Hans Nüsslein (Ger)	Bill Tilden (USA)	6-3, 3-6, 6-3, 2-6, 6-3
1938	No tournament held		
1939	Don Budge (USA)	Hans Nüsslein (Ger)	13-11, 2-6, 6-4
1940–48	No tournament held		
1949	Jack Kramer (USA)	Bobby Riggs (USA)	2-6, 6-4, 6-3, 6-4
1950	Pancho Gonzales (USA)	Welby Van Horn (USA)	6-3, 6-3, 6-2
1951	Pancho Gonzales (USA)	Pancho Segura (USA)	6-2, 6-2, 2-6, 6-4
1952	Pancho Gonzales (USA)	Jack Kramer (USA)	3-6, 3-6, 6-2, 6-4, 7-5
1953	Frank Sedgman (Aus)	Pancho Gonzales (USA)	6-1, 6-2, 6-2
1954–55	No tournament held		
1956	Pancho Gonzales (USA)	Frank Sedgman (Aus)	4-6, 11-9, 11-9, 9-7
1957	Ken Rosewall (Aus)	Pancho Segura (USA)	1-6, 6-3, 6-4, 3-6, 6-4
1958	Frank Sedgman (Aus)	Tony Trabert (USA)	6-4, 6-3, 6-4
1959	Mal Anderson (Aus)	Pancho Segura (USA)	4-6, 6-4, 3-6, 6-3, 8-6
1960	Ken Rosewall (Aus)	Pancho Segura (USA)	5-7, 8-6, 6-1, 6-3
1961	Ken Rosewall (Aus)	Lew Hoad (Aus)	6-3, 3-6, 6-2, 6-3
1962	Ken Rosewall (Aus)	Lew Hoad (Aus)	6-4, 5-7, 15-13, 7-5
1963	Ken Rosewall (Aus)	Lew Hoad (Aus)	6-4, 6-2, 4-6, 6-3
1964	Rod Laver (Aus)	Ken Rosewall (Aus)	7-5, 4-6, 5-7, 8-6, 8-6

1965 Rod Laver (Aus)	Andres Gimeno (Spn)	6-2, 6-3, 6-4
1966 Rod Laver (Aus)	Ken Rosewall (Aus)	6-2, 6-2, 6-3
1967 Rod Laver (Aus)	Ken Rosewall (Aus)	2-6, 6-1, 1-6, 8-6, 6-2
1968 Ken Rosewall (Aus)	John Newcombe (Aus)	6-4, 4-6, 7-5, 6-4
1969 Rod Laver (Aus)	Tony Roche (Aus)	6-4, 6-1, 6-3
1970 Rod Laver (Aus)	Cliff Richey (USA)	6-3, 6-4, 7-5
1971 Ilie Nastase (Rom)	Rod Laver (Aus)	3-6, 6-3, 3-6, 6-4, 6-4
1972–75 No tournament held		
1976 Jimmy Connors (USA)	Roscoe Tanner (USA)	3-6, 7-6, 6-4
1977 Bjorn Borg (Swe)	John Lloyd	6-4, 6-4, 6-3
1978 John McEnroe (USA)	Tim Gullikson (USA)	6-7, 6-4, 7-6, 6-2
1979 John McEnroe (USA)	Harold Solomon (USA)	6-3, 6-4, 7-5
1980 John McEnroe (USA)	Gene Mayer (USA)	6-4, 6-3, 6-3
1981 Jimmy Connors (USA)	John McEnroe (USA)	3-6, 2-6, 6-3, 6-4, 6-2
1982 John McEnroe (USA)	Brian Gottfried (USA)	6-3, 6-2, 6-4
1983 John McEnroe (USA)	Jimmy Connors (USA)	7-5, 6-1, 6-4
1984 Ivan Lendl (Cze)	Andres Gomez (Spa)	7-6, 6-2, 6-1
1985 Ivan Lendl (Cze)	Boris Becker (Ger)	6-7, 6-3, 4-6, 6-4, 6-4
1986 Yannick Noah (Fra)	Jonas Svensson (Swe)	6-2, 6-3, 6-7, 4-6, 7-5
1987 Ivan Lendl (Cze)	Anders Jarryd (Swe)	6-3, 6-2, 7-5
1988 Jakob Hlasek (Sui)	Jonas Svensson (Swe)	6-7, 3-6, 6-4, 6-0, 7-5
1989 Michael Chang (USA)	Guy Forget (Fra)	6-2, 6-1, 6-1
1990 Jakob Hlasek (Sui)	Michael Chang (USA)	7-6, 6-3

Notes on the pre-1939 Wembley tournament

- The 1934 event was conducted on a six-man round-robin basis, with Vines placed first and Nüsslein second as a result of most victories; the score above is the result when the two met in the round-robin.
- Some accounts suggest that the Wembley Pro Champs took place in 1936 and 1938, but the most comprehensive study yet of the pro circuit, Chris Jordan's *The Professional Tennis Archive*, published in 2019, on pages 24 and 33, confirms that the event did not run in those years.
- The 1939 event took place on a four-man round-robin basis, with Budge placed first and Nüsslein second as a result of most victories; the score above is the result when the two met in the round-robin.

The Royal Albert Hall

The chief alternative to Wembley in offering world-class indoor tennis in London during the early Open years was the Royal Albert Hall. Its involvement began when Rothmans – a leader in providing generous sponsorship for a few years – sought to stage a new tournament aimed at maximising the pulling power of WCT professionals such as Laver and Rosewall. The famous Victorian concert hall proved to be a first-rate setting. By temporarily raising the floor of the main arena some ten feet, a suitable base for a covered court (with a carpet surface) was created, easily visible from all sides of the large auditorium. The hall's reputation and location in South Kensington, moreover, helped to attract large crowds, some of whom were able to enjoy upmarket promotions such as champagne suppers while viewing the tennis from plush side boxes.[6]

The inaugural Rothmans International Tournament in March 1970 was well attended, but not without controversy. In echoes of what took place at Bristol the previous summer, the Albert Hall final was briefly interrupted when demonstrators in the top gallery chanted anti-apartheid slogans. The bulk of the crowd responded by slow-handclapping and before long police arrived to remove the protestors.

On court, spectators were treated to several closely fought contests in the preliminary rounds, not least a marathon encounter between Britain's Mark Cox and American Marty Riessen. With the introduction of tie-breaks still a couple of years ahead, Cox claimed the first set 27-25, but his opponent then squeezed through 8-6, 7-5. Riessen, who later reached a career-high world ranking of 11, became the first Rothmans champion when he beat Ken Rosewall in the final, dropping only six games. The 28-year-old from Illinois enjoyed one of his best-ever weeks on tour: by winning both the singles and doubles, he carried off almost a quarter of the £10,000 total prize pot.

Mark Cox continued to feature prominently at the Rothmans International. He reached the final in 1973, but was beaten in four sets by Brian Fairlie of New Zealand. A year later, by which time the prize money on offer had quadrupled, the Leicestershire man looked set for a big pay day when he reached championship point against the Swedish teenage sensation, Bjorn Borg. Cox was unable to convert, however, and subsequently missed five more chances to take the title. Amid wild cheering for Borg – already attracting an exuberant following among younger fans – the Swede edged to a 6-4 deciding-set triumph. In 1975 the British left-hander was finally rewarded for his tenacity and tactical acumen, extracting revenge with a straight-sets win over Brian Fairlie in the final. With annual schedules in flux, the Rothmans meeting was not held the following year, and it was shifted for a last outing in 1977 to Earl's Court, where Florida's Eddie Dibbs outlasted his heavier-hitting fellow American Vitas Gerulaitis in a final lasting almost two and a half hours. With no fresh sponsorship forthcoming, and with mergers taking place between rival men's circuits, the London WCT – the name adopted at Earl's Court – did not return during or after 1978.

Rothmans International

Men's Singles

Year	Winner	Runner-up	Score
1970	Marty Riessen (USA)	Ken Rosewall (Aus)	6-4, 6-2
1971	Rod Laver (Aus)	Niki Pilic (Yug)	6-4, 6-0, 6-2
1972	Cliff Richey (USA)	Clark Graebner (USA)	7-5, 6-7, 7-5, 6-0
1973	Brian Fairlie (NZ)	Mark Cox	2-6, 6-2, 7-5, 6-0
1974	Bjorn Borg (Swe)	Mark Cox	6-7, 7-6, 6-4
1975	Mark Cox	Brian Fairlie (NZ)	6-1, 7-5
1976	No tournament held		
1977	Eddie Dibbs (USA)	Vitas Gerulaitis (USA)	7-6, 6-7, 6-4

During the first half of the 1970s, fans also flocked to the Royal Albert Hall to watch the denouement of another frontline event: the

Dewar Cup. This initiative arose in the late 1960s out of concern that Britain lacked a consolidated indoor programme to round off the season in the autumn. With the Covered Court Championships at Queen's struggling (it was unable to go ahead in 1966 or 1967), the Dewar Cup was launched in the hope of showcasing international-standard tennis to a wider audience in provincial towns and cities. With generous sponsorship from John Dewar and Sons, a Scottish whisky firm, the inaugural running of the cup in 1968 saw preliminary events held at indoor centres in Stalybridge, Perth, Aberavon and Torquay. These standalone meetings had their own prize money, as well as providing qualifying points to take part in the later finals, incorporated into the BCCC for that year and split between Queen's Club and Crystal Palace. In 1969 the circuit was trimmed slightly – matches at Queen's were scrapped – and home fans were able to celebrate as Mark Cox and Virginia Wade carried off the main singles titles.

In 1970 the finals were transferred from Crystal Palace to the Royal Albert Hall (which had demonstrated its viability with the first hosting of the Rothmans International earlier in the year), and for a few seasons the Dewar Cup flourished. Good crowds turned out for the preliminary stages at most provincial venues, and the switch to the Albert Hall ensured that finals were always a sell-out. British tennis fans, making up the bulk of the audience base, were delighted to see that Virginia Wade, enjoying the fast indoor surfaces, proved an irresistible force in the women's singles. She claimed the Dewar title no less than seven times (four years in succession between 1973 and 1976), with victories over some of her most prominent Australian and American rivals in Margaret Court, Evonne Cawley, Julie Heldman and Chris Evert.

The men's singles also attracted some of the top names of the day. In 1972 Dewar increased the prize pot and the meeting acted as the last of the year in the men's Grand Prix series. The colourful Romanian Ilie Nastase carried off the trophy and £2,000 first prize – a substantial amount compared with other tournaments of the time – after hauling himself back into contention having lost the first set of the final to Tom Gorman 6-0. The 1974 men's field was the strongest yet, spearheaded by reigning Wimbledon champion Jimmy Connors, who overcame fellow American Brian Gottfried in straight sets. The following year, however, both Connors and Nastase were involved in some unsavoury scenes, denting the credibility of the tournament and the sport more broadly.

BAD BOYS BOOED OFF COURT

There was talk of 'uproar' and 'disgraceful' antics at the Royal Albert Hall in 1975. World number one Jimmy Connors ended the year poorly, losing the singles final to compatriot Eddie Dibbs and then incurring the wrath of the crowd during the men's doubles final. Connors and partner Ilie Nastase took to the court wearing bow ties under their tennis shirts and proceeded to sip champagne, but this mimicking of groups in the well-appointed spectator boxes did not go down well. Nor were onlookers impressed by the continued showmanship of the top seeds as play progressed. Their unfancied opponents, Wojtek Fibak and Karl Meiler, stayed calm throughout and brought off a fine victory, after which insult was added to injury when Connors and Nastase left the arena, accompanied by slow-handclapping, instead of waiting for the prize-giving ceremony. After some delay they were persuaded to return by Derek Hardwick, a member of the tournament committee. The formalities were duly completed amid continuing booing. Hardwick, who that year served as president of the International Federation, later condemned the behaviour of Connors and Nastase as unwelcome for spectators and unfair on their opponents; moves were intensified to create a new player code of conduct.[7]

By 1976 the tide had turned for the Dewar Cup. Dwindling audiences at several of the non-London venues meant the preliminary stage had already been significantly curtailed compared with the six-week incarnation in the early years. In deciding to withdraw sponsorship altogether, John Dewar blamed the shrinkage of the circuit on rising costs and on the difficulty of attracting sufficient numbers of world-ranked players at the season's end. Home spectators at the final edition in November 1976 were at least treated to witnessing an emphatic victory by Virginia Wade – probably the most satisfying of her seven titles – when she beat the great Chrissie Evert comfortably, 6-3, 6-1. Wade told reporters that in the past she was often guilty of over-thinking things against Evert, who she said possessed the 'best brain' in the game. This time, Wade said, a simple policy of all-out attack – aiming to hit her opponent off court – paid dividends.[8]

Dewar Cup

Men's Singles

Year	Winner	Runner-up	Score
1968	Stan Smith (USA)	Mark Cox	6-4, 6-4
1969	Mark Cox	Bob Hewitt (SA)	4-6, 9-7, 6-2
1970	John Alexander (USA)	Tom Gorman (USA)	5-7, 7-6, 7-6
1971	Gerald Battrick	Bob Hewitt (SA)	6-3, 6-4
1972	Ilie Nastase (Rom)	Tom Gorman (USA)	0-6, 6-1, 6-3
1973	Tom Okker (Ned)	Ilie Nastase (Rom)	6-3, 6-4
1974	Jimmy Connors (USA)	Brian Gottfried (USA)	6-2, 7-6
1975	Eddie Dibbs (USA)	Jimmy Connors (USA)	1-6, 6-1, 7-5
1976	Raul Ramirez (Mex)	Manuel Santana (Spa)	6-3, 6-4

Women's Singles

Year	Winner	Runner-up	Score
1968	Virginia Wade	Margaret Court (Aus)	6-3, 6-4
1969	Virginia Wade	Julie Heldman (USA)	6-4, 6-1
1970	Francoise Durr (Fra)	Ann Jones	7-6, 2-6, 6-2
1971	Virginia Wade	Julie Heldman (USA)	6-1, 6-3
1972	Margaret Court (Aus)	Virginia Wade	6-1, 6-1

1973	Virginia Wade	Julie Heldman (USA)	7-6, 6-2
1974	Virginia Wade	Julie Heldman (USA)	7-6-6-2
1975	Virginia Wade	Evonne Cawley (Aus)	6-3, 6-1
1976	Virginia Wade	Chris Evert (USA)	6-3, 6-1

Despite the demise of both the Rothmans International and the Dewar Cup, the Albert Hall's association with top-level tennis was by no means finished. Britain's home fixtures in the annual women's team contest against the USA, the Wightman Cup, were traditionally held outdoors at Wimbledon, but American domination was so overwhelming by the 1970s that a rethink was essential if the event was to have any chance of surviving. The LTA decided to prioritise indoor venues, first Crystal Palace in 1976 and then the Albert Hall two years later.

The move to central London yielded immediate dividends for the home team when, in the 50th edition of the competition, Britain scored a rousing 4-3 triumph over a strong American squad that included Evert, Tracy Austin and Pam Shriver. Virginia Wade and Sue Barker both defeated Austin over three sets in singles, and then combined in the deciding doubles rubber to win 6-4 in the third against Evert and Shriver. But this stirring victory was as good as it got. In five subsequent encounters held at the Albert Hall, the Americans were always in firm control (winning 7-0 in 1988, for example), and with crowd numbers falling, a joint statement was issued by the US and British governing bodies in 1990 citing dwindling interest as a key reason for winding up the Wightman Cup altogether.

Some years later, world-class tennis of a rather different variety returned to South Kensington. The so-called seniors tour slowly gained credibility in the 1990s, increasing to about ten meetings worldwide and culminating annually from 1998 onwards in masters-style finals held each November in London. The Royal Albert Hall was often filled once more with crowds of over 30,000, happy to get a glimpse of former legends of the men's game. The seniors tour was packaged on promises of entertainment and nostalgia, although sharp rivalry was also sometimes close to the surface, particularly when former firebrands such as McEnroe and Connors put in appearances. McEnroe, above all, was a mainstay and compelling attraction in London, winning three times in succession at the Albert Hall. In contrast to the days when he was often vilified, fans could not get enough of Mac's tantrums (often now more contrived) while admiring his enduring racket skills. On the basis of annual performance, McEnroe was for several years ranked number one among the so-called 'old timers'.

The O2 Arena

For two decades after the ending of Wightman Cup fixtures in 1990, the same year as the Wembley tournament was wound up, London lacked – for the first time in the nation's tennis history – a major indoor meeting featuring some of the world's elite in their prime, notwithstanding the efforts of the talented seniors at the Albert Hall. This one notable gap in the international-standard provision consistently on offer since Victorian times (recalling here that the Queen's Covered Court Championships attracted top amateurs from inception through to the 1960s) was closed when the O2 Arena on the Greenwich Peninsula was chosen to host the ATP World Finals in 2009. This week-long tournament each November stands at the pinnacle of the present-day men's game outside of the four grand slams. London once more became centre stage, being given the privilege of running the end-of-year championship for the top eight singles players and top eight doubles pairs on the ATP Tour, carrying significant ranking points, not to mention huge prize money (in recent years amounting to about £8m).

A version of the ATP Finals (the official title since 2017) has been in existence almost from the start of the Open era, beginning life under the name of the Grand Prix Masters in 1970. Early on, the event – designed to determine who should be ranked as the world's best at the end of each calendar year – moved between different cities annually before settling in particular locations for more extended periods: Houston and New York in the 1980s, and then Frankfurt and Hanover in the 1990s. For most of the time, including in London in recent years, the singles have been played as round-robin group stages, with top performers qualifying for knockout semi-finals and finals.

The list of tournament winners reads like a roll call of the superstars of the modern men's game. Although 11-time grand slam champion Rod Laver was surprisingly beaten by Stan Smith in the inaugural 1970 final (and never managed to claim the title), since then victors have included many of the greats: Connors, Borg, McEnroe, Becker, Lendl, Edberg, Agassi and Sampras among them. The record for the most victories – six – is currently held by Swiss legend Roger Federer; he first triumphed in 2003 and two of his wins came in London, in 2010 and 2011. John McEnroe and Peter Fleming remain unsurpassed in the doubles, which in the early days was held separately after the singles competition, rather than being an integral part of the main proceedings, as it is today. The formidable American pair took the title on seven consecutive occasions in New York between 1978 and 1984.

The instantly recognisable O2 structure on the River Thames, named after its main sponsor, the telecommunications company, was chosen for this most esteemed of tennis gatherings in 2009 for several reasons. Originally constructed as an exhibition space – the Millennium Dome – the multipurpose O2 was described by the ATP as a 'unique and iconic setting'; one which boasted the second-highest seating capacity of any indoor venue in Britain, capable of accommodating up to 20,000 spectators. London's global appeal, its 'brand' as a city, as well as its reputation for delivering high-class tennis, was also a factor. The capital contained, the ATP believed, 'a vibrancy and energy that makes it ideally suited to hosting this event'.[9] The extent to which such confidence was borne out was shown in 2013, when the initial contract was extended to 2020, meaning that for over a decade the crowds who flocked to the O2 were able to regularly enjoy watching the quartet who for long periods stood above the rest of the pack: Federer, Djokovic (winner four times in succession between 2012 and 2015), Nadal and Murray.

For British fans, Andy Murray's victory over Novak Djokovic in the 2016 final was not especially notable for prolonged excitement or exceptional quality. The match was relatively brief and both men, by their usual high standards, made numerous unforced errors. Rather, it was what the outcome signified that mattered. Murray became the only Briton to win the tournament since its inception; had the Serb legend secured his fifth successive ATP title, he would have seized back the world number one slot that Murray claimed a few weeks earlier following an astonishing run of form. The Scot had won nine of 13 tournaments since April (reaching the final of 12 of them), including a record-breaking fifth title at Queen's, his third gram slam, at Wimbledon, and a second Olympic Gold, in Rio de Janeiro. The capacity crowd at the O2 rose to their feet to provide noisy acclamation when Murray defeated Djokovic in straight sets: his 24th win in a row and the culmination of what turned out to be his most successful year on the circuit.

Since Murray's triumph, the title has gone to a different 'young pretender' each year: Gregor Dimitrov, Sacha Zverev, Stefanos Tsitsipas and most recently, in November 2020 – in the only tournament featured in these pages to go ahead in England that year because of the global pandemic – Daniil Medvedev. This meant that the very last O2 meeting, like the first, was claimed by a Russian; Nikolay Davydenko was the winner back in 2009. En route to the most eye-catching success of his developing career so far, the 24-year-old Medvedev beat both Nadal and Djokovic (Federer was absent), before getting the better of Austrian world number three Dominic Thiem in a close three-set final. Whether this marked a genuine milestone in ending the long ascendancy of the 'Big Three' (who, with Andy Murray sidelined by persistent injury problems, continued to monopolise every grand slam from 2017 through to the 2020 US Open) remained to be seen.

In some ways it was a sad finale to the ATP finals at the O2. Aside from officials and limited player entourages, matches throughout the week in 2020 were played in front of massed ranks of empty seats, in line with government guidelines banning crowds at sporting events owing to the pandemic. For the benefit of TV audiences, artificial applause was provided in the background in an effort to generate some sense of atmosphere in the cavernous arena.

Despite this strange farewell, there was little doubt that, seen in the round, the event had been a great success in and for London. The number of meetings held at the O2, a dozen, had been bettered over the course of the ATP finals hitherto by only one other venue (Madison Square Garden in New York, which hosted 13 editions). And by the time the show left town, scheduled to take place in Turin at the end of 2021, a total of about 2.8 million spectators had flocked to Greenwich to enjoy the proceedings. In contrast to most of the locations featured in previous chapters, the O2 Arena – like Wembley and the Albert Hall – was not a bespoke tennis setting. But all three, in addition to Queen's in earlier years, helped to ensure that indoor venues in London contributed hugely to England's long and richly textured history of 'world-class tennis around the country'.

ATP World Tour Finals

Men's Singles

Year	Winner	Runner-up	Score
2009	Nikolay Davydenko (Rus)	Juan Martin del Potro (Arg)	6-3, 6-4
2010	Roger Federer (Sui)	Rafael Nadal (Spn)	6-3, 3-6, 6-1
2011	Roger Federer (Sui)	Jo-Wilfried Tsonga (Fra)	6-3, 6-7, 6-3
2012	Novak Djokovic (Srb)	Roger Federer (Sui)	7-6, 7-5
2013	Novak Djokovic (Srb)	Rafael Nadal (Spn)	6-3, 6-4
2014	Novak Djokovic (Srb)	Roger Federer (Sui)	walkover
2015	Novak Djokovic (Srb)	Roger Federer (Sui)	6-3, 6-4

2016	Andy Murray	Novak Djokovic (Srb)	6-3, 6-4
2017	Grigor Dimitrov (Bul)	David Goffin (Bel)	7-5, 4-6, 6-3
2018	Alexander Zverev (Ger)	Novak Djokovic (Srb)	6-4, 6-3
2019	Stefanos Tsitsipas (Gre)	Dominic Thiem (Aut)	6-7, 6-2, 7-6
2020	Daniil Medvedev (Rus)	Dominic Thiem (Aut)	4-6, 7-6, 6-4

Abbreviations

PLAYERS LISTED as winners or runners-up in the tournament results found in each chapter are from the United Kingdom unless otherwise stated (including players from Ireland prior to the creation of the Irish Free State in 1922). For players from other nations, the following abbreviations are used throughout:

Arg	Argentina
Arm	Armenia
Aus	Australia
Aut	Austria
Bel	Belgium
Ber	Bermuda
Blr	Belarus
Bra	Brazil
Bul	Bulgaria
Can	Canada
Chl	Chile
Chn	China
Cro	Croatia
Czh	Czechoslovakia
CR	Czech Republic
Den	Denmark
Egy	Egypt
Fra	France

Ger	Germany
Gre	Greece
HK	Hong Kong
Hun	Hungary
Ind	India
Ins	Indonesia
Ire	Ireland
Isr	Israel
Ita	Italy
Jpn	Japan
Mex	Mexico
Ned	The Netherlands
NZ	New Zealand
Pak	Pakistan
Par	Paraguay
Phi	The Philippines
Pol	Poland
PR	Puerto Rico
Rho	Rhodesia
Rom	Romania
Rus	Russia
SA	South Africa
Slo	Slovakia
Spn	Spain
Srb	Serbia
Swe	Sweden
Sui	Switzerland
Tai	Taiwan
Tha	Thailand
Ukr	Ukraine
Uru	Uruguay
USA	United States of America

USSR Soviet Union
Uzb   Uzbekistan
Ven   Venezuela
WG   West Germany
Yug   Yugoslavia
Zim   Zimbabwe

Other commonly used abbreviations in the text include:

ATP   Association of Tennis Professionals
BCCC   British Covered Court Championships
BHHC   British Hard Court Championships
ECLTC   Edgbaston Cricket and Lawn Tennis Club
ILTF   International Lawn Tennis Federation
ITF   International Tennis Federation
LTA   Lawn Tennis Association
WCT   World Championship Tennis

Notes

Introduction

1. F.R. Burrow, *My Tournaments* (London: Hodder and Stoughton, 1922), pp. 6-7, 26-7.
2. Gordon Forbes, *A Handful of Summers* (London: HarperCollins, 1997 edn.), pp. 41-2.
3. Lance Tingay (ed.), *Shades of Gray: Tennis Writings of David Gray* (London: Willow, 1988), p. 134.
4. *Lawn Tennis and Badminton*, May 1967.
5. Ronald Atkin (ed.), *For the Love of Tennis* (London: Stanley Paul, 1985), p. 176.
6. See, for example, Simon J. Eaves and Tom Higgins, 'Lawn Tennis in Ireland: the Untold Story, 1870–1914', in Robert J. Lake (ed.), *Routledge Handbook of Tennis: History, Culture and Politics* (2019).
7. Max Robertson (ed.), *The Encyclopedia of Tennis* (London: Allen & Unwin, 1974), p. 314 (Scotland) and p. 342 (Wales). See also George Robertson, *Tennis in Scotland: 100 Years of the Scottish Lawn Tennis Association 1895–1995* (Edinburgh: Scottish Lawn Tennis Association, 1995).
8. In some cases two category headings are combined into one, and not all categories are included in each chapter.
9. Rex Bellamy, *The Tennis Set* (London: Cassell, 1972), p. 5: foreword by Mark Cox.

[1] Queen's Club

1. *Tennis Today*, 68, 12, 2, March/April 2008.
2. Cited in Roy McKelvie, *The Queen's Club Story, 1886–1986* (London: Stanley Paul, 1986), p. 31.
3. *Evening Standard*, 24 June 1907.
4. McKelvie, *Queen's Club Story*, p. 106. The author later confirms, 'leading players, fearful of injury, did not always try their hardest' (p. 173).
5. Forbes, *A Handful of Summers*, pp. 213-14.
6. Mike Sangster with John Ballantine, *Cannonball Tennis* (London: Arthur Barker, 1965), p. 43.
7. Arthur Wallis Myers, *Great Lawn Tennis* (London: Cassell, 1937), pp. 15-16.
8. Lance Tingay, *The Guinness Book of Tennis Facts and Feats* (Enfield: Guinness, 1983), p. 222 claims that the BCCC 'ranked as the second most important British event after the Wimbledon Championships'.
9. Sangster, *Cannonball Tennis*, p. 145.
10. C.M. Jones, *British Lawn Tennis*, February 1967.

[2] Surbiton

1. Burrow, *My Tournaments*, p. 212.
2. *The Field*, 21 June 1890.
3. Geoff Paish, *Surrey County LTA. The First 100 Years* (Surrey: Surrey LTA, 1996), p. 1.
4. www.surbiton.org.
5. *The Field*, 4 August 1900.
6. *The Field*, 2 June 1906.
7. *Illustrated Sporting and Dramatic News*, 30 May 1925.
8. www.surbiton.org; see also *Surbiton Lawn Tennis and Squash Club. 1981 Centenary Handbook and Rules* (Surrey: Surbiton LTC, 1981).

9. Norman Cutler, *Inside Tennis* (London: Evans Brothers, 1954), p. 110.

10. Andrew Baker, *The Independent*, 6 June 1997.

[3] Beckenham

1. Robertson (ed.), *Encyclopedia of Tennis*, p. 276.

2. *The Field*, 5 June 1886.

3. *The Field*, 5 and 12 June 1886.

4. Cited in L.H.W. ('Nicky') Paine, *Beckenham Lawn Tennis Tournament 1886–1986* (Berkhamsted: Dennis Fairey & Associates, 1986), p. 10.

5. *The (London) Daily News*, 17 June 1907.

6. Burrow, *My Tournaments*, p. 198.

7. Wallis Myers, *Great Lawn Tennis*, pp. 179-83.

8. Paine, *Beckenham Lawn Tennis Tournament*, p. 19.

9. *Western Daily Press*, 12 June 1989.

10. www.beckenhamtennisclub.co.uk.

[4] Eastbourne

1. Fred Perry, *Fred Perry: An Autobiography* (London: Hutchinson, 1984), pp. 16-17.

2. Robertson (ed.), *Encyclopedia of Tennis*, p. 235.

3. *Roller Skates and Rackets. The Story of Devonshire Park and Tennis in Eastbourne* (Eastbourne: S.B. Publications, 1999), pp. 4-5.

4. *Eastbourne Gazette*, 14 September 1881.

5. *Eastbourne Gazette*, 16 September 1885.

6. G.W. Hillyard, *Forty Years of First-Class Lawn Tennis* (London: Williams & Norgate, 1924), p. 82.

7. Burrow, *My Tournaments*, p. 139.

8. Cited in *Roller Skates and Rackets*, p. 32.

9. Dan Maskell, *Oh I Say!* (London: Fontana, 1989), p.177.

10. 'How has Eastbourne become a major part of the tennis calendar?' by James Clarke of BBC News Sussex, www.bbc.co.uk/news, 16 June 2014. See also www.devonshireparkltc.co.uk.

[5] Bournemouth

1. 'LTA celebrates 50 years of Open Era tennis', 'Henman joins 50th Anniversary Celebrations', www.westhants.co.uk, 6 May 2018.
2. F.R. Burrow, *The Centre Court and Others* (London: Eyre and Spottiswoode, 1937), pp. 226-7.
3. Atkin (ed.), *For the Love of Tennis*, p. 183.
4. *Lawn Tennis and Badminton*, 12 May 34.
5. Kevin Jefferys, *Fred Perry. British Tennis Legend* (Worthing: Pitch Publishing, 2017), pp. 166-7.
6. *Lawn Tennis and Badminton*, 12 May 34.
7. Cited in Peter Seddon, *Tennis's Strangest Matches* (London: Robson Books, 2001), p. 124.
8. Mike Davies, *Tennis Rebel* (London: Stanley Paul, 1962), p. 107; *Birmingham Daily Gazette* 28 April 1956.
9. Bud Collins, *My Life with the Pros* (New York: Dutton, 1989), p. 192; Tingay (ed.), *Shades of Gray*, pp. 107-8.
10. Virginia Wade, *Courting Triumph* (London: Hodder and Stoughton, 1979), p. 103.
11. Collins, *My Life with the Pros*, p. 195.
12. *Daily Telegraph*, article by tennis correspondent Simon Briggs, posted online 21 April 2018.

[6] The West of England

1. Burrow, *My Tournaments*, p. 207.
2. Fred Perry, *My Story* (London: Hutchinson, 1934), p. 32.
3. 'For Tim and Andy it all started at the Torbay Open!', *Torquay*

Herald Express, 2 July 2011.

4. *Bath Chronicle*, 31 May 1883.

5. Herbert Chipp, *Lawn Tennis Recollections* (London: Merritt and Hatcher, 1898) p. 60.

6. *Western Daily Press & Bristol Mirror*, 14 June 1937.

7. www.redlandgreen.co.uk.

8. Wallis Myers, *Great Lawn Tennis*, pp. 215-19.

9. *Plymouth Herald*, 16 August 2018 and 28 July 2019; see also www.palacehotelexhibition.co.uk.

10. *Herald Express*, 8 November 1958.

11. Bobby Wilson, *My Side of the Net* (London: Stanley Paul, 1962) p. 137.

12. Davies, *Tennis Rebel*, p. 63, refers to his 'alcoholic haze' of 1955, although the tournament was won that year by Bob Howe; Davies triumphed in 1954.

13. Tingay (ed.), *Shades of Gray*, p. 132.

14. *Herald Express*, 1 November 1958.

15. *Herald Express*, 10 November 1962.

16. *The People*, 31 October 1976, claims her average earnings around this time were c.£1,000 a week.

[7] The Northern

1. Cited in David Allaby, *Wimbledon of the North. 100 Years at the Northern* (Didsbury: E.J. Morten, 1981), p. 6.

2. *The Field*, 17 and 24 June 1882.

3. Cited in Arthur Wallis Myers (ed.), *Lawn Tennis At Home and Abroad* (London: George Newnes Ltd, 1903), p. 55. See also Simon Inglis, *Played in Manchester* (Swindon: English Heritage/Malvern Media, 2004), pp. 22, 26.

4. Jeffrey Pearson, *Lottie Dod: Champion of Champions – The Story of an Athlete* (Birkenhead: Countyvise, 1989), p. 10.

5. *Pastime*, 21 June 1893.

6. *Manchester Courier and Lancashire General Advertiser*, 22 June 1889.
7. *The Field*, 23 June 1894.
8. *Manchester Evening News*, 3 June 1921.
9. Mick Collins, *All-Round Genius. The Unknown Story of Britain's Greatest Sportsman* (London: Aurum Publishing, 2006), pp. 166-8.
10. Allaby, *Wimbledon of the North*, p. 67.
11. *Yorkshire Post*, 17 June 1927.
12. Allaby, *Wimbledon of the North*, p. 87.
13. *Daily Herald*, 7 June 1963.
14. www.thenorthern.co.uk.

[8] Scarborough

1. Burrow, *My Tournaments*, p. 47.
2. *East Anglian Daily Times*, 5 July 2008.
3. *Yorkshire Evening Post*, Friday 21 August 1891.
4. *The Field*, 31 August 1901.
5. *The Field*, 27 August 1910.
6. Burrow, *My Tournaments*, p. 239.
7. *Yorkshire Post and Leeds Mercury*, 23 August 1952.
8. Cited in Tingay (ed.), *Shades of Gray*, p. 9.
9. Fred Perry, *Fred Perry: An Autobiography*, p. 141.
10. Tingay (ed.), *Shades of Gray*, p. 142.
11. Jeannie Swales, *Yorkshire Post*, 7 July 2013. This article cites former club chairman Ian McHale saying that at that time the Scarborough Pindar Tennis Club based itself during the summer on the surviving courts at Filey Road, moving to the Pindar Leisure Centre elsewhere in the town in the winter.
12. Burrow, *The Centre Court and Others*, p. 239.

[9] Midland Counties

1. Steve Beauchampé & Simon Inglis, *Played in Birmingham* (English Heritage/Malvern Media, 2006), pp. 18-20.

2. Matt Cole, *At the Heart of the Game. The History of Edgbaston Priory Club* (Edgbaston: Edgbaston Priory Club, 2013), p. 3.

3. *The Field*, 6 August 1881.

4. *Birmingham Daily Post*, 6 and 9 September 1882.

5. *The Field*, 22 July 1899.

6. *Birmingham Gazette*, 31 July 1905.

7. *Birmingham Gazette*, 26 July 1920.

8. Burrow, *My Tournaments*, p. 231.

9. Duncan Macaulay, *Behind the Scenes at Wimbledon* (London: Collins, 1965), p. 90. See also Ronald Lerry, *Cradle of Lawn Tennis: The Story of Warwickshire and its Clubs* (Birmingham: Stanford and Mann, 1946) p. 54.

10. Tingay, *Daily Telegraph*, 28 February 1958; C.M. Jones, *Daily Mirror*, 28 February 1958.

11. Beauchampé & Inglis, *Played in Birmingham*, p. 116.

12. Ron Worley (compiler), *Warwickshire Lawn Tennis Association. The Centenary Book 1897–1997* (Edgbaston: Warwickshire LTA, 1997), p. 43.

13. Cole, *At the Heart of the Game*, p. 6.

14. *Tennis Today*, 70, 12, 4, July/August 2008: *Birmingham Post* tennis correspondent Brian Dick reported that the club needed to win a bidding process if the tournament was to remain at Edgbaston into a fourth decade. See also www.edgbastonpriory.com.

15. Andy Lusis, *Tennis in Robin Hood Country. The Story of Tennis Clubs in Nottinghamshire* (Nottingham: Andy Lusis, 1998), p. 15.

16. Burrow, *My Tournaments*, pp. 173-5: Burrow describes Nottingham as 'a sort of miniature Wimbledon' before the Great War.

[10] Wembley, the Albert Hall and the O2 Arena

1. The *Daily Herald*, 22 May 1939 described the match as a 'tennis classic'. After the war (in which he served in the German army), Nüsslein continued to compete in pro events and only gave up coaching when he reached the age of 70.
2. Robertson (ed.), *Encyclopedia of Tennis*, p. 281.
3. Cited in Chris Jordan, *The Professional Tennis Archive* (privately published, 2019), p. 62.
4. Joe McCauley, *The History of Professional Tennis* (Windsor: Short Run Books, 2000), pp. 16 and 67-9.
5. *Daily Mirror*, 21 September 1964.
6. Robertson (ed.), *Encyclopedia of Tennis*, p. 309.
7. *Birmingham Daily Post*, 17 November 1975.
8. *Daily Mirror*, 8 November 1976.
9. ATP chairman Etienne de Villiers, quoted in *Tennis Today*, July/August 2007.

Select Bibliography

Details of the range of materials on which this study is based, including newspapers, tennis journals and magazines, autobiographies, individual recollections and online sources, are to be found in the Notes and Acknowledgements. Listed below are a selection of published works that have been particularly helpful in preparing the text:

David Allaby, *Wimbledon of the North. 100 Years at the Northern* (Didsbury: E.J. Morten, 1981)

Ronald Atkin (ed.), *For the Love of Tennis* (London: Stanley Paul, 1985)

Steve Beauchampé & Simon Inglis, *Played in Birmingham* (Swindon: English Heritage/Malvern Media, 2006)

F.R. Burrow, *My Tournaments* (London: Hodder and Stoughton, 1922)

F.R. Burrow, *The Centre Court and Others* (London: Eyre and Spottiswoode, 1937)

Matt Cole, *At the Heart of the Game. The History of Edgbaston Priory Club* (Edgbaston: Edgbaston Priory Club, 2013)

Simon Inglis, *Played in Manchester* (Swindon: English Heritage/Malvern Media, 2004)

Chris Jordan, *The Professional Tennis Archive* (privately published, 2019)

Joe McCauley, *The History of Professional Tennis* (Windsor: Short Run Books, 2000)

Roy McKelvie, *The Queen's Club Story, 1886–1986* (London: Stanley Paul, 1986)

Arthur Wallis Myers, *Great Lawn Tennis* (London: Cassell, 1937)

L.H.W. ('Nicky') Paine, *Beckenham Lawn Tennis Tournament 1886-1986* (Beckenham, 1986)

Geoffrey Paish, *Surrey County LTA. The First 100 Years* (Surrey LTA, 1996)

Max Robertson (ed.), *The Encyclopedia of Tennis* (London: Allen and Unwin, 1974)

Roller Skates and Rackets. The Story of Devonshire Park and Tennis in Eastbourne (Eastbourne: S.B. Publications, 1999)

Lance Tingay (ed.), *Shades of Gray: Tennis Writings of David Gray* (London: Willow, 1988)

Ron Worley (compiler), *Warwickshire Lawn Tennis Association. The Centenary Book 1897–1997* (Edgbaston: Warwickshire LTA, 1997)

Also available at all good book stores

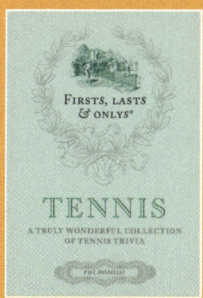

9781785316364

9781785313929

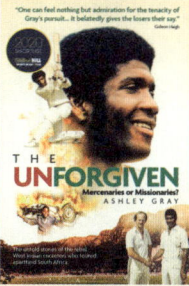

9781785315329

9781785316425

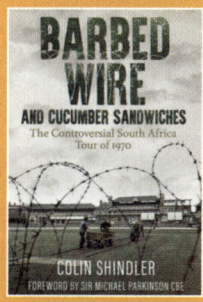

9781785316340

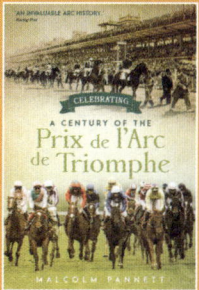

9781785317248

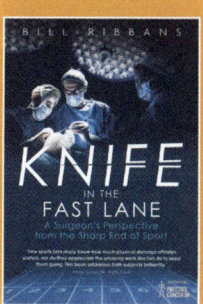

9781785316883

9781785311208

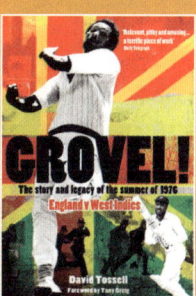

9781908051929